RENOVATING RHETORIC IN CHRISTIAN TRADITION

PITTSBURGH SERIES IN COMPOSITION, LITERACY, AND CULTURE

—

David Bartholomae and Jean Ferguson Carr, Editors

Renovating Rhetoric in Christian Tradition

EDITED BY
ELIZABETH VANDER LEI,
THOMAS AMOROSE,
BETH DANIELL,
AND ANNE RUGGLES GERE

UNIVERSITY OF PITTSBURGH PRESS

Published by the University of Pittsburgh Press, Pittsburgh, Pa., 15260
Copyright © 2014, University of Pittsburgh Press
All rights reserved
Manufactured in the United States of America
Printed on acid-free paper
10 9 8 7 6 5 4 3 2 1

Cataloging-in-Publication data is available at the Library of Congress.

CONTENTS

—

ACKNOWLEDGMENTS

VII

INTRODUCTION
ELIZABETH VANDER LEI

IX

THE RISE OF CHRISTIAN SECTS

1. CONSTRUCTING DEVOUT FEMINISTS: A MORMON CASE
ANNE RUGGLES GERE

3

2. A RHETORIC OF OPPOSITION:
THE SEVENTH-DAY ADVENTIST CHURCH AND THE SABBATH TRADITION
LIZABETH A. RAND

17

THE RISE OF FEMALE RHETORS

3. PREACHING FROM THE PULPIT STEPS:
MARY BOSANQUET FLETCHER AND WOMEN'S PREACHING IN EARLY METHODISM
VICKI TOLAR BURTON

31

4. "WITH THE TONGUE OF [WO]MEN AND ANGELS":
APOSTOLIC RHETORICAL PRACTICES AMONG RELIGIOUS WOMEN
AESHA ADAMS-ROBERTS, ROSALYN COLLINGS EVES, AND LIZ ROHAN

45

5. RHETORICAL STRATEGIES IN PROTESTANT WOMEN'S MISSIONS:
APPROPRIATING AND SUBVERTING GENDER IDEALS
KAREN K. SEAT

59

THE RISE OF ACADEMIC CONCERN ABOUT
AMERICAN CHRISTIAN FUNDAMENTALISM

6. "ATTENTIVE, INTELLIGENT, REASONABLE, AND RESPONSIBLE":
TEACHING COMPOSITION WITH BERNARD LONERGAN
PRISCILLA PERKINS
73

7. "AIN'T WE GOT FUN?": TEACHING WRITING IN A VIOLENT WORLD
ELIZABETH VANDER LEI
89

8. A QUESTION OF TRUTH:
READING THE BIBLE, RHETORIC, AND CHRISTIAN TRADITION
BETH DANIELL
105

RHETORIC IN CHRISTIAN TRADITION

9. THE JEWISH CONTEXT OF PAUL'S RHETORIC
BRUCE HERZBERG
119

10. RESISTANCE TO RHETORIC IN CHRISTIAN TRADITION
THOMAS AMOROSE
135

NOTES
151

BIBLIOGRAPHY
181

CONTRIBUTORS
199

INDEX
203

ACKNOWLEDGMENTS

—

THIS BOOK FINDS its genesis in the scholarly curiosity of five people who, in 2001, applied for a modest Initiative Grant from the Council of Christian Colleges and Universities: Tom Amorose, Beth Daniell, Anne Gere, David Jolliffe, and Elizabeth Vander Lei. When we were selecting readings to discuss and traveling to our first gathering, none of us could have imagined how rich our conversations would be and how deep our friendships would grow. At that first meeting, we talked at length about the scope and, more important, the attitude of our work. To reflect that scope and attitude, we chose the name Symposium for Rhetoric and Christian Tradition—a name that designates the focus of our curiosity and our intent to honor the many historical strands of Christian thought and practice. After the initial three-year grant period, David Jolliffe left the Symposium so that he could focus his attention on his work as Brown Chair for Literacy at the University of Arkansas. Nonetheless, with indefatigable good cheer, David continues to encourage the work of the Symposium. His influence on the scope and attitude of our work cannot be overstated. We are glad for his friendship and support.

After that initial meeting, the Symposium invited other curious scholars to join the conversation. In 2003, Shirley Wilson Logan granted the Symposium status as a Special Interest Group at the Conference on College Composition and Communication; this SIG has been meeting annually ever since, providing CCCC's attendees the opportunity to meet others with a similar scholarly interest and to broaden their awareness of published scholarship and emerging research questions. In 2006, for example, members of the SIG—chaired by Kristine Johnson, Priscilla Perkins, Suzanne Rumsey, Shari Stenberg, and Joonna Trapp—compiled bibliographies of scholarship related to rhetoric and Christian tradition. Over the years others scholars (like Lillian Bridwell Bowles, Keith Miller, Vicki Tolar Burton, and Rebecca Nowacek) have presented summaries of their work at SIG meetings. In 2005 the Symposium hosted a conference at DePaul University that attracted more than one hundred attendees from across the nation for two days of conversation in which we considered further the intersections of rhetoric and Christian tradition. Reverend Dr. John Buchannan, editor of *Christian Century,* and Anne Gere provided plenary lectures. We are grateful to David Jolliffe, again, for his dedicated attention to the local arrangements. We thank Father Dennis Holtschneider, president of DePaul University, for welcoming the Symposium to his campus, and Bonnie Perry, then rector at All Saints Episcopal Church, for her contributions to the conference. And we thank, particularly, all the conference attendees for their willingness to risk time and travel funds on an untested venture, for their openness to varied understandings of both "rhetoric" and "Christian tradition," and for all that they have contributed to the ongoing conversation about rhetoric and Christian tradition.

We are grateful, too, to the authors of chapters in this collection, for the important questions about rhetoric and Christian tradition that they take up and for their perseverance in seeking answers for those questions. We appreciate the work of Josh Shanholtzer at the University of Pittsburgh Press and the anonymous reviewers at the University of Pittsburgh Press for their encouragement and their helpful recommendations for the book as a whole and for individual chapters.

This project was supported by an initial grant from the Council of Christian Colleges and Universities. Elizabeth Vander Lei received sabbatical support from Calvin College to chair the Inquiries into Rhetoric and Christian Tradition conference and additional sabbatical support to prepare the book manuscript for publication. Dean Ward, Jim Vanden Bosch, Bill Vande Kopple, and Becky Moon at Calvin College provided support during the development of the manuscript. Beth Daniell received a semester free from teaching from her chair, Bill Rice, and her dean, Robin Dorff, in order to work with chapter authors.

Our continuing explorations of rhetoric and Christian tradition are enriched daily by the people in our lives. Our students teach us to wonder anew; our families support us as we pursue those wonderments. Tom Amorose is grateful for Victoria's patience with his absences, both mental and physical, related to the development of this book. Beth Daniell thanks Bonnie and Lee, sisters in fact and in spirit, who share the Adventure. Anne Gere's gratitude for an ongoing discussion of homiletics with Budge is matched only by her appreciation for the ways that her three children continue to challenge her rhetorically. And Elizabeth Vander Lei thanks Andrew, Bryant, Maria, and Josie for bringing the circus every day; she thanks Paul for running the show.

INTRODUCTION

—

ELIZABETH VANDER LEI

THIS BOOK GROWS out of and contributes to a persistent scholarly curiosity about the relationship of rhetoric and religion, a curiosity that dapples the history of rhetoric from Augustine's *On Christian Doctrine* to the work of contemporary scholars, a curiosity that persists in part, I believe, because scholars have found that examining this relationship produces useful insights about complex rhetorical acts like argumentation. *Renovating Rhetoric in Christian Tradition* focuses attention on rhetors who press into service an array of rhetorical strategies—some drawn from Christian tradition and some contributing to Christian tradition—to achieve their rhetorical ends. And it gives us more to be curious about: this collection brings together a range of arguments made during times and places of significant social rupture associated with Christian tradition—from the formation of Christianity (Bruce Herzberg) to contemporary questions about religious ways of being (Priscilla Perkins), from colonial Africa (Aesha Adams-Roberts, Rosalyn Collings Eves, and Liz Rohan) to present-day American classrooms (Beth Daniell).

These chapters demonstrate that as rhetors argue, they press into service a variety of strategies, including beliefs and practices that are cultural as well as religious, subtle, multiple, interdependent, and historically situated. Chapters in the first three parts of this collection attend to three particular areas of social rupture: the rise of Christian sects, the rise of female rhetors, and the rise of academic concern about American Christian fundamentalism. In each of these parts, readers meet rhetors who have taken the opportunity to renovate rhetorical resources associated with Christian tradition and, through their use of those resources, reshaped their discourse communities. Chapters in the fourth part, which centers upon rhetoric in Christian tradition, line out the complexities encountered by such rhetors (and those who study them) as they create and resolve moments of social upheaval in Christian tradition.

In the first part, "The Rise of Christian Sects," contributors Anne Ruggles Gere and Lizabeth A. Rand consider how rhetors from "outsider" groups have created arguments with and against Christian tradition to assert the identity of their sect. In this piece, Gere and Rand, like other chapter authors, contribute to a body of scholarship that explores how rhetors have made use of the rhetorical resources available in Christian tradition and how these rhetors sometimes mix those resources with other resources to create hybrid discourses. The rhetorician Patricia Bizzell provides an example of this kind of blending in her analysis of the 1263 Barcelona Disputation, a staged theological debate between the Jewish scholar known as Nahmanides and the Dominican friar Paul Christian.[1]

As a Jew living under the rule of a Christian king, Nahmanides represented religious believers who troubled a culturally promulgated argument for the rationality of the Christian faith because "the Bible was the central holy text for [Jews] but they did not find the same meanings in it that the Christians did."[2] In this contest Nahmanides found himself in a difficult situation: if he won, he risked "offending the high secular and religious authorities in attendance and bringing down more persecution of his fellow Jews."[3] And if he lost, "he risked seriously demoralizing a population who was already under severe psychological and physical assault from the majority culture."[4] Bizzell emphasizes that in this disputation, both Nahmanides and Friar Christian (also a Jew but one who had converted) made extensive use of their knowledge of Jewish and Christian warrants, evidence, and argumentative strategies.[5] Bizzell argues that in rhetorical moments like this, many features of a rhetorical situation—religion and culture, language and argumentation, belief and rationality—intertwine to create a Gordian knot of meaning. Such mingling of features is possible, Bizzell concludes, because "as is often the case when we analyze mixed discourses, we discover that the discourses being mixed were not so separate to begin with."[6] As a result of its long history and global distribution, Christian tradition has been shaped by innumerable mixed discourses like these.

In her chapter "Constructing Devout Feminists: A Mormon Case," Gere studies the rhetorical influence of Mormon women on the arguments for Utah statehood and for the acceptance of Mormonism as an expression of Christianity. She rehearses the terrible social stigma that Mormons, particularly women, endured as a result of the Mormon religious practice of polygamy. She describes how, in the face of this prejudice, Mormon women countered prevalent attitudes toward Mormons by arguing in support of women's suffrage and by getting involved in the women's club movement, even as these women maintained a distinctive Mormon religious identity. In this way they were able to demonstrate their affinity with other American women and their loyalty to American values. More than that, they renovated the concept of feminism to include women like them—deeply religious and passionately concerned about the status of women.

In "A Rhetoric of Opposition: The Seventh-day Adventist Church and the

Sabbath Tradition," Rand considers the oppositional rhetoric of Seventh-day Adventism, a strand of Christianity that defines itself largely through its opposition to the Sunday-worship practices of mainstream Christianity and its critique of the collusion of government and religion, particularly legislation that designates Sunday as a special day for rest, leisure, and worship. Rand notes that as a consequence of their strident opposition to the cooperation of government and religion, Seventh-day Adventists have also critiqued populist ideas of American exceptionalism and the American dream, further isolating themselves from mainstream American culture. This oppositional stance, Rand argues, fulfills an important rhetorical function, what the scholar John Shilb has called a "rhetoric of refusal," and actually demonstrates deep concern for the well-being of their fellow citizens.

The second part, "The Rise of Female Rhetors," offers three chapters that challenge the assumption that religious communities protect orthodox belief and practices at all costs—an assumption rooted in an erroneous idea that for religions (though Christianity and American Christian fundamentalism are pointed to in particular) "'Truth' is static, constant, and universal."[7] Scholars have portrayed orthodoxy as a restricting force on rhetors in religious discourse communities who may be fearful that they will be shut out of the community.[8] For example, in her description of the limits of rhetoric to persuade "apocalyptist" Christian fundamentalists, Sharon Crowley posits that "people who are invested in densely articulated belief systems" are unlikely to respond to rhetorical argumentation—to change their minds—because the cost of changing their belief system is too great, "because it is all they know, or because their friends, family, and important authority figures are similarly invested, or because their identity is in some respects constructed by the beliefs inherent in the system. Rejection of such a belief system ordinarily requires rejection of community and reconstruction of one's identity as well."[9] But are religious discourse communities so rigidly bounded? Are they as static as some have imagined them to be?

While not denying the pressures exerted by all "densely articulated belief systems," be they religious, cultural, or ideological, chapters in *Renovating Rhetoric in Christian Tradition* draw attention to rhetors in Christian discourse communities arguing more freely than some might expect, given their assumptions about the pressures of orthodoxy on religious rhetors. The rhetors showcased in this collection sometimes respect and sometimes challenge orthodox practices and beliefs of their discourse communities. In so doing, they alter those practices and beliefs to serve their arguments and, in the process, they renovate their religious community. Chapters in this edited volume contribute to a body of scholarship that showcases a historical line of rhetors who experience religious belief as a dynamic process of meaning-making—a process that they experience, in part, by making arguments. An example of this kind of scholarship is Lisa Shaver's *Beyond the Pulpit: Women's Rhetorical Roles in the Antebellum Religious Press*. Shaver documents "women's rich, expansive rhetorical legacy"—in particular, the writing that antebellum Methodist women who published "brief everyday descriptions of women's activities" in widely distributed periodicals of the Methodist Church.[10] By studying these publications, Shaver argues, scholars come to understand "how the church provided sites for women's rhetorical development."[11] Shaver documents, for example, women drawing "rhetorical proofs from their own scriptural interpretations," asserting logical conclusions based on Methodist theology, and relying on traditional interpretations to "endorse their public activism."[12] In this process, women reshaped both their religious faith and their religious community.[13] Shaver notes that despite the rhetorical resourcefulness displayed by these humble religious women, they have been overlooked by scholars who "often steer clear of religious institutions."[14]

Like Shaver's research, chapters in *Renovating Rhetoric in Christian Tradition* complicate the idea that to argue successfully in a given discourse community, a rhetor—even one with relatively limited social or political power—is not obligated to adopt unconditionally a community's ways of thinking, believing, and doing in order to gain rhetorical agency within that community. Rather, rhetors can gain rhetorical agency by refurbishing a community's ways of thinking, believing, and doing to suit their rhetorical goals. Three chapters focus on women rhetors in the Protestant tradition of Christianity who altered community-imposed limitations on their rights and opportunities by using the very words, ideas, and rhetorical strategies that had been used to suppress them. These chapters focus particularly on how women rhetors used widely held assumptions about the value of Christian devotion to overcome opposition to their religious, social, and political activism.

In "Preaching from the Pulpit Steps: Mary Bosanquet Fletcher and Women's Preaching in Early Methodism," Vicki Tolar Burton directs readers' attention to a historical and cultural moment during the rise of Protestant sects when a woman's right to speak was under debate. In particular, Burton details Mary Bosanquet Fletcher's argument for Methodist women's right to preach, arguments that rely on an ethos that blends female modesty and sharp (masculine) intellect. Throughout her adult life, Bosanquet put her arguments into action by creating hybrid sacred spaces through her judicious choice of where and when to preach. Furthermore, while Bosanquet willingly preached to those who sought her out, she also pursued approval for her preaching from church authorities, notably John Wesley, who responded favorably to her reasoning.

In "'With the Tongues of [Wo]men and Angels': Apostolic Rhetorical Practices among Religious Women," Aesha Adams-Roberts, Rosalyn Collings Eves, and Liz Rohan describe how four women from different times and places fashioned an apostolic ethos as an alternative to the prophetic ethos available only to men in their culture. Drawing authority from the rhetor's humility and her conversion story, an apostolic ethos enables disenfranchised rhetors like these women to be effective preachers and teachers within their communities. Tracing the various experiences of four women in three diverse historical, cultural, and religious settings, these authors demonstrate that this ethos has been a regular feature of arguments made by Protestant women. This distinctive ethos is underrepresented in scholarship on rhetoric and religion, scholarship that emphasizes instead a prophetic ethos used by socially prominent male speakers.

Karen K. Seat focuses on the rhetoric of American women of the same time period who argued to establish the Woman's Foreign Missionary Society of the Methodist Episcopal Church in her chapter entitled "Rhetorical Strategies in Protestant Women's Missions: Appropriating and Subverting Gender Ideals." Methodist women established this society by altering conservative ideologies of gender—in particular, sexist assumptions about the intellectual capacity of women and the kind of work that was appropriate for them. Because these revised ideologies retained enough of the original thinking to seem familiar, they appeared rational and nonthreatening to initially reluctant male religious leaders. Able to demonstrate success as both social organizers and foreign missionaries, these women shifted Protestant ideas about proper social order and contributed to the liberalizing of mainline American Protestant theology. The women represented in these chapters, as well as other rhetors represented throughout this volume, demonstrate that while discourse communities may provide rhetors with rhetorical identities, strategies, and theoretical frameworks, they are not necessarily constrained by those resources; rather, rhetors can renovate those resources, sometimes in radical ways, refining and adapting the resources to match their rhetorical needs.

As rhetors renovate Christian tradition, they seem to act in some ways that seem similar to those of the student "agents of integration" described by the scholar Rebecca Nowacek in her book of that title. Regarding how people make use of their knowledge and skill to accomplish rhetorical purposes, Nowacek proposes that "as individuals move from one context to the next, they receive cues, both explicit and implicit, that suggest knowledge associated with a prior context may prove useful in the new context."[15] As rhetors in Christian tradition take up rhetorical resources and fit them to argumentative need, rhetors inevitably alter both the resources and themselves.[16] For example, when Martin Luther King Jr. concludes "I Have a Dream" speech with the words of "My Country Tis of Thee," he takes up the song that Marian Anderson sang on the same steps of the Lincoln Memorial in 1939 and fits those lyrics and their rich history to the occasion of the March on Washington.[17] When King follows those words with the "Let Freedom Ring" anaphora, he takes up words that the African American preacher and civil rights activist Archibald Carey spoke to the 1952 Republican Convention, and he refurbishes them by heightening their musicality and matching them to his own speech cadences.[18] When King concludes the anaphora by adding "Let freedom ring from every hill and molehill of Mississippi," he connects Carey's words to contemporary civil rights battles. Immediately following this anaphora, King concludes by imagining heaven as a multiracial choir holding hands and singing a Negro spiritual. This image invokes a Christian theology that was shaped by King's arguments for an experience with nonviolent civic protest. What is true of King and his argument for racial justice is also true of the rhetors and the arguments showcased in this edited volume: as they remake rhetorical resources, they remake themselves.

The experiences of rhetors remaking themselves through argumentation supports Nowacek's more fully embodied model of transfer that "puts the individual as meaning maker at the center of conceptions of transfer and integration" and draws us into the topic of the third part of this book, "The Rise of Concern about American Christian Fundamentalism," a part that features three chapters exploring how teachers of rhetoric and composition might create an environment that would encourage students to become "agents of integration."[19] Assumptions about transfer permeate the composition scholarship about religious students—a body of scholarship that has focused particularly on students who have allegiances to Christian fundamentalism. Early studies presumed negative transfer, specifically that students were inappropriately transferring genre knowledge from their religious experiences, such as witnessing talk, to their academic writing.[20] Later studies suggest the possibility of positive transfer, arguing that students can and should draw on their prior rhetorical experiences in religious communities to solve the rhetorical problems that they encounter in the composition classroom. In this model of transfer, students' religious faith serves as rhetorical resource that they can draw upon when writing.[21] Some research on transfer, however, raises questions about the ease of transferring genres, rhetorical strategies, or even knowledge from a religious community to a composition classroom.[22] Indeed, Rebecca Nowacek's study highlights the varied and subtle factors—religious identity being one—that influence a student's ability to "see" and "sell" connections between even seemingly similar academic contexts to their professor readers.[23] Nowacek describes a student "Betty" as caught in a double-bind, a situation in which "individuals experience contradictions within or between activity systems but cannot articulate any meta-awareness of those contractions."[24] Unwilling to compromise her identity as a Quaker, Betty altered the assignment, writing in a genre other than one the professor describes on the assignment—a decision that carried no small amount of risk. While Betty's instructor rewarded her innovation with an acceptable grade, we are left to consider how easily it might have been otherwise.

Three chapters in this collection explore resources that instructors of rhetoric and composition might draw on when helping students make sense of the relationship of their religious identity and their academic work. In "'Attentive, Intelligent, Reasonable, and Responsible': Teaching Composition with Bernard Lonergan," Priscilla Perkins looks to the work of Lonergan, a Canadian Jesuit philosopher, for an approach to ethos that encourages students to take the time to internalize their argument before they attempt to persuade others. Furthermore, Perkins argues, when students attend to what they are learning and how it affects them, they also learn to attend to the ways their arguments might affect their readers. Perkins describes the difficulties that Tina, a Christian evangelical student, encountered as she struggled against the idea that she might have something to learn from course readings or her classmates.

In my chapter, "'Ain't We Got Fun?': Teaching Writing in a Violent World," I rely on the work of two contemporary Protestant theologians, Stanley Hauerwas and Miraslov Volf, to suggest strategies that teachers and students might use when they encounter ideas that they find odd or offensive. I look to Hauerwas's narrative theology for the idea that when we recognize that our stories are nested in the stories of our communities and when we think of our voice as speaking for, through, and against that community, we find the courage to challenge the power of seemingly univocal stories. I look to Volf's argument against the idea of religion as a private matter to find reasons to enact intellectual hospitality that invites the other in so that we can find a way to talk together and to learn to trust one another. In "A Question of Truth: Reading the Bible, Rhetoric, and Christian Tradition," Beth Daniell considers student questions that might indicate that students are transferring ideas and experiences from fundamentalist Christian communities into the college classroom. Noting that a wide range of students ask the kinds of questions commonly associated with Christian fundamentalist students, Daniell suggests that the study of rhetorical theory draws all students into an exploration of the relationship between language and truth. Daniell lines out strategies that teachers can use when addressing questions that arise during that exploration, strategies that respect the theological and theoretical allegiances of both students and instructors. Drawing on the work of rhetoricians, Christian theologians, and biblical scholars, Daniell considers the rhetorical nature of not only the act of reading but also of Christian tradition itself.

In the final part, "Rhetoric in Christian Tradition," authors Bruce Herzberg and Tom Amorose contemplate the troubled relationship of rhetoric and Christian tradition, tracing the complexities of interpretation and the interplay of religious and rhetorical traditions. In "The Jewish Context of Paul's rhetoric,"

Herzberg demonstrates the Apostle Paul's use of Jewish forms of argumentation, uses that are consonant with the rabbinic tradition that Paul had been trained in. Herzberg lines out scholarship on Paul's rhetoric, scholarship that signals clear allegiance to Christian tradition, that ignores or dismisses the idea that Jewish argumentative traditions could inform our understanding of Paul's argumentative practices. Herzberg clears the way not only for fresh scholarly interpretation of Paul's arguments but also for new consideration of the ways that rhetors who may no longer feel strong allegiance to a particular religious tradition refurbish elements of that tradition to make effective arguments.

Amorose concludes the collection with his chapter "Resistance to Rhetoric in Christian Tradition," in which he provides a clear-eyed review of the challenges faced by scholars who accept Stanley Fish's coronation of religion as the successor of "high theory and the triumvirate of race, gender, and class as the center of intellectual energy in the academy."[25] Amorose develops a convincing case for the argument that Christian tradition has resisted renovating rhetorical practices and consequently missed opportunities to make arguments that can renovate the human heart. Throughout his chapter, Amorose provides an invaluable roadmap for future scholars, pointing out difficulties inherent in any approach that proposes broad and easy intersections of rhetoric and Christianity (and rhetoric and religion generally) and directing scholars toward more productive questions that account for the social, historical, and cultural landscape of arguments.

So although the chapters in *Renovating Rhetoric in Christian Tradition* provoke as many questions (or more) than they can provide answers for, we hope that they fire the curiosity of our readers, compelling them to ask and seek answers for their own questions about rhetoric and Christian tradition.

Renovating Rhetoric in Christian Tradition

THE RISE OF CHRISTIAN SECTS

—

1

CONSTRUCTING DEVOUT FEMINISTS

A MORMON CASE

ANNE RUGGLES GERE

THE FOLLOWERS WHO accompanied Brigham Young when he arrived in the Great Salt Lake valley on July 24, 1847, and declared "this is the place," were the first Mormon pioneers to envision Utah as a location where they could practice their religion with minimal interference. Adherents to this religion, which took shape as Joseph Smith published *The Book of Mormon* in 1830, had moved from Palmyra, New York, to Kirtland, Ohio, to Nauvoo, Illinois, to avoid violence and discrimination, but the 1844 murder of Joseph Smith in Carthage, Illinois, and the subsequent harassment of his followers convinced them to leave Illinois for a better land. Young and his followers moved west to avoid further persecution for the religious differences that raised a mixture of anxiety and hostility in the dominant American culture.

Brigham Young's party included 143 men, 3 women, and 2 children. This gender ratio shifted as subsequent groups arrived, but because of constraints in Mormon doctrine, women remained relatively absent in church governance and leadership. Although women did not take leadership roles in the Church of the Latter Day Saints, as the Mormon church is formally called, women did occupy visible positions in secular society, positions aimed at ameliorating the negative responses generated by religious differences. This chapter uses the term "feminist" to describe the devout Mormon women who helped to transform the State of Deseret, as Utah was originally called, from a territory, subject to frequent federal incursions, into a state that could govern itself and enjoy the increased autonomy that came with statehood, including greater freedom from religious persecution. These Mormon women represent an unusual type of feminism because they both resisted and accepted gendered roles. In the secular context they took up positions and activities that led them to demand rights for women and to take up roles in public life. At the same time, however, these women did not challenge the church's patriarchal power structure and, in fact, they remained deeply committed to its traditions and beliefs. This mixture of enacting and eschewing feminist principles positions Mormon women between 1870 and 1896 as pioneers of a special kind because they entered new gendered territory just as Mormons of both genders entered the territory beyond the Wasatch Mountains.

Mormon women occupied a stigmatized position during the latter part of the nineteenth century because of their religious beliefs. For non-Mormons and particularly for white Protestant women, the bodies and sexuality of Mormon women constituted a site of contest because the Mormon doctrine of plural marriage or polygamy—a signifier of religious devotion among Mormons— took on political significance for non-Mormons. White Protestant women, in particular, saw polygamy as a threat to themselves and the gendered family structure they constituted and were constituted by. Increasingly uneasy about the legal status of women within marriage, these women played out their own anxieties with vicious attacks on Mormon women. As Susa Gates, an active Mormon feminist put it, Mormon women were "even more unpopular in the outside world than the Mormon man. . . . They were actually thought of as debased slaves, ignorant beyond description, and utterly immoral and unchaste."[1] Given such views of Mormon women, it is remarkable that they made concerted efforts to interact with non-Mormon women.

Although women were most concerned about women's legal status in marriage, many Gentiles, or non-Mormons, showed an interest in maintaining the integrity of the gendered family. American national identity narratives depended upon the carefully delineated gender roles of the traditional American family, with the domestic female figure nurturing and influencing male family members so that these males could effect changes in the larger social world. As the Americanist Priscilla Wald has observed, reinforcement of these narratives "used the traditional American family as both metaphor and medium."[2] Fears of "race suicide"—the concern that the combination of immigration and a lower birth rate among resident European Americans would cause the "pure English American" to disappear or at least cease to control the means of cultural production—added significance to the woman's role in maintaining the traditional gendered family. These fears increased hostility toward the aberration of polygamy. The revulsion for polygamy provided a convenient foil for deflecting, as the historian Sarah Barringer Gordon has observed, problems within monogamous marriages because antipolygamists did "not have to examine their own behavior in the course of enacting legislation."[3] The polygamous family, with its reconfigured gender roles and complex questions about sexuality, provided a convenient site onto which anxieties about monogamous marriage could be projected.

Like Mormon polygamy, slavery represented another source of anxiety for many nineteenth-century Americans, and for white women the figure of the female slave raised special concern. Slavery reverberated with Mormon polygamy in the minds of many. Harriet Beecher Stowe's *Uncle Tom's Cabin* was published in the same year (1852) that Mormons first made their practice of polygamy public. As literary scholar Nancy Bentley has explained, both slavery and Mormonism posed problems for the democratic principle of consent—proponents assumed that women in polygamous marriages could not have consented (any more than African Americans) to their status.[4] As the dark double of monogamy, polygamy aroused considerable anxiety about the role of consent in marriage. Before and during the Civil War, anti-Mormon and antislavery movements frequently merged; indeed, the Republican platform of 1856 included a pledge to rid the country of both slavery and polygamy. One manifestation of the anxiety about Mormons appeared in the unwillingness of the U.S. government to accept Utah as a state. The first petition for Utah statehood was made in 1849, and its rejection was followed by unsuccessful petitions in 1856, 1862, 1867, 1872, and 1887. Even though government work, mining, and the railroad brought some Gentiles to Utah, over 90 percent of the population remained Mormon, and concerns about this religious group led to the successive rejections of Utah's petitions for statehood.

Another expression of anxiety appeared in the spate of antipolygamy novels published between 1855 and 1898. With titles such as *In the Grip of the Mormons: By an Escaped Wife of a Mormon Elder*; *Mormon Wives: A Narrative of Facts Stranger than Fiction*; and *Saved from the Mormons*, these narratives were written by non-Mormons who had never been to Utah and detailed horrors including white slave procurers, secret doctrines of organized vengeance, and physical torture of women in polygamous marriages.[5] Although few of these accounts had any basis in fact, they captured the public's imagination, much as Indian captivity narratives had done at an earlier point in American life. Like Indian captivity narratives, antipolygamy novels accomplished purposes that extended beyond their sentimental and sensational accounts of female victims. As the scholar Jane Tompkins has reminded us, the sentimental text achieves its goal by "altering the reader's world view, an alteration that necessarily triggers action in the reader's life."[6]

Such novels also allowed both authors and readers to consider political issues that would have been difficult for them to discuss in other contexts. Antipolygamy novels addressed concerns about the political and moral dimensions of marriage at a time when concerns about the vulnerability of women—bound legally to men whose desires (for sex, gambling, alcohol, or violence) could betray them—ran high. Similarly, anxieties about slavery and, later, the incorporation of African Americans as free citizens found expression in the blurring of concerns about polygamy and slavery, both in the captivity narratives (which portrayed women as unwilling or nonconsenting participants in plural marriages) and in the rendering of the progeny of polygamy as nonwhite. Written mostly by women and addressed to a largely female audience, antipolygamy fiction addressed anxieties while simultaneously arousing popular sentiment against Mormons.[7]

For most Americans, and especially for white Protestant women, the figure of the independent-minded, devout Mormon woman could not be imagined. Gentiles could accept the idea of women entering plural marriages under force or duress, but they could not countenance the idea that Mormon women would willingly enter such unions. It was possible for Gentiles to imagine women accepting the "patriarchal principle," but women who willingly and knowingly embraced Mormon doctrine could not exist in the national imagination because they incited such anxiety among women—and men—from other religious traditions.[8] Greater acceptance of Mormons by Gentiles depended upon repositioning Mormon women in the Gentile mind.

One response of Mormon women was to ally themselves with the cause of woman suffrage, which was granted to Utah's women—for the first time—in 1870. Accounts of how this occurred vary, with some commentators portraying Mormon women as relatively passive and emphasizing the role of non-Mormon women supporting suffrage because they believed that women who could vote would quickly make polygamy illegal.[9] Other accounts describe Mormon women as politically active well before 1870, pointing to their petition to the Illinois state government in 1842, their activism on behalf of the poor, and their continuing defense of their religion.[10]

Both sides agree, however, that Mormon women took public stands on behalf of their religion, including the doctrine of plural marriage. When the legislature voted suffrage for Utah's women, Mormon women called upon rhetorical strategies to argue for statehood in the face of powerful opposition to their religion. In 1870 the poet and LDS leader Eliza Snow addressed an audience of more than five thousand of her Mormon sisters in the Salt Lake Tabernacle, declaring: "Year after year we have petitioned Congress for that which is our inalienable right to claim—a state government; and year after year, our petitions have been treated with contempt."[11] Actually, of course, the petitions had been submitted by Mormon men, but Snow's "our petitions" made a rhetorical claim for the ownership she and her sisters assumed for Utah's political fate. Statehood would give Mormons an autonomy they lacked as a territory, thereby enabling them to practice their religion more freely. In response to this call, Mormon women undertook further rhetorical action by signing and circulating petitions in support of their religious beliefs. In 1871, twenty-five hundred women petitioned for repeal of the Morrill Act, which outlawed bigamy and, after the Supreme Court ruled the act legal in 1879, Mormon women took an even more public rhetorical position by issuing and personally delivering to the White House a series of petitions on behalf of women and children whose legitimacy and inheritance rights were affected by the decision. In their petition drive Mormon women replicated the actions of Gentile feminists, but their goal of protecting the legal rights of polygamous women did not fit comfortably within traditional feminist causes.

With Utah's passage of woman suffrage in 1870, Protestant women confronted the specter of enfranchised women who would not use the ballot to eliminate polygamy. This led them to action. Within Utah, Gentile women organized the Anti-Polygamy Society in 1878 and, with the aid of Protestant women from elsewhere, issued an 1884 petition that Congress disenfranchise Utah women. They succeeded in 1887, when the Edmunds-Tucker law abolished suffrage for women of Utah. Indeed, historical commentators argue that the Edmunds-Tucker law would not have passed without the support of Protestant advocates, a majority of them women.[12] It was a remarkable instance of one group of women undercutting the rights of another. As suffragist Lucy Stone put it: "It is hardly possible that so bold an attempt to disenfranchise citizens who have exercised the right to vote for ten years can be accomplished. It would certainly never have been attempted if these citizens had not been Mormons."[13]

In addition to achieving suffrage, Mormon women used print to ally themselves rhetorically with progressive women, especially on the issue of education. *The Woman's Exponent*, one of three newspapers west of the Mississippi "edited and published entirely by women," including female typesetters, was established by Mormon women in 1872.[14] With a masthead that read: "The Rights of the Women of Zion and the Rights of the Women of all Nations," this paper regularly published articles advocating woman suffrage, reported on the accomplishments of women throughout the world, and self-consciously affirmed the historic importance of women's activities. For example, a significant number of Mormon women became medical doctors, following the example of Romania Pratt, who returned to Utah from the Philadelphia Women's Medical College in 1877. These accomplishments were carefully displayed to an audience beyond Utah.[15] One commentator claimed that "no concentration of women in medicine ever occurred proportionately to the number of women doctors among the pioneers of Utah."

Despite repeated petitions for statehood and despite the woman suffrage, educational and publishing efforts of Mormon women, Utah still remained a territory. The practice of polygamy, which aroused tremendous hostility, still remained an obstacle. Accordingly, on September 24, 1890, the LDS Church president Wilford Woodruff issued a manifesto forbidding plural marriage, and the General Conference of the Church accepted it unanimously on October 6 of the same year. Despite this move, Gentiles remained unconvinced, suspecting that the manifesto might be temporary, "a political maneuver designed to relieve external pressure long enough for Utah to gain entrance to the Union, after which the practice would be gradually reinstated."[16] Whatever the status of its origins or the motivations of those who supported it, the manifesto was a necessary but not sufficient step in Utah's campaign to render a Mormon-dominated territory recognizable as an appropriate candidate for statehood.[17] Since the manifesto by itself was not entirely convincing to Gentile populations, further efforts were necessary.

The next step for Mormon women was women's clubs. The term "clubwomen" may conjure an image of relatively privileged white Protestant women who shared gossip over tea cups or it may call up a turn-of-the-century movement that included working-class, African American, Catholic, and Jewish women in projects of Americanization, philanthropy, and self-improvement, as well as the creation of such institutions as libraries, kindergartens, and schools of social work. Mormons are not typically associated with the women's club movement. In part, this results from the fact that white Protestant clubwomen have been represented as normative in most studies of the women's club movement, much as whiteness has been, until very recently, taken as normative rather than one racial category among several.[18] The unfamiliarity of the phrase "Mormon clubwoman" also results from the stigmatized position of this most American of religions.[19] Despite this unfamiliarity, Mormon women in Salt Lake City organized at least a half-dozen clubs.

Mormon clubwomen were not, of course, the only ones to occupy a stigmatized position. Their African American and Jewish peers faced similar challenges, and these two groups offered compelling examples of how clubwomen could help transform members of their population into fit Americans. Clubwomen affiliated with the National Association of Colored Women not only monitored their own manners and morals to emulate those of the white middle class but also frequently intervened in the lives of their sisters "by whom . . . the world will always judge the womanhood of our race," in attempts to bring them closer to middle-class American norms.[20] In keeping with the National Association of Colored Women's motto, "Lifting as We Climb," these clubwomen helped to constitute members of their race as legitimate Americans.

Jewish clubwomen played a particularly active role in Americanizing members of their community. The rapidly growing number of Jewish immigrants in the 1890s included a significant proportion of women (unlike other immigrant groups, which typically included fewer women) and, as one woman put it in a speech at the 1902 Triennial of the National Council of Jewish Women (NCJW): "We who are the cultured and refined, constitute the minority, but we shall be judged by the majority, the Russian Jews, by the children of the Ghetto."[21] Accordingly, Jewish clubwomen worked to transform these "Russian Jews" into "Americans." Convinced that the "strange ways" of their immigrant sisters might reflect badly on them—particularly if the recent arrivals appeared to present an economic burden—Jewish clubwomen developed a highly efficient and wide-ranging system for acculturating their immigrant sisters. The process designed to transform immigrant Jews included meeting each ship that went through Ellis Island, ascertaining the legitimacy of U.S. family connections claimed, maintaining contact with recent arrivals, and providing educational opportunities such as night schools and summer schools for working women.

Unlike their Jewish peers, Mormon clubwomen lacked an established and assimilated wing that could ease them into public acceptability and, unlike African Americans, they didn't have opportunities for domestic and/or workplace contacts with dominant populations. Their geographic isolation fostered the worst imaginings of misinformation, which in turn were fueled by antipolygamy novels and negative public discourses. Still, however, club work offered what I, following historian Mary Louise Pratt, call a contact zone—a social space where this relatively powerless population and their more influential peers could use literacy to "meet, clash, and grapple with each other."[22]

Mormon women came to clubs later than their peers in other parts of the country and later than Gentile women in Utah, but they entered the movement at a propitious time. Although the larger male culture still remained somewhat hostile toward and suspicious of women's clubs, they had by 1890 become a relatively common social formation.[23] Not only had clubs begun to spring up in cities and towns across the nation but groups of clubs had banded together in national associations. The General Federation of Women's Clubs was founded in 1890, the National Council of Jewish Women in 1893, and the National Association of Colored Women in 1896. Mormon leader Emmeline Wells founded the Utah Women's Press Club (UWPC) in 1891, and both the Reapers Club and Cleofan were established in 1892. Between their founding and Utah's 1896 successful petition for statehood, these clubs carried out rhetorical projects that did much to transform the way Mormon women were perceived. Through clubs, Mormon women engaged in rhetorical exchanges with women who saw them as ignorant and immoral, and such exchanges helped Gentile women to reconsider the identities they had assigned to their Mormon peers.

Like their peers elsewhere, Mormon clubwomen produced and consumed official documents such as constitutions, by-laws, and minutes of meetings; papers written and read at club meetings; as well as letters, articles, and literary texts, thereby signaling their seriousness of purpose. Through publication in *The Woman's Exponent* (which was exchanged for the publications of many other clubs), correspondence with other clubs, state and national meetings where club papers were read, and visits with members of Gentile clubs, Mormon clubwomen circulated their texts to their peers throughout the country, thus countering biased misrepresentations of themselves and their beliefs.

Mormon clubwomen called upon rhetoric to make and circulate overt claims about their relationship to the nation. In a speech given at a reception for members of several clubs and published in the *Exponent,* a Reapers Club member declared: "Politics has been from girlhood an interesting subject to me. . . . I read Daniel Webster's Speeches, the 'Union Text Book' of our American Statesmen including the Constitution and Declaration of Independence . . . the more I read the more I felt the *positive necessity* of woman being not only a wife and mother in name but *in very deed.* Intellectually strong, brave, wise, prudent, efficient and capable."[24] With such statements as "our American Statesmen" and references to the Constitution and Declaration of Independence, this clubwoman appropriates an American heritage for herself and her Mormon audience, using the reading of common texts as a way to show shared values and loyalties. By combining this claim to being American with an affirmation of educated and capable womanhood, the speaker gestures toward a common citizenship that extends both within and beyond the Mormon community.

Another of the "American" virtues displayed by Mormon clubwomen appeared in the causes they supported. For clubwomen in many social locations, moral or social uplift numbered among the most popular causes. In some cases this took the form of attempting to ameliorate poverty or improve the lot of those in less advantaged positions. Although class lines were less well defined in Utah than in the East, Mormon clubwomen took on the burden of "improving" those less advantaged than themselves. A paper given at the Utah Federation of Woman's Clubs by a member of Cleofan, a Mormon club, articulates principles common to clubwomen who supported social uplift projects. Cleofan's membership in the state federation was particularly important since so much anti-Mormon sentiment was generated by Gentiles living in Utah. State meetings provided opportunities for Mormon clubwomen to show members of groups such as Salt Lake's Ladies' Literary and the Woman's Club that religious differences did not weaken patriotism or prevent the flowering of common interests. In her history of the General Federation of Women's Clubs, the founding leader Jennie June Croly affirmed a commonality that extended across religious difference: "No line is drawn in the Utah Federation. Mormons and Gentiles enter on an equal footing, and the work is doing much to break down the walls of ancient prejudice."[25]

In an 1896 paper titled "Social Purity," a Mormon clubwoman argued for the social value of promoting the welfare of all members of society, points to poverty as a cause of social impurity, and urges the assembled clubwomen to help improve "the conditions of those who form the lower classes in society."[26] Moyle, the speaker, goes on to urge that parents provide moral surroundings for children and that men adhere to the same standards of (sexual) purity that they expect of women. In addition to demonstrating how Mormon clubwomen shared the same values as other clubwomen, rhetorical maneuvers like Moyle's offered Mormon women opportunities to redefine themselves as intelligent and moral beings rather than the immoral and ignorant figures anti-Mormon texts made of them.

Another rhetorical alliance created by Mormon clubwomen took aesthetic form. Minutes of Mormon club meetings indicate that members studied literary texts by such American authors as Henry Wadsworth Longfellow, John Greenleaf Whittier, Benjamin Franklin, and Ella Wheeler Wilcox. Like their sisters in the East, Mormon clubwomen accorded even more importance to British literature, lavishing attention on texts by such writers as Chaucer, Milton, Shakespeare, Scott, Byron, Arnold, and Ruskin. Like clubwomen elsewhere, Mormon clubwomen participated in literature-related activities that included writing papers about authors, reading texts aloud or performing them, discussing and interpreting literature, and participating in authors' parties where members dressed like and impersonated literary figures. In choosing to study the same literature and employ approaches similar to those of clubwomen from other parts of the country and in displaying their work in published articles in the *Woman's Exponent* that circulated to their non-Mormon counterparts, Mormon clubwomen constructed another rhetorical connection with American women who occupied less stigmatized social positions.

The circulations of print culture enabled Mormon clubwomen to display rhetorical evidence of their increasing acceptance by non-Mormons. The published minutes of a UWPC meeting included this: "The president stated that she had received a letter from the Countess Annie d'Montaign, asking for information concerning the club, to publish in an Eastern magazine. This shows that the club is becoming well known."[27] In an editorial published by the *Woman's Exponent* in July 1893, UWPC founder Emmeline Wells wrote: "Many times while in Chicago, women whom we had never seen before, said, 'O yes, I know the *Woman's Exponent,* and it has enlightened me greatly on your question, especially concerning the women of your faith.'"[28] Wells published this editorial shortly after her return from the 1893 Chicago Exposition, where she and a delegation of Mormon clubwomen had joined with their peers from all areas of the United States to participate in the Congress of Women as well as other woman-centered activities included in the exposition.[29]

Given their earlier (but later revoked) access to the ballot box, Mormon clubwomen took a clear stance in favor of suffrage. Minutes of the UWPC for April 5, 1895—a time when politicians were debating whether woman suffrage should be included in the forthcoming state constitution—indicate that the club abandoned its planned program to discuss the debate and plan a petition drive in support of including woman suffrage in the Utah state constitution.[30] In reporting on the World's Congress of Women held at the Chicago Exposition in 1893 and attended by more than a dozen Mormon clubwomen, Emmeline Wells asserted that "the woman suffrage question was one of the most popular themes of discussion presented" and described suffragist Susan B. Anthony as the most popular woman of the Congress.[31] When Ellis Shipp, a physician and member of the UWPC, reported on the 1895 meeting of the National Council of Women, a group that favored giving women the vote, she glowed with accounts of having "met some of the brightest women of America" and having seen women "so busily engaged in elevating humanity."[32] Suffrage thus gave Mormon clubwomen a rhetorical platform upon which they could build exchanges with their Gentile sisters.

Records show that Mormon clubwomen measured their own progress in creating linkages with non-Mormon women. In 1894, after attending a meeting of the exclusionary Ladies' Literary Club of Salt Lake, a Gentile group, Emmeline Wells wrote in her diary: "Some years ago, no Mormon could be admitted as visitors even, but now things are different—we [Mormon women] are sought after. . . . We are getting more recognition and stand more on an equality with other women than formerly."[33] Associations with women in the General Federation yielded similar results. Writing from Washington, D.C., where her husband served as representative from Utah, Isabel Cameron Brown described a meeting of the Woman's Press Club in that city. After outlining the papers given by members, she commented: "Nearly every one of the ladies that I met knew Mrs. Wells personally and all said such nice things about her."[34] Emmeline Wells worked with Jennie June Croly, founder of the General Federation of Women's Clubs, and was a guest in her home in New York, an experience she later described in the *Woman's Exponent* after Croly's death. May Wright Sewall, a leader in both the General Federation of Women's Clubs and in the National Council of Women, visited Salt Lake City after statehood had been granted, but her visit was prompted by club friendships that extended back more than a decade. As Emmeline Wells put it in her full-page article about

Sewall's visit, it was "a time we had both looked forward to for many years," and her enthusiastic account of every event in Sewall's four-day stay demonstrates its importance to Wells as well as to the Mormon clubwomen of Salt Lake.

Even as they emulated, exchanged texts with, and became friends of Gentile women, Mormon clubwomen renovated the term "clubwoman." Their identity as *Mormon* clubwomen remained ever-present even though they distinguished themselves from the more overtly religious Female Relief Society. Minutes mention prayers at the beginning and end of some meetings, and members frequently refer to one another with religiously inflected terms like "sister" or "saint." Their reading of British and American literature was interspersed with literature written by Mormon authors like Eliza Snow, Hannah King, Emily Woodmansee, and Sarah Carmichael, whose names appear in club minutes alongside the more familiar American and British ones. A *Women's Exponent* article on current literature listed as "books that can never . . . be surpassed. . . . *The Bible, The Book of Mormon, the Iliad, the Odyssey,* Shakespeare and Milton," asserting: "In the literary world alone were born many most glorious spirits, Hugo, Eliot, Dickens, Bancroft. But the brightest star in all this wondrous constellation, the brightest since the sorrowful Nazarene, was the spirit of *Joseph Smith the Prophet.*"[35] Such readings, claims, and tributes show how Mormon clubwomen reconceptualized literature to include the unique literary contributions of Mormons. In so doing, these women simultaneously affirmed their religious difference and identified themselves with Gentile clubwomen.

In addition, Mormon clubwomen also took advantage of every rhetorical opportunity to represent their religious traditions to non-Mormon clubwomen. The *Women's Exponent* regularly published articles about Mormon theology, paid tribute to church leaders, and affirmed Mormon values. At the World's Congress of Representative Women held at Chicago's 1893 exposition, Mormon clubwomen gave papers outlining the early history of Utah, describing women's achievements, and explaining the differences between first- and second-generation Mormon women of Utah. Whenever clubwomen from other religions expressed interest in the Mormon tradition, clubwomen responded fully. A paper titled "Why a Woman Should Desire to Be a Mormon" was "written by special request and read at Women's Clubs in New York," and club minutes include enthusiastic accounts of opportunities for sharing Mormon theology with other women. One woman, recently returned from a meeting in Washington, D.C., reported meeting with "liberal" women who "found they were dissatisfied with their religion, desiring something that touches the soul. She hoped many would be brought to acknowledge of the truth of the gospel."[36] For this woman, "liberal" means both a supporter of suffrage and someone willing to listen to the Mormon perspective. The networks of associations created by clubs, then, provided Mormon women with opportunities for evangelism as well as interactions with Gentiles.

At the same time that they deployed rhetoric to underscore their similarities with other clubwomen, Mormon clubwomen acknowledged that their religion would always mark them as unlike other Americans. They expressed resentment at the way others represented them. As an editorial in the *Woman's Exponent* put it: "There are still, however, many among the people of the outside world who think Mormon women have no method by which they express their true feelings and are ignorant of all the great questions of the day upon which other women are so well informed. It would be amusing if it were not such a serious matter, to hear how women of the world speak of Mormon women."[37] In describing a character in Sarah Grand's *Heavenly Twins,* a member of the Reapers Club observed: "She holds up a perfect moral, ideal standard to guide humanity, shows that man *must* and *can* bring to the marriage altar as unspotted a record as he demands from the bride. It is the doctrine of our *own* church as well all know, though the world will not receive it from a 'Mormon.'"[38] Although Mormon women were willing to emulate many of the practices of Gentile clubwomen, they remained intensely loyal to their religion and resisted any and all attempts to undermine it.

Mormon women deployed rhetoric effectively to negotiate a complex set of religious and political desires. In entering public life and seeking educational opportunities, they created linkages with their Gentile peers. Although it cannot be definitively proved that Mormon clubwomen facilitated Utah's successful petition for statehood in 1896, they certainly helped to ameliorate the negative perceptions of Mormon women. By becoming active in public life and participating in women's clubs, Mormon women were able to help Gentiles redefine Mormonism. Despite their embrace of liberal causes like suffrage and their willingness to adopt many practices common among Gentile women's clubs, Mormon women were not willing to separate their religious goals from their political aims. Mormon women saw, as Jill Mulvey Derr puts it, "obedience and faithfulness" as inextricably bound to women's cause.[39] Women's clubs consciously distinguished themselves from church-affiliated ladies' societies, but at the same time their rhetoric retained a number of religious markers.

Even though they remained strongly committed to their religion, Mormon women undertook rhetorical practices that allied them with feminists of other religions. Making public speeches, circulating petitions, voting, attending universities, and writing for publication—all these activities distanced Mormon women from the gendered roles assigned them by their religion. Complicating the one-dimensional roles of being Mormon wives and mothers, Mormon women moved outside the domestic boundaries of their lives to take on public positions. In one way these women were collaborating with Mormon patriarchs who supported their participation in public life. No doubt these patriarchs recognized the value of having women promote the Mormon cause. At the same time, however, Mormon women were collaborating with non-Mormon feminists who affirmed woman suffrage and encouraged women to become educated and participate in public life. These alliances probably helped to decrease Gentile anxieties and hostilities, but they also created opportunities for Mormon women to expand their horizons in several directions, including becoming ambassadors for their religion.

To ignore the religious beliefs of women who participate in public life, become educated, or join women's clubs is to miss an important part of their motivations, behavior, and impact. Sadly, the theoretical tools most readily available to scholars do little to help us "see" religion in a secular context, much less to consider the role of religious discourses in nation formation. Among the obstacles to considering the cultural effect of religious discourses are institutional ones. As the historian George Marsden has observed, higher education conflated the disestablishment of Protestant domination—which opened the way for educating Jews, Catholics, and agnostics—with a cultural secularism that banished religion altogether, leading to the "near exclusion of religious perspectives from dominant academic life."[40] A more powerful set of obstacles are the intellectual ones that emerged as the humanities became secularized. Aesthetics were increasingly detached from any traditional religious meaning, creating what the historian T. J. Jackson Lears has called "a surrogate religion of taste well suited to a secular culture of consumption."[41]

This conflation of institutional with intellectual secularization has rendered the discourses surrounding religion stunted, and religion provides, as historian Stephen Carter has put it, a source of embarrassment to American intellectuals.[42] Accordingly, discussions of evangelical Protestant religions are frequently one-dimensional and fail to articulate the internal complexities of specific groups, focusing instead on triviality or extremism.[43] Similarly, representations of contemporary Mormons frequently employ extreme examples and emphasize exoticism without attention to actual doctrines and practices.[44] The paucity of academic language about religion and the normative stance often accorded to mainline Protestant denominations frequently leads to the default view that religion is synonymous with a limited range of denominations. The limited secular academic language for religion means that the agency of rhetors within specific religious populations is often slighted, and that religion is rarely used as a category of analysis. In particular, the impoverished terms of academic discourses about religion make it difficult to perceive and explore the complexities that enable adherents of a given faith to remain completely devout while simultaneously embracing progressive secular causes.

As the case of Mormon women in the nineteenth century shows, although religion is typically conceptualized as personal and private, it can play complex and vital roles in public institutions and issues. Religion's shaping effect on the bodies and sexualities of Mormon women inflected their behavior just as it did the distorting mirror of antipolygamy novels and other anti-Mormon discourses. It inspired the rhetorical stances adopted by these women, and it fueled their emergence into public life. It generated a renovation of a new and more inclusive national identity, and it renovated the concept of "feminism" to include women who simultaneously held deep commitments to religious doctrines and practices *and* determination to take up positions in secular society, both to enhance their own independence and to protect their religion.

In his "Divinity School Address," Ralph Waldo Emerson offers an American perspective on Jesus Christ: "The idioms of his language and the figures of his rhetoric have usurped the place of his truth; and churches are not built on his principles but on his tropes. Christianity became a Mythus, as the poetic teaching of Greece or Egypt, before."[45] Although he focuses on Christianity, Emerson's point can be extended to religion more generally. Religion is always imagined, or socially constructed, and—as is true for constructs like gender, race, and class—it must be continually renovated. This renovation will allow for greater complexity in considering the relationship between the secular and the religious.

2

A RHETORIC OF OPPOSITION

THE SEVENTH-DAY ADVENTIST CHURCH AND THE SABBATH TRADITION

LIZABETH A. RAND

Remember the Sabbath day, to keep it holy. Six days you shall labor, and do
all your work; but the seventh day is a Sabbath to the Lord your God; in it you
shall not do any work, you, or your son, or your daughter, your manservant,
or your maidservant, or your cattle, or the sojourner who is within your gates;
for in six days the Lord made heaven and earth, the sea, and all that is in them,
and rested the seventh day; therefore the Lord blessed the Sabbath day and
hallowed it.

     —EXODUS 20:8–11

THE FOURTH COMMANDMENT, "Remember the Sabbath day, to keep it holy," has
been a central principle of the Seventh-day Adventist (SDA) church, a Christian
denomination with over sixteen million members worldwide, since its beginning. According to Adventist theologian Raymond F. Cottrell, "the Sabbath
was . . . in a very real sense, the unifying factor around which the Seventh-day
Adventist Church came into being, and it is still a potent force that binds together the Adventist people around the world, transcending all barriers of nationality, race, language, political ideology, and economic status."[1] Adventists
worship on Saturday—the seventh day of the week—because this is the day that
they believe God set aside for that purpose, the day that God sanctified and
blessed. Across the nation, and across the world, Seventh-day Adventists spend
the twenty-four-hour period from Friday sundown to Saturday sundown with
their families and friends. Many participate in special religious events on Friday evenings, followed by Sabbath school and Sabbath worship on Saturdays.
They share Sabbath meals and Sabbath rest. Secular talk, secular reading, and
secular activities are also generally put aside.

    The Seventh-day Adventist church, a denomination that developed out of a premillennial movement led by Baptist preacher William Miller in the 1840s, was cofounded by Ellen White and her husband James, along with Joseph Bates, a former sea captain, and shortly thereafter it made Battle Creek, Michigan, its home. The founders built much of the framework of the Adventist movement, with Mrs. White, as she's commonly referred to in Adventist literature, serving as the prophetic voice of the worldwide church. Adventism, both past and present, has contributed most significantly to the American landscape through its message of health and wellness. The Adventist church promotes vegetarianism, funds smoking cessation and addiction recovery programs, and operates a vast network of clinics and hospitals.

It is the Sabbath, however, that shapes the Adventist church's relationship to America more than anything else. For non–Seventh-day Christians (the vast majority of Christians in America), worship on Sunday is such an established custom, so outside of interpretation, that it holds little tension. Seventh-day Adventists, however, define themselves more by their opposition to worship on the first day, and their loyalty to the Saturday Sabbath as sacred time, than by any other moral or religious principle. Founding members believed themselves to be engaged in a cosmic battle against Sunday keepers. Modern-day Adventism in America remains powerfully shaped by a rhetoric of resistance to worship on the first day of the week. For Seventh-day Adventists, the day on which Christians worship (and what, specifically, should occur on that day) is a contested site of both spiritual and political meaning.

THE SABBATH COMMANDMENT IN WESTERN HISTORY: SUNDAY BECOMES SACRED

In his book *Please Don't Wish Me a Merry Christmas: A Critical History of the Separation of Church and State,* scholar Stephen M. Feldman argues convincingly that while America makes strong claims for the separation of church and state, the boundaries between the two are often blurred. The source of these less-than-strict boundaries can be traced back to the early history of the Christian church, as Christianity separated from Judaism and formed a complex relationship with Rome.[2] Christianity and the state "struck a deal for their mutual benefit" for the first of many times in the centuries to come—a deal that clearly privileged Christian identity over all others.[3] At this time, it was Jewish citizens who suffered the most, persecuted for their non-Christian beliefs and practices, including their day of worship.

Making use of the discourse of the New Testament, early Christians "[redefined] Jews as a subcultural Other."[4] Jews were assigned to the realm of the "carnal," the worldly, the flesh, whereas Christians were deemed to be otherworldly, spiritual, and blessed. In this manner, the Jewish faith became a scapegoat, carrying the sins of humanity, so that Christians were free to put their own transgressions aside to pursue a new path toward salvation. Feldman points out that the binary of spirituality versus carnality would become crucial to the development of the doctrine of church-state separation, as religion and laws governing the conduct of citizens were pulled apart from one another: "The Christian rejection of the Jewish Torah, which included laws for all aspects of social and civil life, facilitated this recognition [of two realms of differing authority] and approval of the Roman civil authority. In effect, the Christian repudiation of Jewish law opened a gap where the Roman civil law could legitimately function."[5] It is from within this gap that Sunday worship originated.

Contrary to an often-held assumption that Jesus or his disciples changed the day of worship for Christians from the Jewish Sabbath to Sunday, Kenneth Strand, a professor of Adventist church history, notes that "Sunday was not substituted for Saturday as the Christian weekly day of worship or rest during New Testament times."[6] This change occurred gradually, and from the second to the fifth centuries many Christians still observed the Jewish Sabbath, even as worship on the first day gained influence. In most regions Sunday overtook Saturday as the principal day of Christian fellowship through a two-stage process. Sunday was first treated as a day to hold worship services but also a day to work: "In [this] role, there would be no reason for conflict with the Saturday rest day."[7] Only later did Christians more strongly repudiate Jewish law, collaborating, at times, in unexpected ways with the Roman state to institutionalize Sunday more convincingly as a full day's experience of religion.

It might be surprising to modern-day Christians that Sunday emerged, in part, out of pagan traditions and customs, as a means for the church to establish itself as the dominant religious group. As pagan rhetoric was folded into Christianity, Sunday was transformed into an increasingly sacred and holy day. Samuele Bacchiocchi, an Adventist theologian and author of "The Rise of Sunday Observance in Early Christianity," describes how the early Christian church embraced various features of sun-cult symbolism, and that "Sun worship with its 'Sun-day' was influential in determining the choice of Sunday [as the new day of worship.] . . . [Sunday] provided a fitting symbology that could efficaciously commemorate and explain to the pagan world two fundamental events of the history of salvation—*creation* and *resurrection*."[8] It is no coincidence, Bacchiocchi argues, that Sunday was viewed by the early church as the day that God created light in addition to the day that God's son or "sun" was risen. Bacchiocchi describes church leaders' logic as follows: "'If it is called day of the Sun by the pagans, we most willingly acknowledge it as such, since it is on this day that the *light of the world has appeared* and on this day the *Sun of Justice has risen*.'"[9]

Early Christian church leaders defined Sunday using increasingly devout language, heightening the contrast between Sunday and the Jewish day of worship. Strand identifies the Council of Laodicea, a Roman Catholic council, as issuing in 364 AD the first ecclesiastical Sunday law, decreeing that Christians should treat Sunday as a day of rest, and they should work instead on Saturday: "'Christians shall not Judaize and be idle on Saturday but shall work on that day; [and] the Lord's day they shall especially honour, and, as being Christian, shall, if possible, do no work on that day.'"[10] Fourth-century Christian leaders did not completely prohibit work on Sunday because, they claimed, the Jewish practice of Sabbath rest led people to "wicked idleness."[11] In obvious contradiction, Christians also characterized the Sabbath as too exhaustive and strict: by the end of the sixth century, Pope Gregory worried that Jewishness was negatively impacting the church by shaping Christians' attitudes about what could or could not be done on Sundays. "This paradoxical caricature by Christians of the Jewish Sabbath as both too rigorous and too idle," writes Craig Harline, professor of history at Brigham Young University, "would persist for centuries."[12]

Although the term "blue law"—"the colloquial term for state statutes that regulate or prohibit entertainment and commercial activities on Sundays or religious holidays"—was not used until much later, the actions of the early church clearly set the stage for such restrictions.[13] British colonists brought blue laws with them to America: "Blue laws in colonial America were both widespread and frequently enforced, most commonly through the levying of substantial fines."[14] Even our first president was reprimanded for ignoring a Sunday restriction: as George Washington traveled to New York from Connecticut in 1789, he was stopped by an official for unnecessary travel on the Lord's day; he was allowed to continue after vowing to go only as far as his immediate destination (which was, after all, to attend a worship service).[15] The lawyer Lesley Lawrence-Hammer has observed that "colonial blue laws survived the American Revolution and the enactment of the First Amendment relatively unscathed."[16] In the nineteenth century, blue law enforcement was intensified, including a successful campaign to end Sunday mail delivery. Seventh-day Adventism was founded at the height of moral sentiment over proper behavior on the first day of the week. It would respond by constructing its own distinct culture, running parallel to but separate from the American way of life.

THE SABBATH COMMANDMENT AS
RESISTANCE TO AMERICAN TIME

In coauthors Malcolm Bull and Keith Lockhart's groundbreaking study of Seventh-day Adventism, *Seeking a Sanctuary,* they point out that the American dream, if it were to be described, would include the following components: "(1) the belief that the American Revolution created a state uniquely blessed by God in which human beings have unprecedented opportunities for self-realization and material gain; (2) the conviction that the American nation, through both example and leadership, offers hope for the rest of the world; and (3) the assumption that it is through individual, rather than collective, effort that the progress of humanity will be achieved."[17] According to Bull and Lockhart, the early Adventist church boldly rejected the American dream as popularly defined and offered a different narrative for its followers, one that depended on the rejection of Sunday and all that it symbolized as the most sacred day of the week: "[SDAs] did not accept that the republican experiment would lead to the betterment of humanity or that it would be a lasting success. They consigned America to eventual destruction, and in place of the nation, they daringly substituted themselves as the true vehicle for the redemption of the world."[18]

Most American Seventh-day Adventists still believe that the Sabbath will be the defining issue in the last days before Christ's return, and that the state (this time in the form of America) will once again join hands with powerful religious forces in what will ultimately be a futile (though deadly) attempt to disparage the seventh day. They believe that Seventh-day Adventists will combat these forces, emerge victorious, and bring forth God's salvation. In Seventh-day Adventist founder Ellen White's *The Great Controversy*, a widely known and frequently quoted text within both historical and modern Adventism, she traces the battles between Christ and Satan throughout history, describing in great detail the final war to be waged over good and evil.[19] In the last days, Mrs. White admonishes, Satan will try to persuade as many human beings as he can to worship on Sunday, even going so far as to institute Sunday laws that only the most faithful of God's people will refuse to obey. America, along with Sunday-keeping Protestant and Catholic churches, will attempt to enforce these laws. "In this scenario," Bull and Lockhart point out, "the division between the saved and the damned hinges on which day of the weekly cycle is considered more important. The essential criterion of salvation is a correct apprehension of temporal sequence. Time, the least visible of divisions, is the basis for an irreversible separation of good and evil."[20] In other words, only those who accept the seventh-day Sabbath and remain loyal to it will be a part of God's remnant group.

Persecution is a recurring theme in Adventist literature; clearly, it served as a means for the church to shape its own identity and to differentiate itself from the mainstream Christian world. In the early days of the Adventist movement, SDAs were taunted by rock-throwing mobs, their property was destroyed, and of course they were jailed for working on Sunday (fines, jail, and job termination emerged as the primary means of penalizing modern SDAs for Sabbath observance). In *The Great Controversy*, Mrs. White warns her fellow Adventists that those who uphold the "measure of light" granted to them will necessarily face trial and tribulation: "Opposition is the lot of all whom God employs to present truths specially applicable to their time."[21] During Mrs. White's many years as an influential public speaker and writer whose message circulated widely in the church, she repeatedly characterized Advent followers as an "unpopular little company" of commandment keepers spurned by the world's multitudes. Denounced as "enemies of law and order" who cause "anarchy" by means of their loyalty to the Sabbath, SDAs, according to Mrs. White, would eventually be "misrepresented and condemned. A false coloring will be given to their words; the worst construction will be put upon their motives."[22] Mrs. White exhorted SDAs to think oppositionally, independent of social norms and despite worldly contempt—a principle of Adventism that is deeply embedded within the modern-day church.

SDAs believe that it is Satan in whose hands the true Sabbath was corrupted. For Seventh-day Adventists, Satan's presence in the world—historically and presently—is palpable and startlingly real. In *The Great Controversy,* Mrs. White describes Satan as the most nefarious enemy of Christ (and therefore of all that Christ represents), both an external being and an inner force who can find his way deep into people's hearts and minds. Mrs. White warns that the devil takes pleasure in spreading the belief that he is merely a scary, childish invention of the imagination who does not really exist: "He is well pleased to be painted as a ludicrous or loathsome object, misshapen, half animal and half human. He is pleased to hear his name used in sport and mockery by those who think themselves intelligent and well informed."[23] Rather, Seventh-day Adventists describe Satan as an insidious master of deception, a skilled rhetorician who works to infiltrate people's thoughts, words, and actions (although, finally, not without their consent).

According to Mrs. White, SDAs were to be "soldiers" prepared to do battle against him—the "mighty general" whose aim is to wage war against the authority and supremacy of God: "He seeks to draw away the soldiers of the cross from their strong fortification, while he lies in ambush with his forces, ready to destroy all who venture upon his ground."[24] Early Adventists believed that the most effective way for church members to defend themselves against Satan, and against Sunday—to build a powerfully resistant critical stance—was to acquire reading, writing, and thinking skills. Publishing and printing companies were quickly established by the church. Soon, Adventism became a champion of the first amendment, asserting its viewpoint that the state should not legislate matters of worship. The first Adventist journal to focus on church-state separation, an Adventist publication still in existence, was called the *Sabbath Sentinel* (1884), later changed to, simply, *Liberty.* The church also created a Department of Religious Liberty at the beginning of the twentieth century, in addition to spearheading several other groups, all of which promoted the cause of religious freedom around the world.[25] When the church determined that conflict with the government was unavoidable, the Adventist church, through these organizations, took a strong oppositional stance.

The tension between Seventh-day Adventism and the government heightened in 1863–64 when the National Reform Association (NRA) was created—a group representing numerous Protestant denominations intent on forging a more obvious relationship between church and state. The NRA promoted a constitutional amendment that identified the United States as a Christian nation and, consequently, a nation that should follow Christian principles like worship on the first day of the week.[26] The NRA critiqued, for example, immigrant Roman Catholics for spending too much time on Sunday in secular pursuits, even if they did attend church; it critiqued businesses for requiring their employees to work on that day. Seventh-day Adventists strongly opposed the amendment as they suspected it would lead to Sunday worship being required by the state. They feared that the amendment would instigate a battle that they were not yet prepared to fight, believing that too many of the churched and unchurched had not heard the Adventist message nor had the opportunity to embrace it. Congress eventually rejected the amendment.

In the United States, Adventist opposition to worship on Sunday focused on opposing state-legislated Sunday observance—and church-state collaboration in general. During the late nineteenth and early twentieth centuries, for example, the church fought Sunday blue laws in such states as California, Colorado, Maine, Missouri, New Jersey, Ohio, Pennsylvania, and Tennessee, as well as congressional rulings such as the mandate that the 1893 World's Fair in Chicago be shuttered on Sunday. It should be noted that Sunday laws were opposed by non-SDA citizens as well; one can find such non-SDA signatures as Clarence Darrow's and Thomas Edison's on anti–Sunday-closing petitions. The rationale for blue laws often referenced the need of the American worker for a day off, an argument that appealed to many: "Promoters [of Sunday laws] increasingly associated the needs of the new industrial proletariat for a day of rest with the voices of the traditional religious emphasis. Thus Sunday enforcement was given an idealistic humanitarian guise."[27] The Adventist church opposed such thinking by arguing that Sunday laws were never merely civil in nature, but always also religious (a position that is hard to refute, at least in part because a different, nonreligious day of the week was never proposed as an alternative day of rest in place of Sunday). Adventists were undoubtedly unpopular because of the position that they took (fulfilling Mrs. White's prophecy that they would be an outsider group). The historian Craig Harline, in his book *Sunday*, notes that anti–Sunday keepers "were often labeled as un-American, even secularist, atheist, or Communist, for wanting to open on Sunday. That Christian and other merchants who opened as usual on Saturdays had an unfair advantage over Jewish [and Adventist] merchants, who closed two days a week, usually went unmentioned."[28]

Seventh-day Adventists and others who opposed blue laws also argued that these laws were defined inconsistently and enforced in a less-than-predictable manner. Exemptions for the purpose of commerce or entertainment (which were invented almost immediately after blue laws went into effect) often seemed arbitrary from state to state: "[In Pennsylvania, one] could buy tricycles on Sunday but not bicycles, [in Philadelphia, one] could buy seat covers for a car but not slip covers for a couch, and a real football for teens but not a toy football for kids. . . . [In Massachusetts], one could dig for clams but not dredge for oysters."[29] Jews and Christian Sabbatarians, rather than contributing to an increasingly confusing array of exemptions, challenged blue laws on constitutional grounds. Despite this opposition, in 1961 Sunday laws were upheld by the United States Supreme Court in several important cases, including *Braunfeld v. Brown* and *McGowan v. Maryland.* The scholar Stephen Feldman notes that, of great significance, Chief Justice Earl Warren, writing for the majority opinion in *McGowan,* argued that blue laws—despite their religious origin—did not violate the Establishment clause, since there were, in fact, compelling secular reasons to maintain them. Feldman quotes Warren's words:

> It is common knowledge that the first day of the week has come to have special significance as a rest day in this country. People of all religions and people with no religion regard Sunday as a time for family activity, for visiting friends and relatives, for late sleeping, for passive and active entertainments, for dining out, and the like. . . . Sunday is a day apart from all others. The cause is irrelevant; the fact exists. It would seem unrealistic for enforcement purposes and perhaps detrimental to the general welfare to require a State to choose a common day of rest other than that which most persons would select of their own accord.[30]

Warren's discourse effectively dismisses arguments made by the religious minority over the meaning of Sunday (and the Saturday Sabbath): it is "common knowledge" that Sunday is a day set apart from all other days of the week; people of "all religions" and "no religions" treat Sunday as a day of leisure; the cause of Sunday exclusivity is "irrelevant." "Constitutional rhetoric," according to Feldman, "effectively neutralizes or normalizes many common forms of Christian societal domination by declaring or coding them to be secular."[31] Today, Sunday closing laws still exist, preventing such things as liquor sales and the purchase of automobiles from car dealerships, though fewer laws remain in effect and these laws have less overall impact. It is certainly the case that as an "experience," Sunday remains for most American citizens a day "apart from all others," whether it be a time for religious observance or the last day of "the weekend," a time to rest, relax, shop, entertain, travel, and so on. Seventh-day Adventists have "recreated America within America" because "while forced to share American space . . . [SDAs try to exempt themselves] from American time (a time bounded by annihilation)."[32]

Worship, enacted in time, is a site of rhetorical tension, highlighting the opposition to a sacred Sunday that Seventh-day Adventists have expressed in both their words and their actions, and their indignation (though it is mostly a quiet indignation, which has allowed Adventists to coexist peacefully along-side non-SDAs) over the perceived lack of respect that America has shown for the true Sabbath, Saturday. As a non-Adventist who has studied Adventism for more than a decade, five of those years in an ethnographic context, I feel fairly certain that a majority of SDAs in America do, in fact, firmly believe that worship on the Saturday Sabbath is a necessary condition (though not the only one) for salvation. Still, as is the case in any large religious group, differences do exist within the ranks of its members, and even something as central as the seventh day is not outside the boundaries of dispute among Adventists themselves.

On the periphery of Adventism are SDA institutions run by laypeople outside of strict governance by the denomination.[33] These institutions form a movement, though a loosely organized one: "an interlaced network of people, places, and publications that share certain ideals and have a common heritage. . . . [permitting] adherence to the Adventist denomination through partial op-position to it. In this it may be seen to function in relation to Adventism in precisely the same way that Adventism functions in relation to the mainstream of American life."[34] I have interviewed members of this movement, generally the most conservative members of the church, who are not afraid to express their conviction that most SDAs themselves do not practice the Sabbath as se-riously as they should. Because this movement does not challenge the sanctity of Sabbath keeping itself, mainstream Adventism permits its resistant rhetoric, even though the resistant rhetoric is aimed at the denomination itself.

Law professor Stephen L. Carter, in his book *Civility*, has noted that "in a democratic polity, religions serve the important societal function of resistance: standing up for the possibility that life itself has different meanings than those the dominant culture tries to create."[35] The fact that Seventh-day Adventists devote a twenty-four-hour period from sundown on Friday to sundown on Saturday to spiritual study and practice, rest, nature, family, and volunteer-ism, resisting time as it has been defined by mainstream Christianity and the state is, I believe, to be regarded positively (as is, of course, many aspects of their health message and their growing concern and respect for the environ-ment). Nonetheless, it is the case that the Sabbath serves as a barrier between Seventh-day Adventists and a vast majority of other Americans. One does not have to search very hard for evidence that this barrier remains firmly intact within the twenty-first century church.

In February 2012 the former general secretary of the National Council of Churches—a non-Adventist—was invited to speak at Andrews University, arguably the premier institution of higher learning in the Adventist educational system. His presentation was titled "The Ecumenical Movement and Why You Should Be Involved." Given the Adventist metanarrative laid out so forcefully by Mrs. White in *The Great Controversy*, the significance of such an event is more than noteworthy (one SDA website calling itself "The Third Angel's Message" described it as "a grand seismic spiritual event"). The speaker was friendly and complimentary in his remarks, as suggested by *Spectrum* writer Landon Schnabel's coverage of the event: "'I like who you are and it's a joy to be here.'" He also, however, urged Adventism to become more engaged in the interchurch movement, holding on less tightly to the truth that separates it theologically from other Christians: "'My concern, if I can put it that way, is with your grammar. 'Adventist' is a wonderful adjective, but an idolatrous noun. You are not Seventh-day Adventists, but Seventh-day Adventist Christians.'"[36]

That Andrews University had anticipated the controversial nature of this event is obvious, given the statement that it issued prior to the speaker's visit. The dean of Andrews Theological Seminary reassured the community that distinctive Adventist beliefs were not under siege: "This invitation and lecture should not be perceived or crafted as an attempt at rewriting our historical Adventist faith. We believe in the Three Angels' Messages and the other tenets of our faith. We continue to promote religious liberty and the freedom of conscience. This is not a first step to join the NCC or any other such organizations and we are not promoting ecumenism." The dean continued, though, by reminding Adventists that they were "no longer a small, unknown denomination" and that "it's vital for [SDAs] to learn how to dialog and relate to others despite having a different theology. The ability to understand other viewpoints, including differing religious views, is an essential part of a good education."[37]

After the event, an Andrews Seminary professor was asked to respond to the guest speaker's presentation. The text of his response suggests that he tried to model the kind of rhetorical sensibility recommended by the dean. He concedes that some Adventist worship practices "have been adapted from our Christian friends" and that "Seventh-day Adventists are themselves the result of a truly ecumenical movement." The Sabbath, however, is the fundamental obstacle to full participation in an interfaith effort: "The Sabbath provides practical, historic/prophetic, and theological barriers to our fully joining the modern ecumenical movement. . . . We are . . . sensitive, maybe at times overly so, to projects that wish to seek unity by playing the game of doctrinal or theological minimalization."[38] In a rejoinder, the non-Adventist guest speaker expressed his interest in a discussion of the Sabbath but asked if Seventh-day Adventists are willing to put the issue of the specific day of worship aside.

An observer of the event described the almost visceral reaction of the audience to his query: "The tension in the room rose and a resounding 'no!' could be heard throughout the auditorium."[39] This response on the part of the Adventist community might best be described as a rhetorical refusal—a term used by composition scholar John Schilb "to denote an act of writing or speaking in which the rhetor pointedly refuses to do what the audience considers rhetorically normal. By rejecting a procedure that the audience expects, the rhetor seeks the audience's assent to another principle, cast as a higher priority."[40] Schilb wishes to distinguish acts such as these from simply rebellious behavior (although they may be viewed as such by some); instead, rhetorical refusals are "actively aimed at persuading their audience of something. . . . they are not indifferent to the audience. Rather, they are efforts to shape its thinking, however unusual the means."[41]

Adventist opposition to Sunday as the Christian day of worship is such a refusal: SDAs are not indifferent to their non-Adventist audience; quite the contrary, they believe that their audience's very salvation depends upon the articulation of a higher principle. Schilb points out that "rhetorical refusals can also serve to illuminate dynamics of power. Consciously or unconsciously, often the refusers contest hierarchies that would otherwise govern their utterances."[42] Seventh-day Adventists contest the American manifestation of time, viewing the seventh day to be sacred when the majority of citizens around them treat it as "Saturday," a secular day tied to nonreligious pursuits. Adventists and Sunday keepers have "[occupied] separate paradigms" since the church's beginnings in the nineteenth century.[43] Today, Adventist institutions—mostly hospitals, vegetarian food manufacturers, and other wellness-based businesses—have earned the respect of many non-Adventist citizens who rely on their services and buy their products. Nonetheless, Adventism maintains a distinct identity and an oppositional discourse at odds with the American way of life.

THE RISE OF FEMALE RHETORS

—

3

—

PREACHING FROM THE PULPIT STEPS

MARY BOSANQUET FLETCHER AND WOMEN'S
PREACHING IN EARLY METHODISM

VICKI TOLAR BURTON

ON FEBRUARY 2, 1773, Mary Bosanquet (1739–1815) recorded in her journal: "I went this day to A—. Had a good time in speaking from those words, 'O Nebuchadnezzar, we are not careful to answer thee in this matter.'"[1] Situated in her journal between an entry on being in bad spirits and another on a road trip during which the horse grew ill, this passage seems quite ordinary. But the passage is in fact extraordinary, for it is considered the first written record of a Methodist woman's sermon and signals a historic time, when a movement was enacting rhetorical change from preaching as a genre always gendered male to preaching as a genre open to use by women.

Mary Bosanquet (later Fletcher) was one of the leading women preachers of the first generation of British Methodism, with a preaching career that spanned more than fifty years and influenced thousands of people, many of them poor and otherwise unchurched. She was a close colleague and friend of Methodism's founder, John Wesley (1703–1791), and the power of her preaching and her written defense of women's preaching were crucial in convincing Wesley to alter his position on women's preaching from opposition to qualified approval.

Preaching by women was not a common practice in the Protestantism of the

---

eighteenth century, though there were scattered examples among the Quakers and Anabaptists.[2] Early Methodists considered themselves a part of the Church of England, a denomination that did not allow preaching by women. How did women come to preach in early Methodism, and what persuaded Wesley to support them? I address these questions by examining the rhetorical practices and writings of Mary Bosanquet Fletcher, drawing insight from rhetorical genre theory as it applies to both speech and writing.

Using insights from Kathleen Hall Jamieson and Karlyn Kohrs Campbell's article "Rhetorical Hybrids: Fusions of Generic Elements," I argue that women's preaching entered Methodism through a blending or hybridizing of rhetorical genres used to support a rapidly growing movement that needed more religious leaders but found traditional male leadership in short supply. According to Jamieson and Campbell, rhetorical hybrids are "dynamic" responses to situation and audience, responses that combine elements of two or more genres.[3] In Mary Bosanquet's defense of women's preaching and in her experience as a preacher, we see the fusion of features of various genres. Methodist women hybridized both speech genres and written genres in ways that opened preaching as a genre to women with an "extraordinary call." Bosanquet's hybridizing rhetorical strategies included construction of an ethos that blended female modesty with sharp (masculine) intellect, a sense of what might be called *kairos* in choosing where and when to speak, collaboration with those who could negotiate opportunities for her to speak, and blending of sacred rhetorical space with ordinary spaces of life.

This use of rhetorical hybrids occurred in a social context in which the disruption of traditional preaching as a genre had already begun. Unable to attract enough ordained Anglican clergymen to sustain his followers, Wesley began to allow preaching by laymen who had experienced what he identified as an "extraordinary call" from God. This employment of laymen as preachers began the process of genre disruption. Because most preachers in early Methodism were not ordained, they typically were forbidden to preach in Anglican churches, and so for many years their preaching was not pulpit-centered. Rather, it might occur out-of-doors, with the preacher standing on a hillside or a stump or a wagon, or it might occur in a home, a rented room, or a barn.[4] The pulpit as a location of rhetorical authority was traditionally gendered male, but what about preaching spaces like the wagon, the hillside, or the home?

SPEECH GENRES OF METHODIST WOMEN

Compared to the limited opportunities for public speech generally available to women in eighteenth-century British culture, Methodism offered a remarkable array of ways that women might gain rhetorical experience. This is not surprising since women easily outnumbered men in the movement. Historian

Earl Kent Brown's study of the forms of public utterance available to early Methodist women offers a useful frame for understanding the emergence of women's preaching and the process of genre fusion. Brown says that all Methodists, including women, were expected to engage in spiritual conversation with one another and with non-Methodists. They were also encouraged to speak and pray aloud in classes and bands.[5] (While bands were groups of ten or fewer separated by gender and marital status, classes were larger neighborhood groups of both men and women).[6] In fact, public prayer in class or band was the usual entry to public speech for women, followed by testimony—the most common of women's public discourse. While most women might testify, fewer women would move to the next levels of discourse: exhorting, expounding, and preaching.[7] The subtle differences among the genres of testimony, exhorting, expounding, and preaching in various contexts led to the possibility of fusing features of these genres.

A woman giving testimony to a band meeting of other women, to a mixed class of men and women, or to the larger local Methodist society would stand and tell the gathering about her private spiritual experience. In Methodism, testimony was not a onetime test for membership but rather a frequent spiritual sharing, or what Wesley often called, "declaring what God has done for your soul." Through the experience of giving testimony, women learned to identify their own spiritual stories, to tell them aloud before others, and, most important, to value their own spiritual experience.

In Methodism, exhortation was a special speech genre, in many locations open to both men and women. Its goal was motivational. In exhorting, a speaker would stand before gathered listeners, usually after a sermon had been delivered by someone else, and fervently urge those gathered to embrace the message of the sermon, to employ it in their lives, and to "go on to perfection," that is, to seek union with God's will. Some preachers traveled with their own favorite exhorter. Others relied on local talent. When no preacher was available for a service, as was often the case in rural Methodist societies, a man or woman (perhaps an exhorter) from the society might read aloud one of Wesley's published sermons and then exhort the listeners to apply it to their lives.[8] The historian John H. Wigger has observed of early American Methodism: "Since a thin line separated much of early Methodist preaching from exhorting, Methodist female exhorters undoubtedly used their public speech opportunities to preach what were, in effect, sermons."[9] As historian of rhetoric Lisa J. Shaver has noted in her work on nineteenth-century American women's oratory, some Methodist women acted as exhorters even on their deathbeds.[10]

The last two speech genres—expounding and preaching—were more contested in terms of who might freely perform them. "Expounding," which is interpreting a text and explaining its meaning to a group, is both an intellectual activity and a rhetorical one. Speakers expounded not only scriptural passages but also other religious texts. Because Bible study was common in Methodist bands and classes, it is likely that ordinary women and men expounded in small groups. But exposition (the product of expounding) was also part of preaching, as the preacher "took a text" from scripture and constructed a sermon that interpreted and applied it to the lives of listeners.[11] While Brown's construct of women's rhetoric is positioned within the specific structure of Methodism, an alternate, more broadly focused interpretation of women's preaching across denominations is offered by rhetoric scholar Jane Donawerth. She has argued that women's rhetoric from 1600 to 1900, including preaching, can be theorized as conversation rather than public discourse.[12] Donawerth's definition of a sermon does not appear to require that it be based on a biblical text, as was the practice in Methodism.

Constantly in play in early Methodism were the situations in which each of these rhetorical genres might be practiced—the setting (public or private?), the size of the group (when does a small group become a large group?), the relationship of genres to each other, even the spontaneity with which the events arose. The experience of Mary Bosanquet demonstrates how women's preaching emerged in Methodism by an organic fusion of genres in irregular settings.

CARING FOR THE POOR, SPEAKING FOR GOD

Born in 1739 to a wealthy Anglican family near London, Mary Bosanquet was converted to Methodism at age seven by a family servant who was a Methodist.[13] Through a Methodist lens, Mary came to see her family's privileged lifestyle, their elaborate balls in London and holidays at Bath, their fancy clothes and obsession with the theater, as excessive, frivolous, and un-Godly. At age seventeen, according to historian D. R. Wilson, Mary experienced a call from God, which she described to Sarah Crosby in a letter. Mary dreamed that a bright cloud descended and a voice called to her: "Thou shalt walk with me in White, for I will make thee worthy."[14] By age twenty-two, Bosanquet was so openly hostile to her parents' lifestyle that she took her inheritance from her grandmother, left home, and set up life on her own in London. There she lived in Christian community with other women, joining a group of Methodist women that included Sarah Crosby (1729–1804), the first Methodist woman to preach, and Sarah Ryan (1724–1768), former head mistress of Wesley's school at Kingswood. In this community Bosanquet practiced Christian conversation, prayed in public, gave spiritual testimony, and studied and interpreted Scripture. When at age twenty-four she came into the full possession of her grandmother's home and property, "The Cedars" in Leytonstone outside London, she established a residential school for orphaned children and a home for sick, elderly, and destitute women. The school thrived for five years in Leytonstone and then for thirteen more at Cross Hall near Leeds, where she moved to avoid the criticism that had grown in Leytonstone.[15] Bosanquet's journal records that the children who came to them were often "naked, full of vermin, and [. . .] afflicted with distemper."[16] Her household grew until it contained ten or twelve women and eighteen to twenty children, all supported by Bosanquet's ever-dwindling inheritance.

Having refused suitors chosen by her parents, Bosanquet created for herself a life that was stubbornly single but never solitary. Those she gathered became an impressive, if needy, family. As a head of household with clear spiritual responsibilities, she offered her charges not only food and shelter but also maternal care that included care of their souls. Bosanquet's method of discerning prayer suggests why she was so beloved by her ragtag household of orphans and needy women:

> I will call over each member in my mind with solemn prayer, and search out every perfection of every kind, every trace of the image of God which I can discern in each, and enter them on paper, adding thereto every fresh discovery; and then to each name affix a plan, denoting what is the best method of helping the infirmities and strengthening the virtues of that person. If I do not thus study the tempers and dispositions of my family, how unlike will my carriage be to that of my heavenly Father towards me![17]

With Bosanquet employing this profound and loving model of parenting and pastoral care, it is not surprising that John Wesley considered Bosanquet and her household a pattern for others to follow.

Caring for her household led Bosanquet to public discourse and eventually to preaching. She and Sarah Ryan gathered their "family" for evening prayers and spoke with them about the condition of their souls. These services included spiritual conversation, prayer, scripture reading, and exhorting. In response to requests from poor neighbors in the area, Bosanquet initiated a Thursday-evening prayer meeting for her large household and for neighbors, subtly transforming her role from a woman leading her own family in religious devotions to a woman leading a community in public worship. Even after John Wesley answered Bosanquet's request that he send Leytonstone a male preacher for Sunday worship, Mary Bosanquet and Sarah Ryan continued their evening services.

Gradually, Bosanquet began receiving—and judiciously accepting—invitations to speak to other Methodist groups, and at some point her public prayers, scripture reading, and expounding blended in the context of new rhetorical situations into what was clearly preaching. Her ethos, her skills in exegesis, her delivery, and her evangelical effectiveness grew with experience. Although hundreds gathered to hear her speak, others—including some Methodist preachers—objected strongly to her public address. As Bosanquet was to learn, bringing good news to the poor has its perils: as it attracts multitudes, it also attracts censure from those whose view of the truth is threatened.

A DEFENSE OF WOMEN'S PREACHING

In 1771, in an attempt to relieve her own distress over the attacks upon her, Mary Bosanquet wrote to John Wesley describing her dilemma and the opposition she was experiencing.[18] She laid out her arguments in favor of women's preaching and asked for his guidance. Her letter is considered the first defense of women's preaching in Methodism, and the letter's effectiveness can be understood by looking at both its rhetorical genres and its appeals. As Jamieson and Campbell demonstrate, rhetors can blend genres to achieve more than one purpose. A prime example is Bosanquet's letter defending women's preaching. Blending the genre of the spiritual letter with a forensic apologia for her own preaching, Bosanquet embeds within the apologia a deliberative turn that justifies not only her own preaching but also that of other women with an extraordinary call.

The first section of the letter contains markers of the spiritual letter. Bosanquet begins by establishing a personal connection to the addressee, John Wesley, through the salutation, "Very dear and Honoured Sir." Apologizing for not writing sooner, a move that immediately places this letter in the context of a larger correspondence between Bosanquet and Wesley, she increases intimacy by connecting her own struggles to those Wesley has experienced, writing: "How painful it is to be forced to contend with those with whom one desires above all things to live in peace, is well known to you, Sir, by experience."[19] A second marker of the spiritual letter is that Bosanquet explicitly seeks Wesley's spiritual direction, saying she is confident "God will make you my director in these things." Knowing Wesley will not be happy that she is in conflict with the Methodist preachers, she confesses her extreme suffering in this situation and promises "my soul desires peace, particularly with those that act as heads among us." Through all of these moves, Bosanquet constructs an ethos of pious suffering, humble willingness to submit to Wesley's will, and concern for peace within the larger institution of Methodism.[20]

Before moving to the explicit defense or apologia for her preaching, Bosanquet sets it up by creating a negative ethos for her opponents. She tells Wesley that the cause of her internal suffering is an external exigence situated in the attacks and reprimands she has suffered from various Methodist preachers because of her preaching. In a brief narrative she describes how she has been attacked and accused of violating the Pauline prohibition against women's preaching. One male preacher "thought it quite unscriptural for women to speak in the church and his conscience constrained him to prevent it." She associates her attackers with "Satan" because they tempted her to deny her call. Throughout the narrative she skillfully strengthens her ethos by offering evidence that she has met Wesley's tests for a preacher: evidence of faith and devotion to God ("I believe I am called to do all I can for God"); gifts for the work including the ability to speak publicly with clarity and justice ("Hundreds of unawakened persons were there, and my heart yearned over them"); and evidence of success in converting hearers ("hundreds of carnal persons [were] coming to my prayer meetings, who would not go near a preaching house; and it is enough to say God was with us and made it known by the effects in many places").[21]

Midway through the letter, Bosanquet makes an abrupt shift of tone and genre, adopting the form and voice of a defendant responding to charges in a court. In this forensic apologia her ethos changes from humble sufferer to accomplished forensic rhetorician. She labels the accusations made against her "Ob" (objections) and her answers "An," and her text reads like the transcript of a trial, with her defense based upon a sophisticated exegesis of both Old and New Testament scripture. For example, she answers the charge that speaking in public is immodest for women by offering a parallel case argument through rhetorical identification with biblical females who spoke in public:

> Now I do not apprehend Mary sinned against either of these heads [purity and humility], or could in the least be accused of immodesty, when she carried the joyful news of her Lord's Resurrection and in that sense taught the Teachers of Mankind [the apostles]. Neither was the woman of Samaria to be accused of immodesty when she invited the whole city to come to Christ. Neither do I think the woman mentioned in the 20th chapter of the 2nd Samuel could be said to sin against modesty, tho' she called the General of the opposite army to converse with her, and then (verse the 22nd) went to all the people both Heads and others, to give them her advice and by it the City was saved. Neither do I suppose Deborah did wrong in publicly declaring the message of the Lord, and afterwards accompanying Barak to war, because his hands hung down at going without her.[22]

Bosanquet's elegant exegesis adds a new aspect to her ethos: pious and humble, yes, but also learned and insightful with regard to biblical teachings. Facility with scripture adds to her qualifications to preach under Wesley's rules. As she constructs her case, she also enacts it.

An obvious model for Bosanquet's forensic defense lies in Wesley's published minutes of the annual conference of Methodist preachers, which served as the official record of policies established at the conference and often contained sections composed in the style used by Bosanquet. Wesley would state a question or objection that had been raised at the conference and follow it with his version of the appropriate response, which became official policy. Further, within Wesley's published journals are numerous examples of apologia in which Wesley defends his own conduct or, more generally, practices of the Methodists.[23]

Within Bosanquet's forensic argument, another rhetorical move is the attempt to establish common ground with her opponents, thus portraying herself as one aligned with the good of the movement. Bosanquet's strategy is to grant to her male opponents the existence of some circumstances in which women should not speak, thus establishing as common ground the point that women's speech is limited. Yet with each concession, she points out the parity of men and women who are called by God to preach:

> Ob: But a worse consequence than this is to be feared: will not some improper woman follow your example?
>
> An: This I acknowledge I have feared; but the same might be said of preachers that come out, will not some improper man follow them?
>
> Ob: But if an improper man goes out, the Church has power to stop his mouth, but you will not let yours be stopped.
>
> An: Yes, on the same condition I will. You would not say to him, no *man* must speak, therefore be silent; but only, *You* are not the proper man. Now allowing women may speak, prove to me, it is not my personal call, and I will both lovingly and cheerfully obey.[24]

At the same time Bosanquet has sought common ground, she has slipped in the deliberative argument, "Now allowing women may speak."[25] From that point her argument turns from a defense of her own speech to a larger defense of women's preaching. The ground she claims is only (!) the right to speak publicly for God.

WESLEY'S RESPONSE

To Bosanquet's request for guidance, John Wesley responded with a brief letter that not only offered scriptural endorsement for women's preaching but also placed this "irregular" rhetorical practice within the irregularity of Methodism itself. In the letter Wesley forms an argument that places a woman's call on equal footing with a man's, saying that the "strength of the cause rests" on her having an "extraordinary call," just as every Methodist lay preacher has an extraordinary call. He continues: "It is plaine [*sic*] to me that the whole Work of God termed Methodism is an extraordinary dispensation of His Providence. Therefore I do not wonder if several things occur therein which do not fall under ordinary rules of discipline." By "ordinary rules of discipline," he means the rules of the Anglican Church, of which he still considers himself and all Methodists a part. He points out, almost as an afterthought, that even Paul let women speak in Corinth.[26] It appears that Wesley has endorsed all of Bosanquet's arguments, accepting that women might have an extraordinary call to preach, beyond Pauline limits.

Wesley's response, though positive, was not an all-out endorsement of women's preaching. He still struggled to find a balance between objections voiced by male clergy and the positive results he was seeing from the preaching of women like Mary Bosanquet. He did not argue that women are equal to men under God but rather that Methodism itself is so odd that no one should be surprised by one oddness or another, including seeing a woman with an extraordinary call preach.

Although Wesley affirmed rhetorical space for women, defended preaching women from attacks by male preachers and others, and protected women's right to preach until he died, it is important to note the ways in which Wesley's approval of certain women's preaching differed from the path he set out for male itinerant preachers (called "helpers"). In the Methodist movement male candidates for preacher went through a formal process of nomination, review, and formal acceptance of doctrine and policy as well as a probationary period. At the annual conference in a formal examination, with Wesley as one of the examiners, candidates were questioned about their religious experience, faith, and spiritual life to determine whether they met the criteria for Methodist preaching. After the oral questioning, candidates were asked to write down their reasons for wanting to preach the Gospel. This may well have been a tacit test of their literacy as well as their call. If accepted, they were required to follow a strict schedule of study and self-education prescribed by Wesley (which he compared to gaining a university education) and to keep an hour-by-hour spiritual diary, as John and Charles Wesley had done at Oxford.[27]

Wesley's letter to Bosanquet did not allow women to enter this system, to be put forward as helpers or educated as probationary preachers. Women remained outside the institution of preachers who traveled in established circuits, outside the prescribed course of study and examination, outside the gathering of preachers at the annual conference. Some women preachers did travel from place to place, and they were often in great demand. But they were not part of the regular order of things.

Even more important is the fact that Wesley expressed his approval of women's preaching in private correspondence, not in public at the annual conference or in official minutes. In 1765 the question of even encouraging women's speaking in bands and classes had been raised at the annual conference by opponents who cited Paul's claim in I Corinthians 14: 35: "It is a shame for women to speak in church." As recorded in the minutes, Wesley replied by offering an interpretation of the verse in question, saying that Paul refers only to the great congregation, not to small gatherings and thus "no authority either over man or woman is usurped, by the speaking now in question."[28] Wesley here creates a blended speech genre in which the content of one genre, preaching, is not forbidden to women if they are in a smaller space, with fewer listeners. This interpretation is congruent with Donawerth's argument that women's preaching was modeled on conversation.[29]

Following Wesley's exchange of letters with Bosanquet, no official documents regularized the process for women to become preachers, nor was there a provision that other preachers might put forward or recommend a particular woman as a good candidate for preaching. Wesley did not publish Bosanquet's defense of women's preaching, which he easily could have done, given the resources of his active press at the Foundery. (He had in fact published in 1766 a letter Bosanquet wrote to her female students articulating the advantages of a single life for women.)

Public endorsement of women's preaching might have been the final straw that separated Methodists from their Anglican roots and might have indeed been more than some male Methodists could tolerate. In light of Wesley's belief in the persuasive power of experience, he may have been strategizing that his private approval would give more Methodists exposure to the power of preaching by women with an extraordinary call, like Mary Bosanquet, and this experience would turn the hearts of resistant listeners. Late in his life, he arranged for the Manchester conference of 1787 to issue a note approving the preaching of Sarah Mallet, but it was approval for her alone and entailed certain restrictions.[30]

PERSUADING HERSELF TO PREACH

Having obtained Wesley's private approval, Mary Bosanquet circulated copies of her defense of women's preaching among female colleagues, including Sarah Crosby, who copied it into her letter book. But the defense was not published until after Bosanquet's death, when in 1820, Zechariah Taft (1772–1848), Methodist minister and well-known defender of women's preaching, included Bosanquet's letter in *The Scripture Doctrine of Women's Preaching*.[31] Taft's wife, Mary Barritt Taft, along with Mary Bosanquet Fletcher, was one of the few Methodist women who continued to preach after Wesley's death in 1791 and after the formal ban on women's preaching in 1803 by the Annual Conference of Methodist ministers.

Bosanquet was sometimes asked why, if she were going to preach, she did not join the circuit with the male preachers. It does not appear that she ever wanted to itinerate on a regular schedule with the male preachers. She wrote in her journal: "If I could come into a prayer meeting and speak when I am led to it without being looked for or expected, I could more easily do that. But the appearance of preaching is an awkward thing and yet the Lord is great with me when I do it. At home I have not that difficulty in so great a degree. Lord make me willing to be vile."[32] The public censure for a woman preaching was so acutely felt by women like Mary Bosanquet that it was only a clear call from God on each occasion that gave her the courage to step before the crowd and speak. So part of the extraordinary nature of women's preaching was that they were not to preach as a regular occupation, like the male helpers who were expected at a certain village at a certain hour, often preaching four times on a single day. Rather, preaching women could answer individual invitations and turn down others, preaching as they felt called.

The feminist historian Phyllis Mack has argued that despite Methodism's patriarchal control of women's public speech, these women still possessed spiritual agency. Expanding the definition of agency beyond the idea of individual freedom, Mack posits: "Methodists and others defined agency not as the freedom to do what one wants but as the freedom to want and to do what is right," which includes acting according to conscience and to God's will, as the individual understands it.[33] In a similar vein, the historian Brett C. McInelly has noted: "Unlike women novelists [of the eighteenth century], who were anxious about assuming a public voice, Methodist women worried more about the consequences of *not* speaking. To not speak was to ignore the command of God."[34]

Much of Mary Bosanquet's angst over the agency of preaching was revealed and worked through in dreams, which she recorded in her manuscript journal. Henry Moore, the editor who published her journal after her death, often omitted these dream passages from the published text. Bosanquet claimed that one dream in particular helped her come to terms with the necessity of preaching. She writes:

A few nights ago I dreamed a man came to me and brought a young child saying it is the will of God you should take and suckle this child. I took it in my arms saying, I will feed it. No replyed [sic] he "you must give it suck" that answered I is impossible—but in obedience I will try on which I put it to my breast—but it gave me so much pain—I drew it back—and said to the man in much distress—do take and feed it til my milk comes and then I will give it suck. He replied that is not the way, you must let it to draw, and fear nothing, and then all will be well. I thought I did so in obedience and immediately two streams of milk began to flow from me . . . on which with astonishment I cryed [*sic*] out—Bring me all the children in the world for I have milk enough for them all. . . . The man and the child then disappeared and I said (in my sleep) O now I know the meaning of that word. Let it draw for I see I have been quite wrong, thinking I must wait for more grace and gifts . . . for the way is to let them draw i.e. To be ready to assist and with joy receive every one who would apply to me for help either public or private using the little I have and then God will increase it.[35]

Bosanquet's dream image of herself as a mother nursing one child and then desiring to nurse all the children in the world is poignant. She is a single woman, approaching the age of forty with no apparent plans to marry. The preacher as mother, nurturer, sustainer is an image that is not available to male preachers. Through her dream Bosanquet transformed the role of preacher from one of masculine power to one of feminine abundance. Preaching is the fruit of Mary Bosanquet's body. She does not have to perfect her preaching before she preaches. Rather, the needs of her "children" will draw the preaching from her, like mother's milk, and increase its quality and its flow.

As Bosanquet's preaching drew ever larger crowds, with people coming from farther away to her farm at Cross Hall, she notes in her journal that she encouraged them to form small societies of their own, promising that she would travel to meet with them from time to time. Her rhetorical activities extended beyond praying, testifying, expounding, and preaching. At people's request, she published a list of guidelines for forming a successful society, encouraging her followers to seek the will of God, "bear with each other's mistakes or infirmities in love," beware of evil-speaking, gossip, and criticism of the preachers, and remember their union to God and each other in holy covenant.[36] Clearly, she became a wise pastor as well as a powerful preacher. In 1779 the famous John Fletcher, vicar of Madeley and Wesley's heir apparent, wrote to Mary Bosanquet, affirming her call and drawing parallels between her work and the work of women leaders in the Bible.[37] It was almost as if John Fletcher had read her letter in defense of women's preaching.

After years of living a decidedly single life and rejecting all suitors, in late 1780 Mary Bosanquet became personally reacquainted with John Fletcher (they had obviously corresponded before this meeting), and they fell in love. Fletcher stayed in her home for a number of weeks so that they could deepen their knowledge of each other. About six months later they were married. The groom was fifty-two and the bride forty-two. Fletcher recognized his wife's gifts as a preacher, and they became full partners in ministry, offering a new pattern for Methodist preachers, male and female. Both were sensitive to the furor that might erupt if Mary preached in the Anglican sanctuary. To create a space for her preaching, she and Fletcher renovated the vicarage's tything barn, installing a pulpit and benches. It is said that Mary Fletcher rarely stood in the pulpit to preach, but rather she spoke from the pulpit steps or sat on a stool while delivering her sermons. She thus created a hybrid sacred space for herself that was above the congregation, but she did not physically usurp the pulpit space of male preachers, again blurring the generic lines between preaching and something less threatening, like testimony or expounding.

The marriage appears to have been a source of amazing joy for them both, but it was to last less than four years, for John Fletcher died in 1785 after a brief illness. At first Mary's grief threatened to end her active life, but soon after the funeral she saw that hope lay in renewing her ministry. Speaking of the Methodists in Madeley, she wrote: "I saw there were many things to settle among them respecting the work of God; some dangerous rocks to avoid, and some needful plans to propose. Therefore, before another week passed, I saw I must act among them and meet the people the same as before, and though very ill and filled with sorrow, the Lord enabled me to do so, showing me the only way to bear the cross profitably, was to carry it as if I carried it not."[38] Mary Bosanquet Fletcher continued to live in the Madeley vicarage, to minister to the society there, to teach classes, and to preach several times a week in the tything barn as well as to travel and preach in other locations, until her death in 1815.[39] She is the only woman preacher in early Methodism for whom we have published sermon texts. The bulk of her sermons, called *Watch Words,* exist in manuscript notes at the John Rylands University Library at the University of Manchester. Some *Watch Words* have been edited by David Frudd and published under the name Mary Bosanquet-Fletcher in the *Asbury Journal* in 2006.

Although John Wesley supported Mary Bosanquet Fletcher and other women preachers until the end of his life, his failure to formalize his approval of women's preaching and articulate a process by which women might fully enter the ministry left them vulnerable after his death. In 1803 the annual conference voted to forbid women's speaking except to members of their own sex—and that only after obtaining extensive permission.[40] This effectively curtailed the growth of women's preaching in Methodism and silenced all but a few die-hard women with their own power base, such as Mary Bosanquet Fletcher with her preaching barn at Madeley.

Among the lessons of the women preachers of early Methodism is the notion that genres change slowly, but they can change, especially as rhetors blend approved genres with those that are contested. Mary Bosanquet Fletcher chose to work for change within the institutional church. To expand the notion of who could speak for God, she spoke. She blended genres approved for women with those that were forbidden, finding just the right moment when her preaching seemed all but required. Her rhetorical choices and actions blurred the public with the private, the community with the family, the activity of the priesthood with metaphors of motherhood. She blended the spiritual letter, humble and modest, with classical apologia and biblical exegesis to justify women's preaching. Had John Wesley chosen to publish his approval, it might not have taken another two hundred years for Methodist women to gain the official right to preach.

4

"WITH THE TONGUE OF [WO]MEN AND ANGELS"

APOSTOLIC RHETORICAL PRACTICES AMONG RELIGIOUS WOMEN

Aesha Adams-Roberts,
Rosalyn Collings Eves,
and Liz Rohan

IN 1804 AN African Caribbean Methodist woman, Anne Hart Gilbert, wrote a history of Methodism that sought to correct circulating histories of the Antiguan Methodist church (written by white men) by exposing corrupt practices of some white missionaries and inserting black women into this history.[1] Yet in order to reimagine her community, she had to adopt a voice that would grant her religious and rhetorical authority. Her efforts to come to voice raise the question: How can we best understand the ethoi of Hart Gilbert and women like her, women who grapple not only with the masculine norms of rhetorical practice but with the masculine frameworks of traditional Christianity? Some women within Christian traditions have used an apostolic rhetoric to speak authoritatively and simultaneously to foster a sense of community within their religious groups. Specifically, we explore the apostolic rhetoric of four historical women within three distinct traditions of Christianity and across three centuries: Anne (1768–1834) and Elizabeth Hart (1771–1833), late eighteenth- and early nineteenth-century African Caribbean Methodist missionaries; Eliza R. Snow (1804–1887), nineteenth-century Mormon woman and president of the

Female Relief Society; and Janette Miller (1879–1969), a white middle-class evangelical missionary who grew up in the American Midwest.

This apostolic rhetoric is a powerful lens: it explains the rhetorical ethoi of women in Christian traditions across race, geography, and time. Unlike a prophetic voice, in which the prophet-speaker is positioned above and outside his audience, an apostolic voice positions the speaker within a spiritual community. In many ways this apostolic ethos is a paradoxical one. It draws its authority from both divinely issued spiritual calls as well as physical lived experiences.[2] It frequently relies on a humility topos or claim of personal deficiency precisely to establish authority and sufficiency as a spiritual leader through whom God speaks.[3] And by establishing spiritual conversion, an apostolic ethos allows former outsiders to become insiders. Where prophets historically concerned themselves with spiritual reform, apostles combine this spiritual concern with a pragmatic bent: where John the Baptist speaks as a voice in the wilderness, Paul attends to the needs of a growing congregation. Invoking an apostolic model allowed the women to strengthen their communities through three distinctly apostolic rhetorical practices: translating the word of God for community members and helping them understand the practical implications of the word; regulating local affairs by calling for reform and identifying those who fall short; and teaching appropriate Christian behavior through example.[4]

"WHO IS SUFFICIENT FOR THESE THINGS?": THE HART SISTERS' HISTORY OF METHODISM

Anne and Elizabeth Hart labored among Antiguan slaves, educating and evangelizing them. These two sisters, born to an African Caribbean slaveholding father and a devout Methodist mother, occupied complex positions within their colonial society. As members of the free colored community, they "occupied a critical intersecting zone" between the white elitist landholders and the enslaved Africans, for while they were granted limited political power, they still were not viewed as equals.[5] Nonetheless, the Hart sisters held privileged positions in their community: they were directly related to two of the four founding families of the Methodist movement in Antigua; they both married white men and eventually founded the English Harbor Sunday School and the Female Refuge Society, where they taught hundreds of men, women, and children—both slave and free, black and white—to read. As preaching missionaries in charge of the spiritual instruction of hundreds of women and children, the Hart sisters exemplified a reliance on alternate sources of power.

Both sisters were solicited by the Reverend Richard Pattison, an English missionary to the West Indies during the late eighteenth century, to write a history of Methodist activity in Antigua.[6] Both sisters completed their books in

1804, and both used the title *History of Methodism.* But these texts are remarkably different in terms of their self-representation, means of asserting authority, and ostensible ends. While Anne Hart constructs herself as an apostle with the authority to oversee missionary activity in Antigua, Elizabeth Hart uses her personal conversion to implicitly argue for both the spiritual and *moral* equality of black people. Despite these differences, both sisters use apostolic strategies to describe themselves as "spiritual mothers," moral exemplars with considerable authority to refigure their communities by challenging dominant notions of race and womanhood that were entrenched in prevailing Christian discourse in the eighteenth century.

ANNE HART'S APOSTOLIC EPISTLE

Anne Hart Gilbert begins her *History of Methodism,* written in epistolary form, from a position of deference, acknowledging that her version of Antiguan Methodist history differs from the dominant discourses circulating in Europe: "I feel some reluctance to giving you the information you require of me, lest the testimony of those that have gone before should render my time so employed, uselessly disposed of."[7] As a member of a well-read Methodist family, Anne was most likely aware that current reports from white English missionaries such as Thomas Coke, the first bishop of the Methodist Episcopal Church, and John Baxter depicted the black community (both the slaves and the free blacks) as heathens in need of civilization and "spiritual taming."[8] However, her stated reluctance is merely a rhetorical move, for Anne's goal for her own epistle to England is to "answer back to all those who cast aspersions on the intellect of African Caribbeans."[9] Using apostolic rhetoric, Anne assumes a position of authority from which she indicts the hypocritical actions of immoral white missionaries, constructs a model of appropriate missionary behavior in Antigua, and elevates the work of black women.

Anne's letter provides the necessary token of her apostleship. Her description of her conversion experience employs language reminiscent of the Apostle Paul's Damascus Road conversion, in that she claims "the scales of pride, ignorance & unbelief, fell from my eyes, by the light & power which accompanies the Gospel faithfully preached."[10] Like Paul, Anne depicts herself as a humble yet worthy laborer among the Antiguan enslaved community, a person able to effectively evangelize and unite the black community where white male preachers fell short. As the historian Sandra Hack Polaski has pointed out, the apostles' references to deficiency supported apostolic claims that the Spirit of God spoke through them. Moreover, Anne's very effectiveness as an evangelist provides validation for her apostolic authority, as one of the foremost duties of an apostle was to establish and maintain churches.[11]

In her apostolic position, Anne sets herself up as a regulator of missionary activity in Antigua. As Polaski argues, apostles served as ambassadors for Christ, speaking on His behalf and empowered with His authority, and were able to identify fellow laborers and uproot false apostles. Gilbert praises the work of Thomas Coke, "Mr. Graham, Mr. Black, Mr. Cooke, Mr. McCornock & Mr. Ray" because they were adept at "stirring up those that believe to press after the full image of God"; she then unmasks the apostasy of other missionaries, calling them "messengers of Satan disguised as preachers" whose secret sins (perhaps sexual sins with female slaves) have misled their charges.[12]

In addition to critiquing false laborers, Anne Hart Gilbert utilizes apostolic rhetoric to construct a model of appropriate missionary behavior in Antigua. Only "humble, judicious men; who [are] well disciplin'd in the school of Christ, & have only one single aim in view" are qualified to work with the black community.[13] Gilbert exhorts Reverend Pattison to imitate the qualities she enumerates: "Be not easily discouraged but labour on in patient humble love; and if only one sinner, among many be saved from the guilt, & power of sin, & escapes the wrath to come; be thankful, and rejoice with Host above."[14] Through the mimetic relationship she establishes with the Reverend Pattison, she enacts the apostolic authority reflected in the relationship of the Apostle Paul and his protégé Timothy.[15]

Having differentiated the true apostles from the false, Gilbert's apostolic rhetoric clears a space for her to insert black women into Methodist history and by so doing, to reimagine the Methodist community. Embedding her celebration of black women's labors between a comparison of the faithful white preachers' efforts and the apostate preachers, Gilbert constructs black women as honorable and dignified Methodists. She venerates "Mary Alley a Mulatto Woman & Sophia Campbel a black," as "leaders" of a faithful "praying remnant" of black women: "tho' it cannot be said, that they abounded in knowledge, brightness of reason or soundness of speech, yet I say would to God there was the same simplicity, purity & love of the cross in only one half of our greatly increased Society now. . . . They met together for reading, singing & prayers & with many prayers watered the seed sown by the fathers in the Gospel."[16] Gilbert's discourse is significant on several levels. First, as the scholar Moira Ferguson has noted, "she marks and affirms black women as upholders of the faith and mothers of spirituality, legitimate public authorities."[17] Anne implies that black women have remained constant and diligent even when they did not a have preacher to watch over them. Second, she demonstrates the ways in which the liberalizing tenets of Methodism disrupted social class distinctions. Mary Alley and Sophia Campbel are *both* esteemed as leaders even though they occupy distinct social positions.[18] Finally, Gilbert rejects constructions of black women's immorality by contrasting the "simplicity, purity & love" of black women with the "vain [white] Women of the World." She vehemently indicts the white missionaries' wives' flirtatious behavior, hidden under the guise of hospitality, and shows that white women are "destitute of every principle of vital piety."[19] As a speaker from a subordinate position, Anne Hart Gilbert deploys an apostolic rhetoric to gain access to multiple levels of authority, shape the moral behavior of her fellow missionaries, and improve the position of black women within her spiritual community.

ELIZABETH HART'S CONVERSION NARRATIVE

Elizabeth Hart Thwaites also wrote a letter to Reverend Pattison expounding upon Methodism in Antigua; however, unlike her sister Anne's more explicitly regulatory rhetoric, Elizabeth focuses on the more personal aspects of an apostolic rhetoric to critique Antiguan slaveholding society; her text doubles as a conversion narrative, a sanctioned form of public discourse for women.[20] The historian Judith Weisenfeld has reminded us that the conversion experience gave black women "entry to a different realm of power . . . and connected them to a different sort of lineage from the ones which had been denied them."[21] To be able to testify to a conversion experience, black women confirmed their humanity and linked themselves to authority that transcended earthly realms. In terms of apostolic rhetorical practices, conversion narratives allow rhetors to link spiritual directives with embodied experience to strengthen their authority.[22]

Elizabeth's foregrounding of her conversion experience is significant because it supplies her with the necessary tools to critique slavery in Antigua. As the literary theorist Joycelyn Moody has asserted, black women's spiritual autobiographies permitted them to "simultaneously pursue those political and social rights they were routinely denied as poor black women. Clearly, for black holy women both the personal and the *spiritual* are political."[23] Although philanthropic missions among slaves, such as attending to their physical needs, were deemed acceptable, the Hart sisters' work, which was interracial, was suspect. Methodists were often suspected of being abolitionists because of the egalitarian and revolutionary impulses of Methodist doctrine that proclaimed that all people, regardless of their social status, were eligible for salvation.[24] Such themes threatened the social order of Antiguan slaveholding society. Suspecting Elizabeth Hart of participating in antislavery activities, Antiguan officials summoned her to appear before a committee of the House of Assembly, where she refused to answer the committee's questions.[25] Only when threatened with imprisonment did she assert that "there was no law to punish persons for giving charity to slaves, and she had done no injury to their proprietors" and was promptly released.[26] Although some scholars question the degree to which Elizabeth challenged the system of slavery, claiming she was more of a meliorationist and not an abolitionist, her conversion narrative legitimates her authority as a Methodist spiritual leader and allows her to implicitly critique slavery by making social equality an important condition of the ideal religious community.[27]

A conversion narrative typically chronicles the wretched sinner's struggle to accept grace and enter the community of believers. What is particularly significant about Elizabeth's conversion narrative, however, is the implicit claim that discrimination against slaves is sinful.[28] As her story progresses, Elizabeth depicts herself as one rejected by her family but unwilling to fully enter the community of the (enslaved) believers. She juxtaposes her inability to convert with her reluctance to associate with the community: "Contrary to my intention, I became a constant hearer. There were no young persons, that I knew of, who were in Society at this time, that were not Slaves; on this, and some other accounts, I proudly held out as long as I could, from wholly joining them, tho' I gain'd admittance to many of the private meetings."[29] As a privileged member of the free colored community, Elizabeth resisted associating with "Slaves." However, she quietly acknowledges their moral superiority: they were already converted members of the Society while she struggled to repent of her sins. Even when she joined the Society and served as a spiritual leader of the enslaved women, she retained her sense of social superiority:

> I constantly felt for every deviation from the self-denying path, but had not power to overcome. I often wept, and prayed and strove, revived and was slain; alternately hoped and despaired. I used all the means of Grace, and never came under Church censure, during this time I met a Class of young women who were Slaves and to whom I said nothing of my then experience, which, when at the worst, did not prevent my enforcing upon them the necessity of a present Salvation. I abated in nothing my severity against Sin, and continually enjoined upon them to avoid the very appearance of evil.[30]

Although her class produced some converts who were "still in the good way," Elizabeth identifies her lack of personal and cultural identification with the black women through personal disclosure that signified her incomplete conversion. Only when she was fully converted would she fully share in the life of her community of believers. In this way Elizabeth uses the genre of the conversion narrative and her eventual immersion in the black (enslaved) community as a way to link spiritual maturity to an acceptance of social equality.

MOTHERS OF THE FAITH

Both Anne and Elizabeth Hart were committed to preaching about black female identity, particularly black female sexuality, in the context of their religious community. The sisters' primary concern with slavery was not its suppression of economic and political liberties, but its impact on moral behavior.[31] Slavery disrupted the black family by forcing women to choose between emancipation and their own responsibilities to be examples of morality and purity for their children. Polaski has argued that an apostle inspires community members to act in a particular way by modeling appropriate behavior and vouching for the rightness of that behavior.[32] Thus, as apostolic rhetors, the Hart sisters taught that black women should seek after the freedom from "degradation and impurity" so that they could teach their daughters appropriate moral behavior.[33]

The sisters construct themselves as spiritual mothers in their texts, both literally and figuratively, as a way to frame their instruction on morality and challenge racist conceptions of black families as inherently pathological.[34] Respected and venerable women in black religious communities, often denoted by the title "Mother," wield considerable authority within their "women's worlds" and are able to negotiate shared power with the dominant culture.[35] Anne and Elizabeth Hart served as leaders of same sex "bands" of Methodist societies that functioned as "surrogate families for the alienated poor."[36] As leaders of these bands, the Hart sisters served as immediate mother figures to enslaved women, providing instruction in virtuous living to "orphans" and children with "fallen and depraved relatives."[37] This construction was particularly efficacious in the sisters' quest to secure funds for their Female Refuge Society. Elizabeth's descriptions of the Society circulated among "many benevolent Societies and ladies, who liberally sent aid in money and clothes from time to time."[38]

The Hart sisters were never employed or recognized as preachers by the Methodist Mission Society, even though they evangelized slave quarters often with more success than their white male counterparts and traveled as much as any itinerant missionary. This exclusion is evident through the records left by white male Methodist preachers in Antigua. In a letter to Joseph Benson in England in 1804, the same year the Hart sisters wrote their *History of Methodism,* the Reverend John Baxter claimed that there were "no intelligent persons" to provide accounts of the experiences of the converted slaves.[39] Even though he acknowledges that "colored women"—women like Anne and Elizabeth Hart—outnumber the men, both black and white, he hesitates to attribute them leadership or significant roles. In fact, because these women do not fit his conceptualization of religiosity, they are ignored. It is characterizations such as these that have worked to write black women out of Methodist history. Anne and Elizabeth Hart refused to remain silent, however. In the midst of prevailing ideologies that constructed blacks as spiritually, morally, and intellectually deficient, the Hart sisters used apostolic rhetorical strategies to garner spiritual authority, strengthen the Methodist community they worked in, and create a space for themselves in the history of that community.

"TO BE A HOLY WOMAN": THE RHETORICAL
IDENTIFICATION OF ELIZA R. SNOW

Eliza R. Snow, president of the Mormon women's Female Relief Society for more than two decades in the mid- to late nineteenth century, was arguably "the female voice heard more widely, clearly, and consistently than any other" in Mormon communities during the 1870s and 1880s.[40] Following the Mormons' mass migration to Utah in 1847, Snow became increasingly prominent, through her marriage to Mormon leader Brigham Young as well as her role as president of the Relief Society, a benevolent society that "achieved for Mormon women a power base and a degree of public influence unequalled by [non-Mormon] women on the frontier" through charitable projects such as home industries, women's health education, and the organization of a hospital for women.[41]

Snow was also regarded as a "prophetess" for her manifestations of Pentacostal gifts such as healing and speaking in tongues. Much of Snow's speaking and writing is addressed to her "sister saints" in the Mormon church, who faced the challenges of self-definition within their own religious community and widespread cultural disparagement. Like many other nineteenth-century religious women, Mormon women practiced their faith within a religion structured according to a masculine hierarchy.[42] Outside Mormon communities, popular sensationalist novels of the era routinely depicted Mormon women as victims. The historian Julie Roy Jeffrey has explained that "their stories assumed that only religious trickery, outright oppression, or female depravity could account for women's acceptance of a religion encouraging plural marriage."[43] As the scholar Anne Ruggles Gere has pointed out, Mormon women engaged in literacy and rhetorical practices calculated to address both the gender constraints that faced them within their religious communities and the prejudice facing them outside their communities.[44]

In speeches given to congregations of Mormon women and republished in the *Woman's Exponent* during the 1870s, Snow utilizes apostolic rhetoric to re-envision her spiritual community. She uses extensive first-person plurals to establish a particularly sanctified sense of community among Mormon women. She then offers this communal identity as a hortatory model to call Mormon women to repentance and to promote particular pragmatic and spiritual roles for women within their community. Just as apostles frequently negotiated their authority in relation to other leaders within their community, Snow exercised authority among women without challenging the authority of her church's male leadership, particularly that of Brigham Young.[45] As the historian Jill Mulvay Derr has noted, Snow's public rhetorical strategies involved a complicated balancing act as she sought "for ways to wholly honor the authority and power of the holy priesthood without attributing to men superiority and diminishing herself."[46]

Unlike many of her contemporary women preachers, Snow spends little time justifying her right to speak: most of her addresses to a Mormon audience presume upon her already established reputation as a leader of women. She speaks as an insider, frequently using first-person plurals to evoke a sense of community. Although she does not, like the Hart sisters, draw upon an explicitly maternal ethos, she utilizes a familial role and was known among her contemporaries as "Sister Eliza." She uses her authority in an apostolic manner, regulating communal behavior through consistent exhortations to Mormon women to identify themselves more strongly as a community of holy women: "It is the duty of *each one of us* to be a holy woman. . . . There is no sister so isolated and her sphere so narrow but what she can do a great deal towards establishing the Kingdom of God on earth."[47] By naming herself and her audience as "holy women," Snow identifies with and exhorts her audience. As the literary theorist Kenneth Burke described it, naming is a "somewhat hortatory device" that indicates more what things or individuals should be than what they are; naming tells individuals who they are and what their place is in society.[48] Snow's naming project enhances her audience's sense of Mormon women as a community; in using first-person plural pronouns, Snow unfolds this project as an extension of her own ethos.

As a spiritual leader (apostle) invested in cementing the bonds of a growing spiritual community, Snow reinforces a sense of community by couching her rhetorical admonitions in first-person plural terms, including herself in the rhetorical "ought." Like the audience she seeks to exhort, she acknowledges her own struggles: "I try never to allow myself to do anything for a selfish gratification. Still we are all frail and weak mortals, of the earth, earthy."[49] In a characteristically apostolic practice (and like many women religious speakers, including the Hart sisters and the American missionary Janette Miller), Snow invokes her own experience to exemplify appropriate behavior, explaining: "When I am filled with [the spirit of God] my soul is satisfied; and I can say in good earnest, that the trifling things of the day do not seem to stand in my way at all. But just let me loose my hold of that spirit and power of the Gospel, and partake of the spirit of the world, in the slightest degree, and trouble comes."[50] This personal identification allows her to counsel her audience to set their ambitions on spiritual aims, rather than merely temporal ones, as befits the "holy women" she wants them to become.

As an apostolic rhetor, Snow also uses her authority to call the sisters to repentance when they deviate from her model of holy womanhood. Although a prophetic ethos also includes calls to repentance, Snow's calls for reform are part of an apostolic model because she speaks as a community insider, and her calls for reform often include injunctions for pragmatic action. For instance, in the 1870s Snow and other church leaders were concerned about Mormons' dependence on outside commerce and their excessive consumerism. In 1875, Snow rebuked a congregation of women: "I humbly call on my sisters to reflect, and to reflect seriously. There must be a stop to our waste of energies, and waste of substance by useless expenditures, and, especially on superfluities. . . . Let us assist with all the energies of our souls, in breaking the chains with which we, as a people, are bound; for just as long as we are in debt to or dependent upon our enemies for the necessities and comforts of life, we are virtually their slaves."[51] She went on to encourage women to establish home industries like silk and straw manufacture. As an apostolic authority, Snow blends a call for repentance with the promise that the fruit of such repentance will be stronger bonds within the community.

Snow's apostolic practices also include a kind of spiritual translation: perhaps because the scriptural records contain few specific injunctions to women, Snow frequently articulates a clear spiritual vision for women in the Mormon community that connects their spiritual and secular lives: "Let your first business be to perform your duties at home. But inasmuch as you are wise stewards, you will find time for social duties."[52] Snow consistently links woman's domestic work with her divine role in building a kingdom of God on Earth: "In this great Work, woman has much to do—not only in giving birth to, and training those who shall be the mothers of future generations, . . . prophetesses and holy women . . . but she also has much to do in [building the Kingdom of God]."[53] Snow advocated the education of women as a means of deepening women's abilities and contributions, particularly encouraging women to study medicine.[54]

Throughout her speeches Snow draws on an apostolic rhetoric that allows her to work within (rather than against) her religious tradition to reimagine that community through identification, hortatory admonitions, calls to repentance, and a vision for spiritual and pragmatic action. Perhaps ironically, by using an apostolic rhetoric within a masculine tradition, Snow does not abrogate her authority, but enhances it, by maintaining the widespread community support necessary to make her spiritual and pragmatic aims a reality.

JANETTE MILLER: AN INSIDER/OUTSIDER IN TWENTIETH-CENTURY COLONIZED ANGOLA

Like the Hart sisters and Snow, American missionary Janette Miller relied on apostolic rhetorical strategies to create her discursive space and strengthen a community of believers during her sixty-year-long career in Portuguese-controlled Angola. Specifically, she linked spiritual concerns with pragmatic ones, urged religious reform on her Congregational community, and acted as a translator of Christian principles as a writer and teacher of the Angolan language Umbundu. Miller, also a preacher, poet, and artist, became a missionary in 1910, at the peak of the missionary movement, when she joined a Congregational mission and, after some training in the United States, was sent to Angola. As support for women missionaries virtually dried up in the late 1920s, Miller decided to leave the Congregational church in 1929 and joined a Swiss Mission, the Phil African League.

Like many others at the time, Miller was caught up in a profound conflict within the Protestant churches that began in the 1920s, between the liberals, or Christian modernists, and the conservatives, known as Christian fundamentalists because of their dedication to Bible teaching. Not a proclaimed fundamentalist, Miller nevertheless continued to embrace evangelism as a primary goal for missionary workers and sought to use the Bible as a primary text for missionary teaching—goals that separated her ideology from her fellow Congregational missionaries working in Angola. Miller's later rhetoric was shaped by this controversy as she articulated her disagreements with Christian modernists and lamented that her fellow missionaries no longer took seriously the evangelical project of mass conversion as a means for bringing about personal and societal change.[55]

Like the Harts and Snow, Miller used apostolic rhetoric to encourage religious faith and strengthen religious community among those with whom she worked. An American in Africa, Miller served two communities simultaneously. For example, when she wrote home to those in the United States who supported her financially, Miller wrote as an American to Americans, translating the lives of Africans for American audiences at home, first with articles and newsletters that she wrote for the Congregational missionary magazines and later with her own newsletters, in which included poems and photographs of members of her Christian community. For her American readers, Miller fulfilled the apostolic function of translating the word of God into real-world examples from the lives of the Africans whom she served. When Miller chose to teach and write for her African community, the Ovimbundu, in their native language, Umbundu, she again used apostolic rhetoric, literally translating the word of God into the language of her religious community. Overall, Miller had the privilege of class and race in a colonized Angola. But as a woman, she lacked the power. When she embraced translating and teaching in the Ovimbundu language, Umbundu, she flouted Portuguese policies on language instruction that forbade the use of native languages in mission schools as few other white and Westernized missionaries dared to do.

Miller was foremost a translator, which highlights her investment in methods of apostolic rhetoric. Translation, for Miller, was apostolic because it allowed her to build a community of believers among native Angolans. This investment in translation, while building community with Angolans, challenged Miller's position in the missionary community. In 1921, the same year that Miller published a textbook for those teaching the Angolan dialect Umbundu, Angolan colonial leaders passed a law prohibiting missionaries, both Western and native, from teaching native languages in school.[56] Under the law, languages like Umbundu were to be used only orally and for Bible study. These policies had clashed with those of the Protestant missionaries who historically taught their students in their own native language, believing that the ability to read the "Word of God" in one's own language orchestrated a more genuine conversion.[57] However, despite the efficaciousness of reaching out to potential converts in their own language, Angolan colonialists considered teaching in the native languages to be subversive because they worried that the missionaries' knowledge of the native language gave them undue influence.[58]

As a teacher of young children, Miller saw firsthand the difficulties that the decree created for children's learning. Thus, despite this decree, she continued to write and teach in Umbundu; by refusing to abandon either her students or their language, Miller embodied an apostolic call for reform. Eventually she decided to leave her post as a Congregational missionary so that she could maintain a linguistic community with the Ovimbundu. After World War II and until her death in 1969, Miller ran the Ebenezer Orphanage, a school and home for up to 150 children. She ran this orphanage with help from two women, one Portuguese and the other African American, until her death at eighty-nine in 1969. This project was a physical manifestation of turn-of-the-twentieth-century women's missionary movement ideology that foreground the home and motherhood as a site for sanctity and the seat of evangelistic endeavor via international cooperation between women. In this project Miller created a religious and linguistic community that translated the word of God for the children of her community and taught her constituents what she considered to be appropriate Christian behavior through example. This apostolic role was so profound for Miller that she chose to write her poetry in Umbundu under the pen name, Maikula ("great grandmother" in Umbundu).

When writing in an apostolic mode, Miller often fused the social with the mystical, a key component of an apostolic rhetoric, according to scholar Elisabeth Ceppi.[59] Miller's ethos as "Maikula" emphasized not only her community with the Ovimbundu but also her apostolic authority, an authority based in her command of Umbundu, divine authority as practiced in her role of missionary, and her lived experience. Through her rhetoric Miller encouraged the development of two communities—a spiritual community, which might continue in the next world, and a material community of believers who could live and work together in *this* world.

One of Miller's poems highlights how she used an apostolic ethos to foster a spiritual and material community with her American readers and members of her Ombundu community. Miller originally published the poem in *Mission Studies* in 1917, so her first readers were Americans. But Miller presumably added the first italicized stanza some years later as she reflected on her life and her career, and after adopting the ethos of "Maikula," the great-grandmother.

Long years since the school ma'am came, with wonder in her eyes:
Not many more perhaps before she'll reach the greatest prize
Of our high calling: flowering lives of converts changed in heart.
Failing oft and stumbling much, she chose the better part.
Today my boys to give to me aid stopped short in boist'rous play;
But still, not love to me but Christ is proof of Jesus' Way;
At morning prayers in earnest gaze I saw an answering look.
The fruit of toil in the field of souls is writ in the Angels' book.
Obscure and modest place is mine, no rapturous converts kneel,
But day by day small feet to guide in paths of righteous zeal;
So pray I Lord, for dear brown youths, Oh Thou to bring them up,
And when they reach the heavenly home, how full shall be my cup.[60]

The final lines of the poem first suggest Miller's evangelical beliefs, those that shaped her work as a writer and teacher, and also mark the difference she recognized between herself and her African constituents, workers, and companions. In these lines her ethos is that of a white, Western outsider, acting with the apostolic ethos of teacher and translator of Christian principles for "dear brown youths." It was important to Miller that the children under her guidance "reach the heavenly home," by becoming converted, by reading the Bible, and by circulating its message. And yet, in Miller's description of Ovimbundu children as "my boys," she describes a familial bond of community with the Ovimbundu. Conversion in this context promotes a type of multigenerational and multiracial fellowship that can be the ultimate goal of apostolic work. Miller's apostolic rhetoric thus encourages the fusion of the spiritual and the material through a community that she led not only as a white outsider but also as a motherly insider, looking out for her children's best interests.

APOSTOLIC RHETORIC AND COMMUNITY IDEALS

These disparate yet comparative historical case studies of the Hart sisters, Eliza Snow, and Janette Miller emphasize the ways that Christian women were able to draw on what we call an apostolic rhetoric not only to create physical and discursive spaces for themselves but also to call into being particular ideals of community. Community is essential to both the idea of an apostolic rhetoric and to these case studies, as apostolic rhetors focus their rhetorical practices on creating, shaping, and maintaining communities. Moreover, each of these women used her rhetoric to find a place for herself within and against her religious community and its concomitant rhetorical and spiritual traditions: the Hart sisters utilized apostolic rhetoric, conversion narratives, and personas of spiritual motherhood to place black women at the center of Methodist history (and communities) and challenge slavery in Antigua. Snow used a rhetoric of reform and personal example to exhort Mormon women to find a central spiritual place in their religious community, despite ostracism by the wider Anglo-American community. In her translation, teaching, and poetry, Janette Miller used her insider/outsider ethos to strengthen transatlantic spiritual communities: first, by translating the lives of her African converts for the Americans back home; and second, by translating doctrinal concepts into Umbundu and encouraging spiritual conversion among the Ovimbundu. In the hands of these women, an apostolic rhetoric takes on a distinctly feminine cast, as their authority is used to build and nurture community; in the cases of the Hart sisters and Miller, the ethos that emerges is clearly maternal.

This research also has important implications for our own community of researchers. Although none of these women would likely identify herself as a radical, all of them worked to build communities among women and people of color; in so doing, they challenged the dominant white, Western patriarchy. And yet these rhetors have received little of our scholarly attention. In her work on Christian African American women, scholar Joycelyn Moody has addressed a general neglect and misreading of religious discourse in women's writings. She suggests that many feminist scholars resist or are afraid of examining Christian discourse in these texts because they fear being identified with their subjects—that is, thought to be Christians, Mormons, Methodists, or Evangelicals (along with whatever stereotypes are associated with these identities and beliefs).[61] Moody argues that the "personal faith or political identification of any individual scholar notwithstanding," if we do not account for the rhetorical effects of some subjects' Christian beliefs, we risk marginalizing, and in some cases discarding, these subjects and the agency they achieved through enactments of those beliefs.[62] Moody asserts that "by ignoring or depreciating the *theology* of these women's spiritual autobiographies, contemporary scholars perpetuate the academy's proclivity toward keeping the personal and the private outside its walls, as if it *were* possible to sever the personal from the professional."[63] Moody suggests that if scholars centralize matters of faith and spirituality when they appear in the writings of a women rhetor, they will have access to a more diverse and complete set of analytical tools to better understand her means of persuasion, her identity, and her communities. We hope that our work with apostolic rhetoric demonstrates how more complete methods for studying the rhetorical practice of religious women produces a more complete history of rhetoric.

5

—

RHETORICAL STRATEGIES IN
PROTESTANT WOMEN'S MISSIONS

APPROPRIATING AND SUBVERTING GENDER IDEALS

Karen K. Seat

Between the Civil War and World War II, millions of Protestant American women took up the cause of missions, creating their own woman-run missionary societies and sending unmarried women to countries around the world to work as professional missionaries.[1] The pages of women's missionary literature from this era brim with the rhetorical prowess of those involved in the movement. Chronicling the rise of the United States' largest and most active women's missionary society, Frances J. Baker's 436-page volume *The Story of the Woman's Foreign Missionary Society of the Methodist Episcopal Church, 1869–1895*, published in 1896, highlighted the dramatic achievements of women who ventured into the public world of rhetoric. Baker described how in March of 1869, a band of Methodist women began gathering support for women's missions by giving speeches at small church meetings in Boston, in which they revealed "in a thrilling and impressive way the need the women of India had of the gospel, and why it could only be brought to them by women."[2] Within days the Woman's Foreign Missionary Society of the Methodist Episcopal Church (WFMS) was formed, and by November of the same year the WFMS had sent its first two missionary women to India. That year the WFMS also began publishing its monthly magazine, *The Heathen Woman's Friend,* at a time when "papers and magazines conducted by women were something of a novelty, the field new and untried.">[3] The husband of one of the founding members of the WFMS promised five hundred dollars "to meet deficiencies" if the magazine did not generate adequate revenue, but the women proved themselves perfectly competent at marketing their new publication. They ended the year with four thousand subscribers and a profit. Three years later, they could boast of twenty-five thousand subscribers. The women who were first involved in this mission movement surprised even themselves with the extent of their success; as one woman exclaimed four years after the WFMS was founded: "How much talent has this infant society already called out! What able essays have been written and eloquent speeches made by women unused to this exercise of pen or tongue!"[4]

The success of women's missionary societies was by no means a foregone conclusion when mission-minded women began their project. From the start, the women were confronted with sexist and racist opposition to their work. One of the most formidable obstacles they faced was the widespread notion that woman-run organizations were antithetical to women's nature. Not only did conservatives within their denominations oppose women's public activities as ungodly and unwomanly, but it was generally assumed that women had neither the discipline nor the business sense necessary to carry out a major international enterprise. Meanwhile, vocal racists of the day charged that the missionary enterprise itself was futile because nonwhite people were incapable of changing their "debased" natures. In order to promote their work, women in missions had to challenge deep-seated beliefs that women and people of color were by nature fixed at a subordinate position to men of Anglo-Saxon stock. Women in missions met these challenges through renovating traditional rhetoric about gender, civilization, and Christian redemption.

The women who built what would become a vast network of missionary organizations were successful, in part, because their rhetoric simultaneously appropriated and undermined dominant gender ideologies of the day; they used gender ideologies that seemed familiar and reasonable to American Protestants to promote innovative activities for women and to kindle interest in improving the lives of women around the world. While early advocates of women's missions embraced mainstream Protestant commitments to women's domesticity and Western expansionism, over time the women's mission movement challenged Protestant ideologies regarding the proper social order. Women's missions ultimately had a liberalizing influence on mainline American Protestantism and paved one path toward women's suffrage.

Thus, while nineteenth-century missionaries were often the purveyors of sexist and imperialist ideologies, the mission movement was much more complicated and much less predictable than any such one-dimensional depiction. In fact, missionaries' very appropriation of these ideologies proved most useful in the dismantling of them. Because missionaries often used conservative rhetoric, ordinary Protestants trusted that missionaries shared their values and saw them as a reliable source of information about the changing world. Foreign mission societies ultimately brought alternative visions of the world and gender into their denominational discourses. Church visits by missionaries on furlough and widely popular mission publications, to which missionaries contributed articles about their experiences in non-Western lands, exposed ordinary American Protestants to new ideas and a more global worldview.[5] As a whole, Protestant missions were an important influence on American culture in the late nineteenth and early twentieth centuries—and women's missions were particularly influential. As they became more established, women involved in missions chafed against the very gender norms they had sought to universalize through missions, and this was reflected in their evolving rhetoric as they more directly challenged patriarchal Protestant paradigms.

According to the dominant gender ideology of the nineteenth-century United States, which the historian Barbara Welter famously termed the "Cult of True Womanhood," a woman's role was to be strictly relegated to a private sphere of domesticity and religion, removed from the brave new world of industrial-age waged labor and politics.[6] Women were to influence American society indirectly as religiously pious mothers and wives, creating a domestic haven that would safeguard their virtue and submissiveness. However, while many nineteenth-century men and women, especially of the middle class, believed the sexes ought to occupy separate spheres, this was never a universal reality or even an ideal for all women. As the "separate spheres" ideology was embedding itself in the popular consciousness of the United States, women's movements arose that challenged it, including campaigns for broader political rights and economic opportunities.

Protestants interested in promoting women's missions found that they were entering turbulent waters, as any direct challenge to prescribed gender roles drew the ire of leading Protestants. For example, in 1891 James Monroe Buckley, editor of the influential Methodist periodical *The Christian Advocate*, cautioned in one of his editorials that women who campaigned for expanded rights and roles in religious and civic arenas would bring down the wrath of God. He claimed: "imperious women, cursing the day they were born because they were not made men, have rebelled against their own nature, and therefore against God's law. Ambitious women, seeking to rival men, because they cannot bear to see them possess a kind of power denied to them, have sought to wrest dominion. . . . [they] have sought pre-eminence through means condemned by the law of God."[7] Declaring that "every man who understands the

Gospel finds no difficulty in wishing his wife, mother, sister, and daughter to be subject to himself and other men in the sense in which the Gospel requires it," Buckley warned his audience that the moment women gained equal rights in Church and society, "the *Christian family* is gone."[8] According to Buckley, women who truly sought to promote Christianity and the family would accept biblical mandates regarding women's silence and obedience, and acknowledge that theirs was "a noble sort of disenfranchisement," which included the "right" to "live under the protection of a stronger arm than her own. . . . and to look to that head to plan for her well-being."[9]

The women who first organized women's missionary societies sidestepped much criticism from conservatives by rhetorically embracing gender ideals like Buckley's, which deflected attention away from their nondomestic pursuits. Protestant women involved in missions did not set out to prove that women should have a voice and a profession in the public sphere; the fact that they demonstrated women's capacity for public engagement was initially a mere by-product of their larger religious goals. When American women began to organize their missionary societies after the Civil War, most were themselves firmly rooted in white Protestant domesticity and ethnocentricity. As the United States entered the world stage as a global power, the fervent desire of most Protestant women was to domesticate savage cultures through introducing the "Christian home." They were as passionate as Buckley about the importance of the "Christian family," and they were so committed to this ideal that they were willing to "sacrifice" their own place in the domestic sphere to help the heathen learn about true familial bliss. "Our Bible gives us the home,—that one sweet bit of paradise that has survived the fall," an early article in the *Heathen Woman's Friend* proclaimed: "Dare we, Christian women, withhold the cup of cold water from those who perish with thirst?"[10]

Like other nineteenth-century pioneers who had promoted women's involvement in higher education and social reform, advocates of women's missions also justified their cause through building on the widely held Victorian belief that women had a God-given role to be the moral anchors of their families. By extension, they argued that women could anchor civilization itself. Precisely because of women's natural propensity for piety, they asserted, Christian women had a responsibility to elevate not only their own nation but also all the nations of the world through evangelizing "heathen" women. Catherine Beecher, a prominent advocate of this ideology, proclaimed that the United States was called to be involved in "the destiny of the whole earth," and thus "to American women, more than to any others on earth, is committed the exalted privilege of extending over the world those blessed influences, that are to renovate degraded man, and 'clothe all climes with beauty.'"[11]

Women's missionary societies began their work in Burma, China, the Congo,

India, Japan, Turkey, and numerous other places with enthusiastic proclamations that the key to converting these societies to true Christianity and civilization was the conversion of women, who would then instill the values of middle-class American Protestants in their own families. As the Presbyterian publication *Woman's Work for Woman* stated, the evangelization of women was uniquely important in "that it touches society at all of its most sensitive points. It concerns the sacredness of womanhood and motherhood. It molds the plastic character of the young. It exalts and sanctifies the home."[12] The Congregationalist women's mission magazine, *Light and Life for Heathen Women,* identified the conversion of women as a path of salvation for whole societies: "The degradation and oppression of woman is the stronghold of heathenism; and when the lever of the gospel has raised HER, then the whole structure of superstition and idolatry falls."[13] Summing up the motivating logic of the women's missionary movement, one missionary simply stated: "You cannot evangelize a country until you convert the women."[14] In their campaign to support "woman's work for woman" in the mission field, American Protestant women embraced the ideal of a private, female sphere of domesticity but renovated this concept to place this female sphere at the center of civilization. Having given women such an exalted status, it logically followed that women's missionary work with women was the most important missionary venture of all.

This sense of importance that women gained through their role as moral guardians in the domestic sphere emboldened them for action in the public sphere, even when they did meet resistance from fellow church members. The secretary of the General Mission Board of the Methodist Episcopal Church, John Price Durbin, attempted to stop the creation of the denomination's Woman's Foreign Missionary Society in 1869. He chided the women who had resolved to organize the WFMS, stating: "Could you ladies make the necessary arrangements for Miss A. to go to India, obtain bills of exchange, take care of her on the voyage, provide a home when she arrives at her destination, and so forth? No, your work is to forward the money for Miss A. to [the General Board headquarters in] New York."[15] Despite such opposition, the women were determined to create their own missionary organization because, as the WFMS advocate Frances Baker pointed out in her 1896 history of this society, even though they "had not been trained in business methods . . . they realized they were being divinely led."[16] The founders of the WFMS responded to Durbin's objections by declaring their submission to his General Board while simultaneously defying his wishes, stating: "We will be as dutiful children to the Church authorities, but through our own organization we may do a work which no other can accomplish."[17]

Along with opposition to their work because of their gender, women in missions also faced racist skepticism about the project of foreign missions itself. Prominent racial theorists mocked missionaries in general, stating that they were misguided in thinking that any fundamental change could be brought about among nonwhite populations around the world. The influential nineteenth-century racial theorist Josiah C. Nott stated:

> All the historical records of the past tell us of the same moral and physical differences of races which exist at the present day, and we can only judge the future by the past. The numberless attempts by the Caucasian race, during several thousand years, to bring the Mongol, Malay, Indian and Negro, under the same religion, laws, manners, customs, etc., have failed, and must continue to fail. . . . What has been the result of missions to Africa, to China, to India, to the American Indians, &c.? Much as we may lament such a result . . . these philanthropic efforts . . . do more harm than good.[18]

Nott argued that missions were, in effect, an attempt to alter a natural order created by biological differences. Contradictorily, he suggested that such efforts were doomed to failure because of the intractability of biological differences but also that such efforts were a danger to the social order. As Nott and others like him popularized scientific theories justifying racism—and purported that it was essentially a biological impossibility to transfer the "white man's religion" to nonwhites—missionaries in the nineteenth century had to defend the Christian tradition of evangelization.

Similarly, anti-immigrant propagandist Montaville Flowers campaigned against the threat that foreign missions posed to white supremacy, denouncing "missionary enthusiasm" for non-Western peoples. A vocal opponent of Asian immigration to the United States, Flowers feared that misguided activities like foreign missions would give white Americans the false impression that the "yellow race" and Caucasians could live together harmoniously. Revolutionary American notions of equality and human rights only made sense, according to Flowers, when they were applied to the men who founded the Republic and their descendants, because these men "were the warp and woof of a new human fabric woven from the richest materials of the superior nations of the white race."[19] Only the white race had the innate abilities to perpetuate the achievements of Western civilization, in the view of racist propagandists such as Flowers, and missionaries thereby threatened Western civilization itself by attempting to school nonwhites in Western values. In seeking to save the souls of nonwhites, Flowers warned, missionaries were on a slippery slope toward embracing people of color as social equals in addition to spiritual equals.

Rejecting racist ideologies such as those perpetuated by the likes of Nott and Flowers, women in missions renovated the rhetoric of domesticity not only to justify their own public activities as women but also to champion the mission movement as the antidote to racism and racial divisions. Instead of fixating on supposed racial differences, they rhetorically erased difference through cultivating a vision of a worldwide Christian family. Building on the evangelical Protestant belief that the perceived "degradation" of foreign cultures was caused by false religion—not by inherent racial characteristics—advocates of women's missions placed the blame for the "inferiority" of non-Western cultures on the absence of Christian homes at the core of their civilizations. Women in missions countered racist opposition to their work by referencing, again, the Protestant belief that the creation and maintenance of a "Christian family," where godliness and virtue were instilled and nourished, was at the core of *any* civilization's strength. They insisted that ethnic and racial "deficiencies" would be overcome by the propagation of Christian virtue through Christian wives and mothers. That theirs was yet another kind of ethnocentric, imperialist project did not seem to occur to them, at least during the early years of the women's mission movement.

Although the mission movement's representation of non-Western cultures would become more respectful and nuanced over time (later mission literature even featured multiple perspectives of non-Western women), in the early years mission supporters portrayed non-Western women as victims in need of the physical, mental, and spiritual salvation that American Christians could offer.[20] In 1875 a missionary wife wrote: "I have often been questioned in regard to the characteristics and capabilities of the women of India, and have endeavored, in a book that is now going through the press, . . . to show that Hindostanee women posses powers of mind equal to those of the women of Christian lands, and that they only need the inspiration of Christianity to raise them to an equality with ourselves."[21] Conversion to Christianity offered to all races a path to the heights of human civilization, which many missionaries unquestioningly identified with Western culture. Such portrayals were successful in convincing many in their denominations that it was worthwhile for Christian women to give up their own domestic roles and present themselves as "a whole burnt-offering" to help other women in need.[22]

In their efforts to globalize their notions of proper Christian womanhood, American Protestants opened up a space of legitimacy for women who did not fulfill domestic roles. Protestant mission boards employed unmarried women to convert other women to Christianity and proper domestication. They reasoned that only women could do the work of converting non-Christian women, since male missionaries were unable to cross into the female sphere of other cultures that also maintained distinct gender divisions. According to missionary William Butler, who strongly supported the creation of the first independent women's missionary societies in the late 1860s, men "faced a shut door and the key was not in their hands. Only women could enter there. . . . to reach the women who fled from the [male] missionary himself."[23] Moreover, they stressed that only "single women could give themselves completely to the needs of in-digenous women" because "missionary wives in the field were overwhelmed by family responsibilities."[24] Ironically, then, it was the ideology of domesticity, as well as the patriarchal arrangements of many non-Western cultures, which provided the justification for Protestant women to forgo a life in the domestic sphere to build their own mission movement.

Not only would Christian homes save future generations from incivility, according to the rhetoric of the women's mission movement, but Christianity would also save women in foreign lands from their bondage within a system that degraded them. While women in missions eventually began to criticize the patriarchal social arrangements of Western civilizations as well, initially they portrayed the American domestic ideal as a form of emancipation for women. Many American Protestants believed that the value placed on motherhood and domesticity in the Victorian West resulted from Christianity, and thus when other cultures adopted Christian values, women around the world would rise from their status as "slaves" to become "queens" of their homes.

With the Civil War behind them and American slavery abolished, many northern evangelical women saw foreign missions as the new abolition-ist movement and drew on the recent rhetoric of that movement to bolster women's missions, as they urged white women to continue to work against women's "slavery" around the world. An 1869 issue of the *Heathen Woman's Friend* informed the women of the Methodist Episcopal Church that "almost universally, the bearing of the [Hindu] wife is that of complete subjection and subserviency—that of an abject menial. . . . The same degradation and social oppression exists among Mohammedan women; they are also *slaves*. . . . It is a fact, that every Christian woman should bear in mind, that no less than 300,000,000 of women are still in the condition of slavery."[25] Now that the work against slavery in the United States was technically over, a whole world of "slaves" was waiting for the saving influence of Christian women.

White women were called upon to free these "heathen" women, as one mis-sionary periodical stated, from the "lying, thieving, and women-flogging, the licentiousness and infanticide of all pagandom."[26] Like many white leaders of the abolitionist movement, leaders of the women's mission movement com-bined their outrage over the oppressive lives of people in their world with a hefty dose of paternalism. The *Heathen Woman's Friend* proclaimed:

> God has put a new work in the hands of the women of the Methodist church.
> He has committed to our care millions of our dusky sisters. . . . The sick, the
> ignorant, the degraded, the helpless, stretch out their hands to us who are
> rejoicing in the light and glory of our Christian civilization. . . . Shall we be
> deaf to the cry of thousands? Shall we be preoccupied and careless, when

God in answer to our prayers has opened to us such precious opportunities of extending His kingdom?[27]

The early publications of the women's mission movement presented a nearly monolithic portrayal of women in non-Christian lands: universally oppressed and without the means to save themselves. The task of their salvation was placed squarely on the shoulders of Western women, a burden evangelical women took upon themselves with exhilarating displays of strength, courage, and confidence. Postmillennialist hopes melded with imperialist fervor in the early days of women's missions, a marriage that broadened white women's horizons like never before. By embracing the responsibility for their degraded "heathen sisters," Western women fashioned for themselves an identity as global rescuers and caretakers, which significantly undermined America's separate spheres ideology that promoted women's submissiveness and seclusion in the domestic realm.

Just as the abolitionist movement had led an earlier generation of American women to work for the political emancipation of women in addition to the abolition of slavery, the mission movement was extremely effective in bringing late nineteenth- and early twentieth-century women into the cause of women's rights.[28] As they became more established, women's missions helped develop women's professional skills in previously male-dominated arenas, leading to more overt confrontations with traditional gender ideals. Women's missionary societies were among the first organizations to support and hire female physicians, and hundreds of these doctors worked in mission fields during the heyday of the movement. Women missionaries also had professional opportunities to serve as executive directors of schools and benevolent organizations; and they could work as preachers overseas, even if their denominations back home prohibited women's ordination.

Mission magazines demystified these pursuits for their reading audience in the United States, as they proudly featured stories about successful missionary women. Unmarried women in the mission field often expressed much satisfaction over their choice of career, and they communicated to women back in the United States their exceeding pleasure at their accomplishments and adventures. As one missionary woman stated: "The Lord has given me so much to be thankful for lately, that I would like to transfer a little of it to America, and let you share it with me." Suggesting that her call to a public life of missionary work was even more worthy than a life of motherhood and domesticity, another missionary woman wrote: "I feel quite sure there can be no happier person, nor any more blessed work than mine."[29] Far from the pathetically unwed and childless women imagined by the early critics of the women's mission movement, unmarried missionary women communicated to women back in the United States that life in the public sphere as educated, skilled professionals could be profoundly rewarding.

As missionary women themselves embraced their opportunities for public leadership, their visions for emancipating women around the world became more radical, and their rhetoric more bold. Over time, Protestant women broadened their goal of reshaping the domestic realm of foreign lands, as they began to envision new freedoms for women outside the home. By the early twentieth century, mission literature highlighted women's entry into public arenas around the world as a sign that Christianity was in fact influencing "heathen" cultures. A 1907 issue of the *Woman's Missionary Friend* featured an article on progress in China, which began with the quip: "'A girl is no good—only to get married.' Familiar? Oh, no, that's 'heathen Chinese,' not even modern China." While the "heathen China" of the past had no roles for women to play other than wife and mother, the article proclaimed, as a result of mission schools, "each burning a hole in the dark that is causing the whole system of heathenism to break into pieces," the women of "modern China" now had a myriad of new paths open to them. In particular, the article highlighted Chinese graduates of female mission schools who went on to study medicine in the United States, returning to work in China as doctors.[30] Another article stated that because of Christianity, a "spirit of rebellion is working among the Japanese, who are refusing to be kept at home practicing obedience to their husbands and fathers," and that in China "one will find plenty of high-spirited feminists . . . in the mission schools."[31]

Clearly, by the twentieth century some women began to understand the mission movement as a part of the larger movement for women's rights. Women's experiences in the mission movement ultimately strengthened their resolve to gain more ecclesiastical and political power in the United States itself. As early as 1896, Frances Baker pointed out in her book that "there were 'oppressors' in the West as well as in the more conservative East . . . ministers and laymen in the church who said: 'Let your women keep silence in the churches.'" The women's mission movement gave women a voice in the church as "workers" who were "intelligent and self-respecting"; Baker quoted a preacher from Indiana who quipped: "You call your paper the *Heathen Woman's Friend*. . . . You would better call it the Christian Woman's Friend. See what it is doing for the women in our [American] churches."[32] In subsequent decades, mission women's rhetoric succeeded in making women's political emancipation a respectable topic in mainline American Protestant circles. Women like Helen Barrett Montgomery, one of the most well-loved speakers and writers in the Protestant women's mission movement during the early twentieth century, found mission supporters to be quite receptive to her liberal religious and political views. Montgomery's seminal book *Western Women in Eastern Lands* (1910)—a text that women in all the major Protestant denominations studied in their educational programs—openly connected the women's rights movement with the work of the women's foreign mission movement.

While an earlier generation of women in missions had used the Cult of True Womanhood to gain rhetorical power, subsequent leaders of the movement, like Montgomery, used that rhetorical power to dismantle the Cult of True Womanhood. Montgomery identified the women's mission movement not as the bulwark of traditional gender ideologies, but as one of the major forces behind the subversion and rejection of the ideology of separate spheres. Montgomery stated: "The organization of the Women's Mission societies is but one of a remarkable series of movements among women that have made the nineteenth century known as the Woman's Century. In it forces long at work crystallized so as to revolutionize many conceptions regarding the proper sphere and activities of women."[33] Montgomery conflated the values and objectives of the women's rights movement with those of the women's mission movement—in short, the elevation of women. Montgomery stated that *Christian* progress throughout the nineteenth century was evident in that

> all the demands made by that ridiculed and persecuted little band of women [i.e., women's rights supporters], in their first convention at Seneca Falls, have since been adopted and embodied in law, save one only. They asked for woman the right to have personal freedom, to acquire an education, to earn a living, to claim her wages, to own property, to sue and be sued, to make contracts, to testify in court, to obtain a divorce for just cause, to possess her children, to claim a fair share of the accumulations during marriage, *to vote.*[34]

Asserting a biblical basis for women's rights, she urged more missionary women to take up the cause of women's political and economic rights. Doing so, they would further their goals in mission work, for if "women fully recognized the emancipatory nature of the pure religion of Jesus, the force of the religious missionary arguments would be tremendously strengthened."[35]

By embracing gender equality as a Christian ideal, Montgomery was more critical of her own society than earlier mission women, and she had to explain why women continued to be oppressed in predominantly Christian societies. She did so by exempting Christianity itself from any role in the oppression of women, even in Western societies; where Western societies failed women, it was because they had not fully embraced Christianity either. While she admitted that "there are terrible wrongs against women in our own land," the difference between "Christian" America and non-Christian lands, she claimed, was that "the wrongs of Hindu, Chinese, and Moslem women are buttressed behind the sanctions of religion, and are indorsed [sic] by the founders of their faith; while in our own land these wrongs flaunt themselves against the spirit and the plain provisions of our religion."[36]

Montgomery went on to say: "Strictly speaking, there is no Christian nation, but only nations in process of becoming Christian. But even so, the steady pressure of Bible ideals, exerted slowly and against tremendous difficulties, has already brought a revolution in the position of women."[37] Dismissing the Apostle Paul's injunctions against women's leadership, so important to conservative Christians like James Monroe Buckley, as biblical passages that were "not at all inspired," Montgomery instead emphasized, like many other missionary women, Paul's words in Galatians 3:28 as "the Magna Charta of womanhood in a Christianity in which there is neither male nor female."[38] Montgomery's grand vision, which ultimately became the vision of many women involved in the major Protestant denominations' missionary enterprises, was to bring all people, regardless of gender or national boundaries, into "Christ's great democracy," a world of both religious and political emancipation.[39]

As the image of the missionary woman working to uplift the status of women around the world became an acceptable trope in the minds of middle-class Protestant America, the women's rights movement began to find more widespread acceptance within the United States' most politically powerful religious group. Through the rhetoric of women's missionary literature, the oppression of women came to be linked to "heathendom," while women's emancipation around the globe was presented as a logical result of enlightened Christian culture. Beginning the women's mission movement in the 1860s through renovating the ideology of domesticity, by the early twentieth century many women involved in missions were champions of woman's suffrage. The growing feminist consciousness of the women's mission movement also reveals that through global expansionism the Western world was itself reshaped and that progressive liberalism in the United States was often built out of imperialist and racist discourses. America's engagement with non-Western countries, such as that of American missionary women, gave rise to new ways of thinking and new self-understanding within the imperialist culture itself.

THE RISE OF ACADEMIC CONCERN ABOUT
AMERICAN CHRISTIAN FUNDAMENTALISM

—

6

—

"ATTENTIVE, INTELLIGENT, REASONABLE, AND RESPONSIBLE"

TEACHING COMPOSITION WITH BERNARD LONERGAN

Priscilla Perkins

If there is a primary vehicle of persuasion, it is not our words, but the persons we have become.

—Kenneth Melchin, *Living with Other People*

For who among men knows the thoughts of a man except the man's spirit within him? In the same way no one knows the thoughts of God except the Spirit of God. We have not received the spirit of the world but the Spirit who is from God, that we may understand what God has freely given us.

—1 Corinthians 2:11–12 (New International Version)

Teaching honors classes used to drive me crazy, at least during the first weeks of the semester. Before I returned the first graded writing assignment, I had to steel myself for the grade-grubbery that inevitably followed, a student ritual I called the "Attack of the Killer B Pluses." Many of the students who enroll in Writing About Ideas, a course for honors students who have transferred from community colleges, have never earned a B before. In my experience honors students are more likely than other students to come into a course so (outwardly) certain of who they are and what they know, and they're the only ones who regularly argue about grades. During a recent semester, therefore, I chose the generic-sounding theme "Identity and Belief," so that students might experience the power of academic discourses, what the social linguist James Paul Gee has called ways of "being, thinking, acting, talking, writing, reading, and valuing," for exploring issues that shape college students' relationships to their learning.[1] In turn, I wanted students to use what they learned about their identities and beliefs as heuristics for assessing the personal usefulness of the discourses they were trying on.

Engaging in interpretive back-and-forth between selves and discourses is, I tell students, both a way of initiating oneself into the academy and a way of using academic tools in the service of personal development. As a progressive Catholic academic working in a secular university, I practice what I teach: I am attracted to thinkers, religious or not, who help me create equitable conditions for learning and justice-oriented action. My pedagogy in this course was strongly informed by the work of the Canadian Jesuit philosopher Bernard Lonergan (1904–1984) and his growing number of interpreters in theology, political science, education, economics, and communication theory. Though Lonergan is little-known among composition theorists, his method of "self-appropriation"—a practice of self-reflexive cognition that urges subjects to "Be attentive; Be intelligent; Be reasonable; Be responsible"—can help student writers ground their analyses more firmly in their own life experiences and values, even as they enlarge their interpretive horizons to include the experiences of others. In the few cases where students have trouble incorporating self-appropriation into their writing practices (including the case of "Tina," one of the students I will discuss in this chapter), Lonergan's theories about the interplay of self-knowledge and ethics help to explain why.

Lonergan has so far not been embraced by American academics because, although his thinking was deeply influenced by developments in many disciplines, his Catholic Thomism (his grounding in Thomas of Aquinas's readings of Aristotelian, Islamic, and Jewish thinking) placed him outside the mainstreams of both the analytic and Continental philosophy of his time. Lonergan's writings articulate ideas about illocutionary power in ways that are familiar to readers of John Searle and John L. Austin, and he questions assumptions about authority as rigorously as Jacques Derrida and Michel Foucault do, but he starts from the theological premise that there is a God-created order to the universe that humans, with deliberate cognitive practice, can discern. Such discernment, he argues, creates opportunities for ethical action and progress toward the goals of social justice; in linking cognition with justice-oriented social action, Lonergan resembles a better-known Catholic educator, Paulo Freire.[2] While Lonergan's Catholic theology, which is fully integrated into an ecumenical Christian philosophy of the self, may be a stumbling block for some academics, many of his perspectives can be readily integrated into secular learning environments. His commitment to helping learners take responsibility for their acts of knowing is especially suited to writing classes that bring together students with diverse beliefs—in the case of my class, Jewish, Evangelical Christian, Hindu, Catholic, and atheist. Like other bridges that make communication across traditions of belief possible, this one doesn't fit perfectly, and the risk of miscommunication is always present.[3] But a pedagogy based on Lonergan's method of self-appropriation presses students and teachers into habits of reflection: they begin to reappraise their earlier thoughts, words, and interactions in ways that enhance the best practices of process pedagogy.

By touting the value of a Lonerganian writing pedagogy, obscure and initially difficult, I call into question a popular way of teaching that has an ancient and respected pedigree, an Aristotelian rhetorical pedagogy that tacitly encourages students to distance themselves from the arguments they make. In countless colleges, including the community colleges that send their graduates to my university, writers are taught that in order to win converts to their arguments, they must project personae self-consciously molded to the messages they want their audiences to accept. Most mainstream college composition textbooks incorporate an at least partially Aristotelian approach, but the best-selling *Everything's an Argument* puts this rhetorical practice in stark terms: "Voice is a choice. That is, writers modify the tone and style of their language depending on who they want to *seem to be*." The coauthors, Andrea Lunsford and John Ruszkiewicz, advise students that "you'll need to change the way you claim authority, establish credibility, and demonstrate competence as you try to convince different audiences of your character."[4] In this representation of ethos, two basic meanings of "character" merge. Character is both "the inherent complex of attributes that determine a person's moral and ethical actions and reactions" and "an imaginary person represented in a work of fiction." As *Everything's an Argument* explains, "there is much to be said for framing arguments directly and confidently, as if you really mean them. (And it helps if you do)."[5] In this representation the effective rhetor is a Method actor.

Such a teetery concept of *ethos* is, well, an ethical problem in the teaching of writing. In the terms that Lonergan offers, however, the problem is cognitive before it is ethical. Teaching writing as a process of persuasive appeals to an audience based on reason, character, and feeling distracts students from asking what they are doing when they know, when they look at themselves and others, and when they respond emotionally to their environments. In other words, this rhetorical pedagogy problematically directs students' attention outward before they have a chance to look inside. As the Catholic ethicist John C. Haughey has written: "We do not do justice to our intentionality if we are led around by ideas and concepts arrived at by others and not personally internalized. So, for example, Lonergan would have been very wary of someone who was a strong advocate of human rights but whose promotion of them disregarded the distinctiveness of subjectivity, one's own or the other's. He disdained a formulaic morality and trusted responses that emerged through the subject seeking to understand the specifics of a given situation."[6]

Too often, rhetorical pedagogy encourages students to take positions on issues without doing the metacognitive work necessary to "own" their arguments. They learn to pretend certainty about issues they don't (perhaps can't) yet understand. When students take an instrumentalist approach to *ethos,* they focus more on managing their reader's responses than on producing knowledge that is new to both the reader and the writer. Conversely, by emphasizing recursive self-appropriation rather than the cultivation of rhetorical *ethos,* a Lonerganian pedagogy suggests that, as they are reading, writing, and rewriting, students must take their own experiences and positions seriously enough that they cannot help but consider how their words might affect—not just persuade—the communities they address. This chapter takes up composition theorist Michael-John DePalma's recommendation that we "invent alternative terminologies with which to talk and think in more complex ways about the relationship between religious faith and composition instruction"—starting, in this case, by turning the rhetorical imperative to *seem* into an epistemological and ontological imperative to *be.*[7]

BE ATTENTIVE, BE INTELLIGENT

In his article on "Casuistic Stretching," the composition theorist Jeffrey Ringer introduces us to an evangelical undergraduate so earnest that he eagerly shares his own psalm-like poetry with Ringer (who also self-identifies as evangelical).[8] Though he has trouble representing his faith to nonbelievers, "Austin" projects a stable, pretense-free sense of "being." By contrast, more than most students I have taught, "Tina," an evangelical Christian business major in platform shoes and low-slung jeans, was visibly torn between "being" and "seeming." When class members discussed their everyday, out-of-school lives—the TV they watched, their ways of getting and spending money, their relationships with parents and romantic partners—Tina treated us to her unvarnished, irrepressible "being": at her most comfortable, she dissected her coworkers' and boyfriend's eccentricities in a rapid-fire patter that made us laugh and like her (even though we knew that, at work and home, she was doing the same thing to *us*). She was quick to announce that the writers we read in class were "stupid whiners." When the class wanted to renegotiate a due date with me, they turned to Tina, whose entrepreneurial wheeling-and-dealing sometimes overwhelmed my ability to protect a carefully constructed syllabus. A kinetic physical presence, Tina inhaled McDonald's fries and chicken sandwiches, bounced between her seat and the trash can, and sometimes disappeared—with no pretense and no apologies—for a three-minute smoke on the sidewalk outside our classroom window. Seated between cerebral humanities and computer science majors, Tina asserted that hard work, not intellectual aptitude, earned her a spot in the honors program and would someday lead her to the kind of income her more brainy peers would probably never attain. No one believed that she wasn't as smart as the rest of the class, of course; her intelligence was not something she could hide, even if she truly wanted to.

The first three essay assignments for ENG 222 challenged students in ways for which their community college writing courses had not prepared them. For their first foray, students had to select ideas from Victor Seidler's "Language and Masculinity" that could help them decide whether postmodern philosophy, as the social critic Neil Postman has argued, really suffers from "serious depression" and a lack of "conviction."[9] This was no easy task, given their relative unfamiliarity with either Enlightenment or postmodern thinking, but in the "mushfake" spirit advocated by Gee, students were assured that the more actively they tried out new ideas and ways of writing, the more quickly they would develop the genuine authority academic writers need.[10] In early drafting activities, students paraphrased Seidler's ideas and tested them against their own experiences; in class discussion, they shared and commented on the informal writing they were producing. Then, with full drafts in hand and a half-sheet of "revision tasks"—questions designed to refocus their attention on the analytical work called for in the essay assignment—they commented on the ideas being developed in two or three of their peers' drafts.

Every step in the process required them to notice their own acts of cognition. In my response to Tina's final draft, I again encouraged her, in Lonergan's terms, to "be attentive" and "be intelligent"—in other words, to "look lively" and ask questions. First, I wrote: "Though you stake your opening and closing on the idea that Seidler and Postman agree on most issues, the body of your paper tells a different (and much more interesting) story." Here I invited Tina to recognize the unexpected knowledge that she had produced but overlooked in her attempt to produce a tidy five-paragraph essay. I also introduced an interpersonal ethic of inquiry for our work in the class: "When you look in the margins, you'll see a number of questions that I've asked you about your ideas. These are *real* questions—I don't know the answers to them, and I'm curious to hear what you'd say."[11] With this comment I let Tina know that, though formative, my questions were not intended primarily to help her internalize the teacher's way of doing things so that she could get a better grade next time. I expected her to answer my questions so that we'd both know more about our work. In her second and third papers Tina often did respond "attentively" to her own ideas and "intelligently" to the questions of her readers, though, like many students, she still tended to short-circuit analysis by relying on formulaic organizational strategies. For example, because she started from the five-paragraph model she had learned in Expository Writing 101, she sometimes stopped working out an idea if it looked like it might take more than one paragraph to explore; or, if she did let her analysis spill over into a second paragraph, she undermined its power by inserting a transitional phrase that didn't capture the actual relationship between the ideas she was working out.

During those first two months of the course, Tina's work was not so different from that of her peers: somewhat more facile, often less patient with nuance, she was generally on the same page as the rest of the class. The fourth essay assignment changed everything. In preparation for this essay, the class had worked with several readings that were at least partly about religious belief; in addition to Andrea Fishman's essay about Amish literacy practices and Jeffrey Weeks's discussion of moral pluralism and AIDS, we talked about Frank Black Elk's "Observations on Marxism and Lakota Tradition," Jennifer Cobb's "Cybergrace: The Search for God in the Digital World," Nawal el-Saadawi's "Love and Sex in the Life of the Arab," and Renato Rosaldo's "Grief and a Head-hunter's Rage."[12] Immersed in the authors' diverse perspectives, and fortified by multiple opportunities to write informally about their relationships to these perspectives, Tina and the rest of the students began work on the capstone assignment for the semester:

> Construct a "narrative" that accounts for the development and current state of your own "big story" in Postman's terms, a story that is "sufficiently profound and complex to offer explanations of the origins and future of a people . . . that construct[s] ideals, prescribe[s] rules of conduct, specif[ies] sources of authority, and, in doing all this, provide[s] a sense of continuity and purpose." Then, using terms and concepts from Black Elk, Rosaldo, and Weeks or el-Saadawi, analyze any tensions, comforts, contradictions, or questions that this "big story" creates for you in your everyday life.

Though the assignment foregrounded Postman's assumption that people's beliefs are enabling fictions, capable of being examined at arm's length and revised as necessary, other readings in the mix suggested that beliefs are inextricable from identity, and that identities, while fluid, are not simply performances. Unlike Postman, who sees Enlightenment rationalism as a force for preventing overidentification with belief, several of the other writers posit that their religious traditions themselves offer tools for thinking critically about beliefs without abandoning them. In keeping with coauthors Elizabeth Vander Lei's and Lauren Fitzgerald's caution against requiring students "to write about their faith when they would rather not," neither the readings nor the assignment specified that the students' "big stories" had to be about religion.[13]

Students responded to this assignment in predictably diverse ways. A twice-married "ex-Catholic" described how she came to trust her own judgment on the rightness of her sexual choices, while an atheist computer major talked about his faith in the scientific method. A Latina Jew, living between the cultures of her biological and adoptive families, preferred what she saw as Jewish tradition over Catholic dogma. An Indian American biology major's models for living came from the Hindu stories of gods and goddesses she had heard as a child. A history major from a conservative Lutheran congregation addressed (though didn't completely untangle) contradictions between her belief in biblical teachings and the pluralistic perspectives she had adopted during three years of college. Except for Tina—the one class member who until this point had regularly offered unsolicited religious advice—everyone in the class engaged comfortably in discussions and revision activities around this assignment.

An exercise in Lonerganian self-appropriation, the assignment worked for most of the students because, in keeping with mainstream academic critical practices, it acknowledged that received meanings and values can't automatically be accepted and that self-reflexive (read: "attentive" and "intelligent") awareness of one's situatedness is a prerequisite for "reasonable" and "responsible" participation in discourse. The kind of thinking required for this assignment was familiar to the students, even though its Christian assumptions about intellectual inquiry might not have been. Lonergan, building on a tradition that predates Augustine, argued that, as knowers created in God's likeness, humans possess a "normative dynamic structure of interior operations"—in other words, a set of innate, flexible thinking abilities that, once trained, requires individuals to be involved in "the outstanding and successful intellectual endeavors" of their time, to use their powers of reason to judge those endeavors, and to make personal moral choices based on those judgments.[14] Within Lonergan's Catholic Christian philosophy, *logos* (or meaning) emerges through knowing ourselves—intelligently, reasonably, responsibly, lovingly—in relation to others, rather than through simply following what the Bible or Church says (as challenging as it can be to follow either of these sources of authority).

"WHEN WILL YOU BELIEVE? WHAT'S STOPPING YOU?"

Viewed from a perspective of Lonerganian self-appropriation, Tina's difficulties with the assignment begin to make sense. Tina had represented herself throughout the course as tolerant and more than assimilated into our secular university; indeed, she characterized her background, her style, and her goals as normative. Once the class started writing about belief, however, Tina's self-presentation changed radically. Her beliefs, she said, were not "a narrative" but "[her] life." If her peers, as they claimed, had had bad experiences with Christians, she explained that those were isolated phenomena or could be attributed to the perpetrator's affiliation with a church that was only "sort of" Christian (Catholic, Presbyterian, and so on), perhaps one, in John Haughey's words, more invested in "Church-ianity" than "Christ-ianity."[15] She jumped anxiously on every chance to demonstrate how her faith in Christ had eliminated worry and uncertainty from her life. She brought her neon-colored *Teen Study Bible* to class so everyone could see that it was as hip as she was. Having shared her personal story of salvation with her peers, she felt empowered (or obliged) to remind them that non-Christians, like homosexuals and other sinners, had a limited window of time within which to change direction. Most exasperating to her classmates, perhaps, was this question, formulated in several different ways during the weeks in which we discussed religious belief: "It sounds like you *understand* the Gospel. When will you *believe*? What's stopping you?" And it seemed that no answer short of "Right this minute!" could satisfy her.

Tina's fellow students understandably began to question how a fashion-forward cultural critic coexisted with a nervous proselytizer. In her writing for this assignment, stylistically tortuous compared to her much more direct writing for other assignments, Tina rejects any suggestion of strain between the two personae: "My beliefs do not really create the tensions in my life; it is my life that creates the problems in which I turn to my beliefs to deal with. I will always be faced with people who do not like me because of what I believe or who do not understand it. But God never said it would be easy."[16] Tina's unwieldy apologia reveals a simultaneously rigid and fragile identification with her evangelical character. Where the "everyday" Tina apparently didn't worry about the disapproval of those she lambasted, laughed at, or unceremoniously walked out on, the evangelical Tina fought off the threat of "people who do not like me because of what I believe," her description of classmates who had either asked for clarifying details about her beliefs or, in at least two cases, asked her politely to respect their own religious beliefs by not aggressively "witnessing" to them.

Conflicts between Tina and her classmates could be blamed on the students' and my failure to adhere to basic rules of cultural pluralism in the class, the "don't ask, don't tell" etiquette surrounding religion and politics in quasi-public spaces like composition classrooms.[17] Catholic theologian Kenneth Melchin, though, urges us to ask the following questions about our secular learning environments, before we conclude that such spaces should be ideology-free zones: "Do you disagree with everyone, all the time, on everything moral or ethical? What about your routines of day-to-day living? Do you not frequently find yourself sharing values, convictions, moral habits, ethical practices with those around you? Even when you disagree, do all your disagreements end in mortal combat? If not, what do you tacitly agree upon that tempers your disagreeing? These, too, are moral agreements."[18]

In most cases our interactions revealed the classroom to be an ethically sturdy space in which people who disagree can still work together effectively. Using what Lonergan defined in *Insight* as the "common sense" of everyday life, the approach to morality whose "concern is the concrete and practical," we repeatedly choose to interact patiently and generously with each other. As Lonergan writes: "Common sense undertakes . . . communication, not as an exercise in formal logic, but as a work of art."[19] The class, like most other small groups, started with a tacit interest in contributing to the "common good" of our learning community, which, in Melchin's terms, "is fashioned by all, sets the framework for meeting the requirements of all, and, when it is functioning well, sustains a high degree of liberty for all."[20] In the face of the "belief-as-narrative" assignment, though, that interest would quickly become explicit.

The class's work with this assignment demonstrated how, in situations of conflict, the common good cannot (according to Lonergan and Melchin) be achieved through the easy operations of "common sense" ethics. "To *choose* the common good," writes Melchin, "we must *know* the common good. Moral knowledge, then, is knowledge of the dynamic structure of the common good, how it sustains all aspects of our living, and the demands it makes on our personal decision-making."[21] While the "belief-as-narrative" assignment at first created "common sense" (or improvisational) opportunities for all students to consider the dynamic ethical content of their interactions, Tina's startling response to the topic sent the rest of the class into a much more self-appropriative mode of communicating with each other. And the self-knowledge they created led to richer writing: other students began to choose words more carefully, with the intent of increasing, not blunting, their resonance and truth-telling power.

"THE RIGHT TO SPEAK AND TO BE LISTENED TO"

Even before I started working with Lonergan's ideas in the classroom, I was committed to a pedagogy that frames writing as a process for creating hermeneutic understanding. Laying the conceptual groundwork for his hermeneutic theories, the philosopher Hans-Georg Gadamer wrote that rhetoric and hermeneutics exist in a "positive/negative" relationship to each other. Insofar as classical rhetoric is based on what Gadamer described as the desire to make arguments "appropriate to the specific receptivity of the souls to which they are directed"—an approach that requires deep knowledge of the other party's beliefs and values—his claim that rhetoric is "essentially prior" to hermeneutics could be true.[22] Because the most common classroom approach to rhetoric focuses, as I have suggested, on the creation of persuasive personae, I prefer to teach academic writing as a process that must start from the writer's cognitive and moral relationships to the subject matter, a hermeneutic pedagogy that is consistent with Lonergan's approach to understanding. In "Understanding as the Transformation of What Is Already Known," Peter Ashworth writes that "an essential feature of hermeneutic participation, is that the individual sees him- or herself as having the right to interact with the subject matter. Usually this means the right to speak and to be listened to."[23] The interaction between Sara, a history major and Evangelical Lutheran, and Shruti, a Hindu biology major, shows how "attentive, intelligent" dialogue created hermeneutic participation in an environment of tension. In her first draft for the assignment, Sara explored her Evangelical Lutheran tradition, which she saw emphasizing the dignity of all humans, through the refracting lens of historical relativism:

> I am inclined to agree with [Frank Black Elk that] the Native American has often been converted to Christianity for the white man's ends, but there may be a middle ground between his view and the missionary's. My former pastor's daughter certainly never used her position as a missionary to steal land or collect booty, but I do think she could have found another way to spread God's love. For example, why not found a public school and bring clothes and food to people who need them in another country?[24]

In her comments on Sara's draft, Shruti tried to "get inside" the Christian beliefs about evangelism that her classmates had discussed and written about, but which Shruti said she still could not understand: "If the pastor's daughter strongly believes in spreading the word of God, as she obviously does, do you think that just setting up schools to provide clothes and food to the needy will satisfy her inner desire to fulfill her duty?" Shruti's comments used terms meaningful to Sara ("spreading the word of God," "fulfill[ing] her duty") to draw Sara's attention to "aporia" in her thinking, those places where "significant meaning is not predetermined, leaving both linguistically grappling for words to conversationally take things forward."[25] Though Tina's proselytizing had clearly aggrieved her, Shruti sympathized with the "problem of meaning" (in Renato Rosaldo's term) experienced by Christians like Sara who could not or chose not to evangelize; having practiced hermeneutic, or interpretively oriented, revision strategies throughout the semester, she easily prompted her revision partner to examine her relativism more self-consciously. Was this relativism, Shruti asked, something that Sara truly wanted to "own" in herself? Was it consistent with the theological beliefs and values with which Sara most closely identified?

Sara's and Shruti's experience of "the dynamic structure of the common good" in the class may have motivated Sara to add a page on what she called "religious diversity" at the end of her final draft. In this section Sara quotes John 3:16—in which Jesus says that "whoever believes in him shall not perish but have eternal life"—and then writes: "Taken literally, this statement means that all those who do not believe that God is the ultimate truth *will* perish. In my daily life, however, I encounter great numbers of people who do not believe in God. Does their unbelief mean that I will go to heaven and they will not?"[26] Sara's carefully considered answer is no.

As though she understood the difficult position her evangelical classmate was, by necessity or choice, occupying in the class, Sara made comments on Tina's draft that were unfailingly polite and supportive, while they also invited

Tina to say more about beliefs that non-Christian (or nonevangelical) class members might be expected to misunderstand. In her final draft Tina appears not to have accepted any of these invitations; though it is likely that she read Sara's draft, she also apparently chose not to comment on it. Intriguingly, however, Sara's final draft responds explicitly to one of Tina's frequently stated concerns as well as to the biblical context from which it ostensibly springs. "As one of my classmates points out," writes Sara, "the Old Testament states that people who are homosexuals will be condemned." Sara's argument against "condemning homosexuals to hell" uses a common nonliteralist strategy for confronting the kind of "proof-texting" that Tina had used in class discussion: she explains that Leviticus, the book that mentions homosexuality, "also includes innumerable laws on cleansing, sacrifices, and rules for eliminating mildew"—most of which are ignored by all "modern Christians."[27] As I have argued elsewhere, this strategy, satisfying as it is to the nonliteralist, tends not to advance dialogue with a literalist believer.[28] So, while she could have stopped there, hoping that her readers' ethical "common sense" would convince them not to pursue an unproductive dispute about homosexuality, Sara chooses instead to respond "attentively, intelligently, reasonably, and responsibly" to Tina's concerns: "God apparently did not feel that homosexuality was an important enough issue to include in the Ten Commandments. Instead, for the First Commandment we have, 'Thou shalt have no other gods before me.' This commandment causes difficulties for many people who put money, a spouse, or work before God. I do not believe that any sin is greater than another, but if a heterosexual can struggle with the first commandment and receive forgiveness from God, then homosexuals can enter heaven as well."[29]

Sara accomplishes a great deal here. Without claiming that she was comfortable with homosexuality (I don't think she was), she encourages her readers, literalist and otherwise, to reflect both on Christian priorities as Christians frequently see them projected in the Jewish Bible and on her readers' own desires to create the "common good" of a tolerant community. There's a gentle nudge to Tina, whose own draft used the example of King Solomon to argue that one can love money *and* love God, but Sara's larger goal is clear: she speaks to Tina as a sister sinner and Christian, and she invites Tina to what Lonergan, in *A Third Collection,* called "affective conversion" or "commitment to love in the home, loyalty in the community, faith in the destiny of man."[30] For Sara, "Christian faith exercises a *heuristic* force that moves moral inquiry in a specific direction, and with a characteristic set of concerns."[31] In her writing, Sara's Lonerganian self-appropriation creates the possibility of persuasion—of Christian renovation, or even conversion—that is based not on a character she projects but on the person she has become.

Why did Tina's investment in her own Christian identity prevent her from engaging her peers on the subject that mattered the most to her? I propose that because "Jesus Christ"—Tina's image of the human incarnation of God as she saw Him represented in selected passages from the Christian Gospels—was experienced by Tina as somehow more real than her physically present, flesh-and-blood peers, she struggled to create authentically ethical relationships with those peers. In a very nearly literal sense, Tina behaved as though the primary audience for her fourth essay (and for her life, at least as she represented it in that text) was Jesus alone, not the fellow and sister humans through whom the Gospel says believers can serve Jesus. Underlying Lonerganian self-appropriation, in which knowledge of God's will is attained only through rigorous practices of self-understanding and ethical encounters with other's selves, is Luke 10:27: "'Love the Lord your God with all your heart and with all your soul and with all your strength and with all your mind'; and, 'Love your neighbor as yourself.'" Tina's selective emulation of Jesus's character led her to devalue both self-knowledge and the meaning-making possibility of interactions with others, especially when those people were questioning her claims to religious and moral certainty. Likewise, Tina's sense of personal agency was straitened by her desire for her will to be subsumed by Jesus's will to the point that she sometimes did not recognize peer-to-peer interactions as *requiring* a discerning practice of ethical renovation.

Ironically, Tina's Jesus-focused ethos orientation—developed through church attendance and guided Bible study, and reinforced by the rhetorical training she received in her first-year college composition courses—made her nearly impervious to either the affective conversion that Lonergan describes or to the intellectual, "metanoic" conversion that I have explored elsewhere.[32] To understand why, it's important to see how an evangelical ethos orientation can differ from the secular kind. In its most general sense, an "ethos orientation" is an approach to communication grounded, explicitly or not, in some version of the rhetorical triangle, "other-focused" mostly insofar as it seeks to win over the audience to the writer's argument or worldview, and supported by the writer's preexisting moral character. In the case of a biblical literalist like Tina, however, the rhetorical triangle is flattened because the rhetor's ethos is necessarily supported by, and sometimes inextricable from, a scripture-centered reliance on logos, considered literally to be the word of God as revealed in the Christian Bible. In other words, the writer writes as though her credibility comes entirely from her reliance on biblical authority. Indeed, in extreme cases evangelical ethos may seem to depend so completely on identification with scriptural logos that ethos loses its humanness. Logos, in its turn, is emptied of what Catholic Christians (among others) think of as incarnational mystery, or the paradoxically close relationship among God, God's word, and God's creation. As the theologian Michael J. Himes has written: "To speak about God who is gift is to speak about the human being who is the object of the giving; to know the Word is to know the one who is called into being into order to hear the Word. . . . The more fully one has explored and cultivated one's capacities as a human being, the readier one is to hear the Gospel, the Word which is God's self."[33] Self-appropriation, reinforced through metacognition and self-reflexive, renovating ethical action, offers one way for humans to experience the "incarnational mystery" of their relationships with God. But the "integral humanism" that, in Himes's terms, develops a person's intellectual and affective ability to enact the Gospel does not necessarily, for literalist believers, coexist with an ethos orientation. The evangelical writer may resist seeing logos as a dynamic force: the Word Is What It Is, and the writer's job is to use her Christian character to convince readers to accept that Word.

Practically speaking, in the evangelical ethos-oriented text, developments in the writer's outlook or understanding are likely to be located textually in the writer's past, usually around the time of her Christian conversion, rather than in the relatively present-tense unfolding—or writing—of her text. Tina's paper title, "John 3:16," fits this pattern. Unlike Sara, who used the same verse within her paper to work out its relevance for her relationships with nonbelievers, Tina uses John 3:16 as a banner that announces her identity and position before she says anything in her own voice. The essay begins by claiming that Tina's reading of Frank Black Elk and Renato Rosaldo, both of whom question the ethics of much Christian evangelism, has helped her "open up my beliefs and explain them more than I already have."[34] Tina's "already" expresses her vexation at being asked by her peers to talk about articles of faith that are, for her, literal, self-evident, and perhaps even predetermined. But in her paper "opening up" these beliefs doesn't mean examining them, using the tools of reason to mentally and spiritually renovate them, or considering what they mean for her relationships with the people around her, as it does in Sara's essay; instead, it means exposing them to nonbelievers' attacks.

When she does try to use course readings to frame discussions of her own beliefs, Tina decontextualizes those writers' ideas so that they seem to apply to her own concerns; at these moments her writing looks like that of novice college writers who are just learning how to create analytical frames for their experiences. For example, Tina harnesses Rosaldo's now well-known idea of the "problem of meaning" (attributed in his text to the clash between evangelical Christianity and Ilongot headhunting) to clichés about sex and the single Christian: "In Thessalonians 4:3–8, God says He wants us to be pure, using self-control over our physical desires. Things like this are hard to deal with especially when I know what God wants me to do. But although this part of my beliefs causes tension in my life, I know God is right, therefore I know what the right thing to do is."[35] Like many biblical literalists, Tina conflates God and the human transcribers of scripture, so that St. Paul's long-distance advice to the early Christians in Thessalonika becomes God's fatherly surveillance of young adults in suburban dance clubs. For Tina the "tension" is sexual temptation, which she represents as a force she resists with the help of scripture, rather than her awareness of potential gaps between her religious beliefs and her sexual choices.

Tina's intellectual engagement in her business classes, combined with her optimism that she would someday earn much more money than her lower middle-class parents had, made her bristle when her classmates pointed out Gospel passages in which Jesus tells the rich to give their possessions to the poor. In her final draft she argues that materialistic people are not "true believers" in Christianity (if they were, they'd "realize that 'things' mean nothing") while she simultaneously foregrounds the Old Testament example of King Solomon as someone who manages to love God and embrace earthly riches (without acknowledging of course that Solomon, unlike Tina, was not a follower of Jesus). I suspect that one classmate who pushed Tina on "the money issue" simply wanted to antagonize her (he looked for buttons to push in all of us), but the other students seemed genuinely alarmed at what they saw as a conflict between Tina's beliefs and her aspirations. They knew the discourses that Tina should have (given her declared identity) found internally persuasive; given her energetic performance of a Christian persona, they were troubled at how she cherry-picked Bible passages to rationalize the conflict away.

Tina's essay does touch what many conservative Christian students readily identify as a distressing "problem of meaning"—knowing that a close relative or friend has died without accepting salvation through Jesus Christ—but, as in other areas, Tina's ethos orientation keeps her from acknowledging this experience as an opportunity for self-appropriation. At least in this assignment she cannot set aside the character of the believer/witness long enough to look carefully at her own feelings or connect with peers who have also experienced deep grief. As she explains: "It is harder for me when a person dies that was not a believer, but all I can do is pray about it. It is hard for me when a person dies that is not a believer, because God says, 'Then they will go away to eternal punishment [hell], but the righteous to eternal life [heaven]' (Matthew 25:46)."[36] As her teacher, I found the repetition in this passage (which first appears in her final draft) painful to read, in part, I confess, because her relationship to scripture is so different from my own. She sounds depleted, not buoyed, by her reliance on biblical authority.

Because she cast her first draft of her essay in relatively inflexible, testimonial terms, Tina's revisions read either additively, as they do in the above example, or defensively, as responses to disembodied questions that she experiences as distractions from the story she is trying to tell. In the following passage, the first two sentences come from Tina's initial draft, while those that follow are her rejoinder to a peer whom had observed that she "make[s] Jesus sound like [her] buddy":

> I do not go through any memorized prayers when I pray. Since I have a personal relationship with God, I pray to Him in a manner that I would talk to anyone else in. This does not mean that I treat God like a "buddy." I mean that I speak to him as if He were sitting right next to me. I do not speak to Him in any fancy manner or use huge biblical terms. When I have something on my mind, I just start talking to Him. That is what I mean when I say that I talk to Him like I would anyone else.[37]

Of course, anyone on the receiving end of Tina's verbal barbs could be fairly sure that she did *not* talk to God "in a manner that [she] would talk to anyone else in."

To observe the discontinuity between the "everyday" Tina and her Christian persona is not necessarily to label her a hypocrite but to point out the difficulties her ethos orientation creates for her on multiple levels—stylistic, rhetorical, even spiritual. If she processes revision-oriented questions as distractions that do not deserve to be integrated into her own utterances, how can her writing attain stylistic coherence? If she feels threatened and can barely contain her irritation at these questions, how can her writing provide the Christian witness that she believes her peers need? Most worrisome, perhaps, for the success of her testimony: what does the discontinuity between flesh-and-blood "being" and textual "seeming" suggest about the God to which she hopes to lead her peers? In her final draft for the class, a self-portrait written as an act of Christian witness but barely resembling the person *we* had come to know, Tina's God looks naive, petty, and faraway —not all-knowing, all-loving, and wonderfully immanent.

Peter Lawler, writing about the evangelical students he teaches at Berry College, has said that "souls full of longing cry out for education, but souls that are flat or believe they are flat are often just too wounded to be able to appreciate liberal learning."[38] I don't believe that Tina was "too wounded to be able to appreciate liberal learning," although I also don't know how she did in the honors classes she subsequently took (most of which would have included her classmates from Writing About Ideas). At the same time, while her classmates and I experienced Tina as a complicated force of nature, by the end of the term I do think she projected a disheartening belief in her own "flatness," perhaps because she felt rejected by peers who would not be converted and anxious about tensions in her beliefs that her ethos orientation discouraged her from naming. When I look at the writing she produced in my class, I see few improvements in her ability to interpret and approximate examples of academic discourse, to organize her thoughts, or even to create navigable sentences. By the standards of my university's Composition Program, which requires students to "recogniz[e] the relevance of one's own experiences for understanding how other people think about the world and their lives," Tina's writing was weaker at the end of the term than it was at the beginning. Ashworth's ideas about "hermeneutic participation" suggest one reason why: "The individual who is able to learn must be able to suspend a central or thematic concern with the self. The truth of this claim is shown by the fact that, if one's selfhood or identity as a worthy participant in learning is seriously at hazard, and one cannot pay relaxed attention to the matters at hand without being distracted with the issue of how one appears in the eyes of the other, then learning is in jeopardy."[39]

Even when we self-appropriatively take responsibility for our own acts of knowing, as I tried to do, and as students like Sara and Shruti did, our "moral horizons often spontaneously screen out the concerns that animate the other person."[40] Tina's "thematic concern with the self," which took the form of an anxious Christian witness that precluded self-appropriation, paradoxically impeded her ability to use her experience heuristically, either to help her become a more confident college writer or, in Lonergan's words, to "[discover] what the fullness of human authenticity can be and [embrace] it with her whole being."[41] I believe that, had she begun to "own" her sharp-tongued, brilliantly funny, entrepreneurial, evangelical self in my class, Tina could only have shown how, in the words of Psalm 139, she was "fearfully and wonderfully made": a work in progress, witnessing to her Lord's power in the free and responsible exercise of her intellect.

7

—

"AIN'T WE GOT FUN?"

TEACHING WRITING IN A VIOLENT WORLD

Elizabeth Vander Lei

> The violence of the world is but a mirror of the violence of our lives. We say we desire peace, but we have not the souls for it. We fear the boredom peace seems to imply. Even more we fear the lack of control a commitment to peace would entail.
> —Stanley Hauerwas, *The Peaceable Kingdom*

> If we are to make rhetoric relevant across not only disciplinary boundaries, but also across the boundary between the university and the "real world," as teachers we have to help people cultivate language and relationships to work though often radical contingencies.
> —Thomas Darwin, "Pathos, Pedagogy, and the Familiar"

It seemed a simple way to have some fun in the last ten minutes of the first class after spring break. After a short lesson on composing styles, I turned to my students, students in a first-year writing class that I considered one of my best ever, and asked them to create a metaphor for academic writing. I expected, and received, typical metaphors of writing as physical adventure. Most students invoked emotions of fear, anticipation, and exhilaration; most described a concluding moment of satisfaction for a difficult job, done well. Three students, however, told of a different kind of experience. John, an earnest, unfailingly nice student, described his writing in terms of disheartening defeat, like that he feels as a fan of his then-disappointing Detroit Tigers. Robin, in the middle of revising one of her essays for publication in the college newspaper, nevertheless compared writing to enduring the shooting pain associated with a rotting tooth.

But nothing prepared me for what I received from Marty: "Writing is like being flogged in a dungeon. It is like this because we're being held prisoner here at school, and we are tortured with writing assignments. Writing is like being flogged, because it is a painful process that can go on for hours, and you just wish that you would die. It is also like being flogged because weeks later you get your grade, and it is like seeing scars on your body that remind you of a past painful experience." I was surprised, embarrassed, disheartened: I thought we had been having fun. While Marty's passive voice verbs de-emphasized my role in the torture, I couldn't help wondering about the violence he ascribed to me—violence that was intellectual, not physical, but violence nonetheless. I held on to Marty's description for a long time, wondering how I had contributed to his pain, wondering if scholar Elaine Scarry is right that "what is remembered in the body is remembered especially well," and, consequently, wondering if this pain would be one of Marty's principal memories of his first and only year of study at Calvin College.[1]

The shootings on college campuses like Virginia Tech, Northern Illinois University, and recently at a Houston community college remind me that violence is not some distant problem and that the students in our classes may be suffering more than we know. Following the 2012 shooting of elementary school children in Connecticut, I concur with the scholar Paul Lynch, writing about the apocalyptic turn, that "ultimately, kairos doesn't matter: there are enough global threats to occasion any essay."[2] To make sense of Marty's experience in my class, I turned to composition scholarship. In *The Peaceable Classroom,* author Mary Rose O'Reilley frames my wonderment into an ambitious research question: "Is it possible to teach English so that people stop killing each other?"[3] O'Reilley's question helps me focus my own question, one that bears some similarity to Lynch's quest for "an apocalyptic turn toward responsibility": how can we teach students to engage (rather than enact violence on) people who offer words and ideas that we may find disagreeable?[4]

My experience with Marty helped me refine my focus even further because I suspect that my response to his religious assumptions—assumptions consistent with Christian fundamentalism—may have been one source of the pain he describes. Two different streams of research have helped me frame an answer to this question. The first is familiar to many of us: the work on violence and incivility by rhetoricians Lynn Worsham and Sharon Crowley. The second stream is likely less familiar, but it may serve us well as we theorize about our teaching of writing: Christian theology, particularly the thinking of two Christian theologians—Stanley Hauerwas and Miroslav Volf. These streams of research share a commitment to an attitude of renovation—that is, valuing what is present and seeking to improve it, over deciding to demolish it and build anew.

In "Going Postal: Pedagogic Violence and the Schooling of Emotion," Worsham describes the violence all around us as being as much a result of the social conditions in which people live and work as it is a result of personal choice:

"Although we may prefer to be comforted by the view that violence is the unfortunate result of individual pathology, we must remember that the phrase *going postal* originates in the objective conditions of the working day in U.S. postal facilities and should tell us something about those conditions: conditions of exploitation and domination; humiliating and alienating conditions that produce rage, bitterness, frustration and indignation."[5] At school, as in the workplace, violence is a hardly surprising response of people who have been made "nobodies" by those with "the power to impose meanings that maintain and reinforce the reigning social, economic, and political arrangements as legitimate when in fact they are entirely arbitrary."[6]

The result of this imposition of meaning, according to Worsham, is an emotional education that teaches "grief, hatred, bitterness, anger, rage, terror, and apathy as well as emotions of self-assessment such as pride, guilt, and shame—these form the core of the hidden curriculum for the vast majority of people living and learning in a highly stratified capitalistic society."[7] Marty's metaphor, as I reread it in the context of Worsham's description, voices the emotions that Worsham describes, particularly trauma.[8] And what of my ignorance of his emotions in a class that I considered a success? Worsham would likely argue that I was surprised because I had not paid enough attention to the emotional aspects of my teaching. Or perhaps I had caricatured and then dismissed Marty as a "nobody," one of those students who seemed uninterested in engaging in college-level critical inquiry or in improving his writing. In fact, Worsham argues, comfortable with the status quo, we are likely to misapprehend student resistance as something other than a response to emotional pain. Or we miss it entirely, as contemporary listeners to the song "Ain't We Got Fun?" likely miss the anger created by poverty-producing economic policies of the 1920s, as overseers listening to the "happy" songs of African American slaves missed enveloping sorrow or plans for running away, just as I missed wondering about Marty's silence in the midst of the repartee that characterized our class sessions.

Intellectual violence also results from people paying a particular kind of attention to each other: the antagonism we direct at our ideological enemies. Focusing beyond the classroom, Crowley characterizes American civic discourse as a pitched battle between equally powerful forces. She opens *Toward a Civil Discourse* by describing the question screamed at her friend who was peaceably protesting the 2003 invasion of Iraq: "Traitor! Why don't you go to Iraq and suck Saddam's dick?"[9] In this case, the invective did not come from a powerless "nobody"; the screamer supported a president who had enough political clout to invade another country despite strong public opposition. Crowley sources this violent hatred to a polarization in American culture that has been described as the "culture wars." In these battles between progressive and conservative forces, religion becomes simultaneously battlefield and weapon;

religious faith is easily reduced, by both sides, to conservative Christian ideals. Crowley claims: "Discussion of civic issues stalls repeatedly at this moment in American history because it takes place in a discursive climate dominated by two powerful, social discourses: liberalism and Christian fundamentalism."[10]

In this hostile environment it shouldn't surprise us that we and our students think of argument as warfare, "a form of intellectual violence. We pile up evidence as the kids in my neighborhood used to pile up snowballs, each with a rock in the middle, on the rims of their forts."[11] Teaching argumentation as war—a familiar enough "conceptual system, in terms of which we both think and act"—we might find ourselves encouraging students to engage the words and ideas of others but to engage with the goal of winning the right to tell others what to do.[12] Teaching argumentation as renovation, we might find ourselves and our students challenged to be willing to change our arguments as a result of encountering new people and ideas, to accept and even value heterogeneity and specificity in our discourse communities, and to evaluate proposed arguments in light of community standards.

One of the two opposing groups that Crowley identifies is Christian fundamentalism, but we in English studies (typically comfortable with the social discourse of liberalism) may find ourselves ill-equipped to model good rhetorical behavior toward students whom we identify as Christian fundamentalists because we have difficulty engaging these students peaceably—at least in part because we find their words and ideas so disagreeable. Rather than examine the source of our disagreeableness, we examine with "fury and ferocity" the weaknesses of writers and arguments that we find disagreeable.[13] The scholar Doug Downs courageously provides a vivid example of his frustration on display in this response to the research and writing of one of his students about gay people adopting children:

> Congratulations! You've just written the most indoctrinated, closed-minded, uncritical, simplistically reasoned paper I've ever read! . . . You haven't deeply examined the situation. You've gone and found the evidence . . . that would support your long-held preconceptions. You didn't talk to any gay people; never met any gay parents; never got critical of straight parents; never sought to see the good things in gay parenting and the problems with the "nuclear" family; never questioned the assumptions you have about homosexuality (how do you picture gays living, for instance?); never questioned why it's okay to make fun of gay kids in school. They're freaks, right? But I thought "the children" were important to you. Not if they're gay? That's very consistent of you, Keith.[14]

Most of us can sympathize not only with Downs's frustration over shoddy academic research but also with his subsequent suggestion that what really bugs us—what leads us into a kind of intellectual violence—is that these students seem unwilling to think as we do. They resist using the methods of academic inquiry to reach the intellectual goals that we have set for them.[15] What we might be less likely to admit is that our frustration with *how* students think is compounded by our distaste for *what* students believe. Emotionally frustrated, ideologically distanced, we may be inclined to imagine them as opponents rather than members of our discourse community who need to experience renovation, as we all do. We may be inclined to theorize and to teach in a way that "trivializes and misrepresents faith-related expression."[16] Given the complexities of teaching, such trivialization may seem a minor fault, but it can be a powerful weapon in intellectual exchanges that turn violent.

In *Toward Civil Discourse,* Crowley analyzes the rhetorical power of trivialization. Noting that "belief systems are social," she describes how communities identify their boundaries—who's in and who's out—by constructing "shared identities," verbal commonplaces that demarcate the furthest extent of the community.[17] Despite the stereotypes that are produced by these verbal commonplaces, Crowley reminds us that communities are actually made up of a wide variety of people.[18] Each community hosts members who cooperate, resist, rename, and reembody the task and the passion of the community. Each community hosts stories that diverge, intersect, contradict. Indeed, heterogeneity is so important that Crowley identifies it as crucial for the survival of the social group: "If a range of possibilities were not available to a community, it could not adapt to changing circumstance."[19] This diversity is so vital that when hostilities break out across community boundaries, Crowley notes, a first impulse of the combatants is to replace this vital heterogeneity with an easily dismissed caricature of the opposing community, an outsider's perspective in which "they all look alike."[20] Reducing our opponents to caricatures, we find it easy enough to dismiss them as uninformed or illogical.

While few of us would intentionally engage in such cross-community misconduct, most of us find it difficult to avoid doing so. For example, Crowley carefully attends to heterogeneity when she works with theories and language of her own community; when she turns her attention to religion, however, she demonstrates just how difficult it is to avoid the impulse to homogenize, exoticize, and thereby trivialize religious communities and those who inhabit them. In her research Crowley ignores "Christians who think of themselves as political liberals and many, if not most, Christians in the academy."[21] And she ignores differences among Christian theologies and between theology and fiction. For example, in her chapter entitled "Ideas Do Have Consequences: Apocalypticism and the Christian Right," Crowley uses "conservative religious belief" as a synonym for "apocalyptic theology," enacting a kind of Russian doll reduction of religious belief to *Christian* belief, Christian belief to *conservative* Christian belief, conservative Christian belief to *fundamentalist* Christian belief, and fundamentalist Christian belief to one of its more exotic features, *dispensational premillennialism* or, in Crowley's terms, apocalyptic theology.[22] It requires no stretch of the imagination to believe that conservative Christians are likely to feel a disrupted "sense of order and rightness," the feeling that results, according to scholar Jacqueline Jones Royster, "when the subject matter is me and the voice is not mine."[23] Crowley relies on rigorous scholarly methodology to attempt to "mitigate the difficulty posed by difference," but she herself notes "extreme frustration" with her "seeming inability to bridge these intellectual differences" between her own belief system and that which fosters books like Timothy LaHaye's *Left Behind* series.[24]

I sympathize with Crowley's frustration; it matches mine at my own failure to bridge my intellectual and theological differences with my student Marty. For example, when the class I described earlier in this chapter began to work on research papers, Marty found it difficult to commit to a topic, choosing and abandoning three or four in the span of two weeks. Finally, when other students were finishing their first drafts, Marty appeared at my office door and announced that in his paper (five to seven pages, typed) he wanted to prove that a worldwide flood had happened exactly as described in the Bible. He excitedly showed me a book that, in his words, compiled all the "physical evidence" he would need to prove his claim. Marty and I argued about topics familiar in first-year composition: that evidence is scholarly if it has been accepted by a scholarly community, that a PhD in one academic field does not make a person a reputable scholar in other fields, that reputable academic research is generally published by academic presses, and so on. Finally, well past five, Marty left my office, defeated. He chose another topic, one I cannot recall, and wrote a paper that I do not remember reading. One week after our meeting, Marty described writing in my class as being tortured in prison.

Thus acknowledging the difficulty of the task, I cannot, in fifteen pages, single-spaced, presume to answer the question of how to renovate our teaching of writing so that, adopting scholar Shari Stenberg's image, we make good use of our hands: "How do we use them not only to challenge, but also to support? Not only to critique, but also to validate? Not only to deconstruct, but also to reconstruct?"[25] The most I can offer is a speculation that the work of two Christian theologians—Stanley Hauerwas and Miroslav Volf—on the social virtues of self-discipline and hospitality might help us begin imagining how to renovate our writing pedagogy so that we can engage people whose words and ideas we may find disagreeable.

Hauerwas's narrative theology resonates with theories that feel familiar to us, such as those in the work of Mary Rose O'Reilley. O'Reilley concedes that "the connections between language and war, between language and oppression are multiple and complex," and she focuses her attention on the rhetorical consequences of trivialization: how reducing individuals to faceless members of a group encourages violence: "War begins in banality, the suppression of the personal and idiosyncratic."[26] To counter the numbing effects of massed humanity and abstracted ideals that can motivate violent acts, O'Reilley champions a writing pedagogy that is rooted in the personal, a pedagogy that focuses both instructor and student attention on individuals and on the writing classroom as a heterogeneous community.[27] Like O'Reilley, Hauerwas locates the root of violence in abstraction; he argues that "when freedom and equality are made ideal abstractions, they become the justification for violence, since if these values are absent or insufficiently institutionalized some conclude they must be forced into existence."[28] Such abstraction is not a normal state, Hauerwas notes, for "freedom and equality are not self-interpreting, but require a tradition to give them content."[29]

Within a given tradition like Christianity, people come to understand concepts like freedom, justice, and mercy as they have been enacted over many years in the lives of members of communities within that tradition. So, for example, if a child has learned in a Christian tradition about Jesus's command to care for "the least of these" and has watched, as I did, her mother travel at night into an urban neighborhood that she feared even in daylight so that she could volunteer with other members of our church at a homeless shelter, that child understands the concept of justice in terms that are not only legal but also social. Had I approached Marty's proposed topic with that memory fresh in my mind and with an attitude of renovation, I would have focused his and my attention to the tradition and personal experiences that shaped his commitment to his topic; as a result, we both might have learned something.

As a Christian theologian speaking to Christians, Hauerwas claims that it is through narrative that religious traditions convey complex ideas, including an understanding of God: "Narrative is not secondary for our knowledge of God; there is no 'point' that can be separated from the story. The narratives through which we learn of God *are* the point. Stories are not substitute explanations we can someday hope to supplant with more straightforward accounts. Precisely to the contrary, narratives are necessary to our understanding of those aspects of our existence which admit of no further explanation—i.e. God, the world, and the self."[30] But while Christians may read the same "narratives through which we learn of God," they certainly do not come to the "same understanding of those aspects of our existence which admit of no further explanation." It seems likely that people understand differently at least in part because they interpret the narratives of God differently—in the context of different communities. Within a given community, according to Hauerwas, Christians can understand governing ideas like freedom and justice only "when we can place ourselves—locate our stories—within God's story."[31]

To avoid living violently, Christians must exhibit enormous self-control: they must remember that they understand and live out these governing ideas in relationship to their community's interpretation of the narratives of God, even when their understanding challenges, resists, or renames how the community has interpreted God's story. To act peaceably, then, they must acknowledge not only that their own stories are rooted in an interpretive community but also that their story exists in a particular kind of relationship to the other stories in that community. It seems likely, given the scholar Christian Smith's description of the fluid state of college students' relationship to the religious traditions they were raised in, that students would welcome the opportunity to consider their relationship to their interpretive communities.[32]

But Hauerwas's ideas challenge his Christian readers to an even greater degree of self-control when he notes that Christians' stories also exist in relationship to the narratives told in other communities—religious orders, denominations, nonprofit groups, and so on—associated with Christian tradition. To acknowledge the nested nature of their story, Christians must acknowledge the governing force of those other narratives on their own. Christians, Hauerwas claims, can't just tell whatever story they want to. Like homeowners hoping to remodel a house in a historical district, they are constrained by the history and standards of their community.

What would happen if we help students, all students, recognize academic writing as renovating a story rather than building one new? We might help them feel that even far from home they are not alone and that their voice speaks for, through, and against a community of voices. So emboldened, they might become writers who are stronger and more effective than the pathetic orphans that O'Reilley imagines: "To teach beginning students to write with a formal, academic dialect is to disable them emotionally and politically. Having made people feel like charlatans, it submits them, half-clad in rags of personhood, bashful and confused, to the dominion of force."[33] So emboldened, they might be willing to engage in what the scholar T. J. Geiger II refers to as "the free exercise of rhetoric" in which students and instructors "engage discourses that compel and repel [them], figuring out together how to deploy ethical writing and research practices in the midst of encounters that unsettle, shock, and confuse."[34] Students who are reminded that they are not alone may feel less like the victims of the pedagogical violence that Worsham describes: "In particular, pedagogy provides and limits a vocabulary of emotion and, especially to those in subordinate positions, it teaches an inability to adequately apprehend, name, and interpret their affective lives. This is its primary violence."[35]

If we help students, all students, recognize that their own stories are nested in larger stories, students may better apprehend the powerful rhetorical effect of those larger stories on their own. As a result, they may interrogate these larger stories and their effects more carefully. What O'Reilley claims for personal writing can apply to all who seriously examine their ideological commitments: "I defend personal writing . . . because I think that some form of self-interrogation is essential to the formation of *le coeur*: personal subjectivity, as Vaclav Havel puts it, becoming the principal link with the subjectivity of the world. Besides . . . it allows each of us to try our one unique experience against the univocal cultural story Western man has made up about the nature of reality."[36] Hauerwas's concept of nested stories encourages students to deconstruct the idea that they themselves, their own communities, and even the nature of reality might be "univocal." Doing so, they may equip themselves to recognize the warrants hidden in such supposedly univocal narratives and to challenge the influence of those warrants on their thinking and their lives.

For example, in his essay "Peaceableness toward Enemies," the writer Wendell Berry critiques American political leaders who publicly claim allegiance to Christians' God but do not demonstrate the self-control to nest the history they are making into the larger story of God:

> In times of war, our leaders always speak of their prayers. . . . These prayers are usually understood to be Christian prayers. But Christian prayers made to or in the name of Jesus, who loved, prayed for, and forgave his enemies and instructed his followers to do likewise. A Christian supplicant, therefore, who has resolved to kill those whom he has enjoined to love, to bless, to do good to, to pray for, and to forgive as he hopes to be forgiven is not conceivably in a situation in which he can be at peace with himself.[37]

In his argument Berry presents Christian peace as the context for violent responses of Christian politicians toward their enemies. To be at peace, to be consistent with their ideological commitments, Berry argues, Christian politicians must value peaceable, loving responses; the peaceableness that characterizes Jesus ought to serve as a governor for the political actions of Christian politicians. But, of course, historically such politicians have not always demonstrated this kind of self-control. Rather, they have justified their use of violence as a necessary evil, a way to stave off even more horrific violence, a common enough claim in the Western version of reality that O'Reilley refers to earlier.

Applying Hauerwas's idea of nested stories to Berry's critique of the prayers of politicians, we might conclude that these politicians have rooted their story more fully in a political and cultural narrative than in a Christian one.

While I savor Berry's challenge to Christian politicians to demonstrate at least enough self-control to be governed by the particulars of the stories of their community, my mouth sours when I think about the discussion Marty and I had about his research topic. I must confess that I relied heavily on the "univocal" story of the academic research paper, a story in which I was expert and Marty novice, a story that as far as Marty knew—and as most of our students presume—is universally true for all people at all times in all places. Had I asked Marty about the relationship of his proposed research topic to his own story and to the communities that have shaped him, I might have understood his motivation for writing on the subject. I wish that I had asked him why this newly found source had captured his interest. Did the source or the methodology help him believe something new, or did it give him a different kind of evidence for what he had always believed? I could have asked him if this source had answered questions he had about the story of the flood or if it had sparked new questions. I could have asked him about the topic—had he always been interested or had something or someone recently caused him to attend to the story more closely? Turning his attention to the community that shaped his beliefs, I could have asked him to explore the range of stories that people in his community tell about the flood and how his source relates to those other stories. I could have encouraged Marty in so many different ways to see this research project as an opportunity to renovate his and my thinking. I didn't try any of them.

Reflecting on my poor performance, I suspect that I avoided asking Marty these questions, in part, because I unselfconsciously enacted another univocal story, one that trivializes religion as a private matter, something off-limits to a teacher. That I (someone who has critiqued this story myself) could enact it at Calvin College (a place that highly values exploratory, open discussion of religious ideas) may indicate just how pervasive and persuasive this univocal story is and how desperately it needs to be renovated.

THE HOSPITALITY TO INVITE THE OTHER IN

The story of religion as a private matter has a long and potentially noble history. The rhetorician Kristine Hansen roots this resistance in Enlightenment ideas of what constitutes public, objective, and rational.[38] The scholar Stephen Carter has suggested that we, like many others, may have acted out this story to avoid community-shattering anger: "One good way to end a conversation—or start an argument—is to tell a group of well-educated professionals that you hold a position (preferably a controversial one such as being against abortion or pornography) because it is required by your understanding of God's will."[39] In a desire to live together in peace, we have sequestered from others both our beliefs and our reasons for holding those beliefs. Miroslav Volf summarizes this common thinking: "The contemporary resurgence of religion seems to go hand in hand with the resurgence of religiously legitimized violence—at least in the public perception. Hence, the argument goes, it is necessary to weaken, neutralize, or outright eliminate religion as a factor in public life."[40] Relying not only on his training as a Christian theologian but also on his experience in the blood-soaked Croatian war for independence, Volf argues that common knowledge has it exactly backward with regards to Christianity: "At least when it comes to Christianity, the cure for religiously induced or legitimized violence is not *less* religion but, in a carefully qualified sense, *more* religion. Put differently, the more we reduce Christian faith to vague religiosity or conceive of it as exclusively a private affair of individuals, the worse off we will be; inversely, the more we nurture Christian faith as an ongoing tradition that by its intrinsic content shapes behavior and in its regulative reach touches the public sphere, the better off we will be."[41] According to Volf, Christian faith *can* foster peaceableness, but only if we find the courage to be hospitable—to open ourselves to accept Christianity as a faith that is heterogeneous: textually rich, theologically complex, and passionately debated among its adherents. Such intellectual hospitality would preclude people, those who profess to be Christians as well as others, from reducing Christianity to an easily wielded sound bite and would discourage the misappropriation of Christianity as justification for violent acts that have everything to do with political power or economic goods and nothing to do with Christian faith as faith.

Such intellectual hospitality would encourage us to attend to arguments within particular religious communities. This kind of attention might help us evaluate the first principles that support those arguments. For example, in late 2002 and early 2003, Christians publicly challenged President George W. Bush's arguments for a preemptive strike against Iraq on theological grounds. In September 2002, Volf used one of his "Faith Matters" columns in *Christian Century* to explore the concept of war in Christian theology: "Over the centuries, Christians have developed two basic attitudes toward war. Both would rule out as immoral a preemptive war against Iraq."[42] In his selection of this publication venue and in his appeal for action, Volf targeted Christians: "Christians must organize demonstrations, the leaders of its churches must make public statements, and individuals must begin collecting signatures—all to prevent the leaders of our nation from engaging in an immoral and unwise war."[43]

In December 2002, Christian theologians took their argument public—in a full-page ad in the *New York Times*. The banner of the ad read "President Bush, Let Jesus Change Your Mind," and the opening paragraph drew the attention of all readers to a first principle of the Christian faith, the authority of Jesus's words and life: "We beseech you to turn back from the brink of war on Iraq. Your war would violate the teachings of Jesus Christ. It would violate the tenets, prayers and entreaties of your own United Methodist Church bishops. It would ignore the pleas of hundreds of Jewish, Muslim and Christian leaders. You've proclaimed the crucial role of your faith in your life, and you've said that people of faith are often 'our nation's voice of conscience.' Listen to our voices now."[44] I do not know, but I suspect that most non-Christians read this more as gladiatorial spectacle than as voices in a deliberative process, informed voices that challenged the legitimacy of Bush's first principles. And I fear that those who do not claim membership in a Christian community did not embrace these arguments because the first principles were not ones that they shared. And yet, as political scientist Diane Mutz has explained, deliberative democracy demands that we embrace what is unfamiliar closely enough for us to see the strengths and weaknesses of particular arguments: "Citizens do need to be skilled at picking among . . . competing arguments, and at circulating them among themselves; trying them out in informal conversation and discarding those that do not ring true."[45] In this case, listening to arguments about religious first principles by those who hold allegiance to those principles might have better positioned Americans to assess the relationship between Christian principles and the violence perpetrated by those who profess to enact those principles.[46]

Despite Volf's careful reasoning, many readers are likely to reject his proposal as dangerous, ill-advised, or at least impractical. After all, if Christian principles have not deterred minds set on mayhem before, could we reasonably expect that they could have done so prior to the start of the Iraq War? Much of Volf's voluminous scholarship attempts to answer this question; his thinking about another first principle of the Christian faith demonstrates why his ideas deserve our attention. Volf believes that the potential of Christianity to foster public good is located in the nature of Christianity's God: three distinct persons who, together, form "a perfect communion of love; the persons give themselves to each other and receive themselves from each other in love."[47] According to Volf, the welcoming hospitality of the persons of the trinity to each other should encourage Christian believers to welcome others, too: "Since the God Christians worship is the God of unconditional and indiscriminate love, the will to embrace the other is the most fundamental obligation of Christians. The claim is radical, and precisely for its radicality, socially significant. The will to give ourselves to others and to welcome them, to readjust our identities to make space for them, is prior to any judgment about others."[48]

Volf argues that this will to embrace, using what he calls the "open arms" of hospitality, can counter the "clenched fist" of exclusivity by pressing Christians to see themselves and their opponents more honestly and more fully: "The clenched fist hinders the perception of the possible justness of our opponents and thereby reinforces injustice; the open arms help detect any justness that may hide behind what seems to be the manifest injustness of our opponents and thereby reinforce justice."[49] Acknowledging the utopian quality of this hospitable embrace, Volf nonetheless argues for its practical application; the goal of offering a welcoming embrace rather than a clenched fist fosters peaceableness across communities: "It translates into the shaping of cultural sensibilities that help people live in a humane way in the absence of final harmony."[50] If we were able to set Volf's metaphor of the welcoming embrace as a rhetorical goal, we might all get along a little better.

Volf's claim seems much less utopian when we look into the political habits of U.S. citizens. In *Hearing the Other Side,* Mutz investigates the political practices of Americans. She finds that when citizens interact with people who hold political views that differ from theirs, they are more likely to collaborate on political solutions: "People who have had to learn to 'agree to disagree' in their daily lives better understand the need to do so as a matter of public policy."[51] As a result of embracing others and their views, citizens become more familiar with "legitimate rationales for opposing views," they talk more with those they might otherwise consider an opponent; they demonstrate "a greater willingness to extend civil liberties" to citizens whose political views they dislike.[52] Considering the case of race in America, the scholar Danielle Allen agrees: "Trust grows only through experience; habits of citizenship are fashioned only through actual interaction."[53] If we hope to work together, we must find a way to talk together and to trust each other, in spite of the experiences and ideologies that may divide us.

Returning to my exchange with Marty, I'm left to wonder what would have happened if I had embraced his enthusiasm for his topic rather than shown it my clenched fist. Might Marty and I have been able to sort out where our ideas about the biblical flood converged and diverged, lining out what the rhetorician Shannon Carter has called the "'rhetorical spaces' of . . . communities of practice"?[54] Was Marty mature enough at that time to put forth this kind of effort? Could Marty and I have renovated his project on the biblical flood into something that would have satisfied both of us? Might I have persuaded him to imagine school as a hospitable place rather than as a prison? And perhaps the most challenging question of all: could I have found the courage to embrace Marty's rationale long enough to understand it—and maybe even to be moved by it?

Imagining taking this approach with Marty, I'm daunted by the hard work it would have required from both of us. Why would either of us expend such effort? Mutz notes that political views are not abstract constructions; they are enacted by individuals, real people with whom we work and play. We engage differing political views, Mutz argues, because we happen to like the people who hold those views, and I believe that Marty's metaphor for writing has stuck with me in part because I liked him so much. I was drawn to his sweet temperament; I noticed and appreciated how he seemed to be the center of fun in the room before class began. Then, I was grateful for his polite respect for my authority when he acceded to my rejection of his topic; now, I wish that we had found a way to have some fun with it.

Before we begin the fun, though, we must understand that Volf's argument for open arms of hospitality does have serious consequences. First, the scholar Jeffrey Ringer has demonstrated how "Austin" "casuistically stretched" his religious beliefs in the process of putting them to use in his academic writing: when students embrace other ways of thinking, being, and doing, they can be changed by that experience in ways that they did not expect and may not even recognize.[55] Second, directing her attention to hospitality to political ideas, Mutz notes that "although diverse political networks foster a better understanding of multiple perspectives on issues and encourage political tolerance, they discourage political participation, particularly among those who are adverse to conflict."[56] That is, as citizens better understand the political views of others, they're less likely to act based on their own political views. So, if we practice the hospitality of Volf's embrace to those not like ourselves, we increase our willingness to deliberate and decrease our willingness to participate. Conversely, Mutz notes that when people talk about politics, they strongly prefer to do so with those who already share their political views; not surprisingly, these conversations encourage people to participate more robustly in politics. Hospitality to those who are like us increases our commitment to our political views and increases our willingness to act on those views. Mutz concludes that the goals of deliberative democracy and participative democracy seem impossible to achieve simultaneously:

> The kind of network that encourages an open and tolerant society is not
> necessarily the same kind that produces an enthusiastically participative
> citizenry. . . . We want the democratic citizen to be enthusiastically politically
> active and strongly partisan, yet not to be surrounded by like-minded others.
> We want this citizen to be aware of all the rationales for opposing sides of an
> issue, yet not to be paralyzed by all of this conflicting information and the
> cross-pressures it brings to bear. We want tight-knit, close networks of mutual
> trust, but we want them to be among people who frequently disagree. And
> we want frequent conversations involving political disagreement that have no

repercussions for people's personal lives. At the very least this is a difficult bill to fill.[57]

If the goals of increasing peaceableness and increasing participation are incompatible, we must choose whether to privilege deliberation or participation.

Applying Mutz's consideration to Volf's argument about religion helps us see that if we approach each other with open arms of hospitality, we will be making a value judgment for deliberation over participation. Decreasing partisanship may seem a good thing if we view partisanship as "the antithesis to open-mindedness and tolerance."[58] In a writing classroom that values deliberation over participation, Marty would do more exploring and less arguing. In public argumentation, at this moment in history I believe that if we cannot have both, we should privilege deliberation. Nationally and globally we face unprecedented challenges that require us to get along with one other—to understand one other, to accept one other, to trust one other, and to have fun together so that we can work together.

Maybe someday in composition classes and in our public discourse we will be able to address the goals of deliberative and participative democracy simultaneously. Maybe someday we will provide what Mutz calls for "instruction, and explicit norms, for how political differences should be handled respectfully in informal discourse. How can one be a successful advocate of political ideas without isolating one's self from those whose ideas differ? Only when such skills are equitably distributed—the ability to build and maintain diverse networks, and to evaluate and promote ideas through them—will the metaphor of a marketplace of ideas ring true for American political culture."[59] We will begin to engage each other peaceably when we are willing to renovate our own ideas, when we learn to value both heterogeneity and specificity, and when we learn to acknowledge the constraints of community standards. We will begin to respect the ideas of others, even the ideas we find disagreeable, when we demonstrate the self-control to remember that their ideas, like our own, are rooted in the story of a life and in a community. For a long time I have appreciated scholar Virginia Chappell's description of "Teaching—and Living—in the Meantime" because her story gave me a glimpse into a way of teaching and living in which we "do the best that we can, in the meantime, with the time and resources that we have. But we do it together."[60] As I considered how I treated Marty, I returned repeatedly to Chappell's essay, reminding myself that I too live in the meantime, "hoping for new motives, clearer commitments, new responsibilities," finding encouragement to hope that, like Chappell, I would be able to "accept the fact that I was not likely to know about the ultimate gleanings of the imaginations I sought to enrich."[61]

Not long ago I typed Marty's name into a search engine. And I found him, showcased in a church newsletter about a transcontinental bike-a-thon to raise funds for an antipoverty program, a program that I had supported financially. Through our mutual commitment to the antipoverty program, rising from differing stories nested within Christian tradition, Marty and I have been able to offer a kind of hospitality to others that I wish we had been able to offer to each other. It may be that the work of rhetoricians on violence and incivility and the work of Christian theologians on self-discipline and hospitality will help me create a composition class that is more fun for all of us.

A QUESTION OF TRUTH

READING THE BIBLE, RHETORIC, AND CHRISTIAN TRADITION

BETH DANIELL

ON THE SYLLABUS for my upper-division rhetoric course is the statement that one goal of the class is to explore is the relationship of language and truth. This topic, I find, very much interests undergraduates. In almost every rhetoric class I've taught, as we review the various stances between rhetoric and truth, a student has asked, indirectly or directly, in a response paper or in class discussion or in my office, some version of this question: "If we create truth or knowledge through language, and it's all persuasion, then how do we know what is right? If rhetoric isn't conveying some big-T Truth but is instead creating many little-t truths, what happens to morality? To the Ten Commandments? To the Bible?"

This is a question college instructors must be prepared not only to respond to but also to respect. The young adults who come into our classrooms are moving into critical thinking and are being confronted with ideas that are new to them and narratives that run counter to the ones they learned in their home communities. Sometimes students respond to these new ideas with resistance: the questions provoked by this new information are just too scary. But sometimes students are not resisting; they're just grappling with unfamiliar outlooks and perspectives, trying to make it all make sense. Many students come to college from conservative evangelical or fundamentalist backgrounds and may be thus concerned about possible challenges to the truth of the Bible. This is true particularly in my part of the country, the South, which, you may remember, Flannery O'Connor called "Christ-haunted."[1] But in my experience many students who voice concerns about the truth of scripture come, as well, from the mainstream denominations—Presbyterian, Methodist, Episcopalian, Lutheran, Church of Christ, Catholic.

The students I am talking about are not the apocalyptic fundamentalists you've met in Sharon Crowley's book *Toward a Civil Discourse: Rhetoric and Fundamentalism,* nor are they necessarily like the conservative young woman named Mary in Nancy Grimm's *Good Intentions: Writing Center Work for Postmodern Times* or other fundamentalist students about whom academics become exercised.[2] These are, rather, upper-division students, some from small towns but others from midsize cities or from one large metropolis, mostly middle class, who have done well in English, history, political science, or communications. They have chosen to take rhetorical theory, and they've been in the class for several weeks when these questions are voiced: if rhetoric isn't just conveying some big-T Truth that already exists out there somewhere but is instead using language to create little-t truths for particular groups in particular times and places, then how do we know what is right?

Our answers should be neither flippant nor disrespectful. I say this definitively, having myself committed both pedagogical sins. The first year I taught at Clemson University in South Carolina, the topic of evolution came up in an advanced composition class. One student spoke aloud the concern of many when she asked, "Dr. Daniell, you don't believe in evolution, do you?" My reply: "Yes, of course I do. I believe in electricity, too." Concern turned to horror as the students realized their professor was apostate. I spent two days explaining what a theory is and what evidence means as well as preaching heartfelt sermons on the importance of intellectual doubt—"There is more faith in honest doubt than in all the creeds."[3] And, though they listened politely, I never quite got that class back. I tell this story when people ask about how to handle questions of faith that come up in class because this narrative is an exemplar of how *not* to deal with such issues. Confronted with that question now that I am older and, I hope, somewhat wiser, I would lose the sarcasm and talk about the relationship of science and faith, hoping to help students recognize that where some people see a conflict, others see complementarities.

The more I've thought about this question of the truth of scriptural texts, the more I've realized that the underlying issue is actually, more often than not, how people read. Despite the fact that most of my rhetorical theory students are English majors, they often seem to have missed the concept that there are many ways to read a text—perhaps they think that literary interpretation is a peculiarity of the professor teaching the class. Once I began to see that the students' concerns about truth were really about reading, I began to consider questions that might call forth substantive responses: What can rhetoric teach us about reading? What does Christian tradition tell us about reading? Particularly, can rhetoric and Christian tradition together offer students ways to read scripture that do not deny their faith as they move from what biblical scholar Marcus Borg has called "precritical naiveté" to more critical reading and thinking?[4]

So in this chapter I discuss strategies and information that might be useful to colleagues confronted with similar questions from students about biblical truth. I am not supplying canned answers to these questions because I trust teachers to reply appropriately as they take into account the complex situation of student, make-up and level of class, and local culture. What I share here is information about the meaning of the term "sacred texts," about rhetorical concepts that offer explanations, about the history of reading in Christian tradition, and about contemporary reading in American Christianity. Long experience has taught me that the more I know, the better.

RECOGNITION OF THE SACRED TEXT

The first thing that professors need to be aware of as we deal with these questions from students is the sacredness of texts—not just in our students' minds but historically, theologically, and culturally. Because texts are central to belief and practice, the Abrahamic religions—Judaism, Christianity, and Islam—have been called religions of the book. As New Testament scholar Bart D. Ehrman points out, Judaism, the common ancestor of both Christianity and Islam, "was unique [among the religions of the Roman Empire] in that it stressed its ancestral traditions, customs, and laws, and maintained that these had been recorded in sacred books that had the status of 'scripture' for the Jewish people."[5] What makes this phenomenon unique, Ehrman explains, is that "books played virtually no role in the polytheistic religions of the ancient Western world."[6] Both Christianity and Islam inherited from Judaism definitions of their texts as holy.

But the texts are not sacred only because practitioners of these faiths believe that the words were inspired by God, whatever the term "inspired" means in specific faith traditions—and indeed that word has many meanings in Christian tradition. The texts are sacred because they have been read for hundreds, even thousands, of years during the worst and best times in the lives of individuals and cultures. I think of one communicant of Holy Trinity, Clemson, who, on hearing complaints about the sterility of the new church building, said, "It will be more beautiful when it has been steeped in prayer, when it has been the site of baptisms, weddings, and funerals." According to this definition, it is not the origin of the text but the experience of it which determines holiness. For believers, the scriptural texts are both reminders of obstacles encountered by ancestors and lessons in how to live a good life. Scriptural texts offer hope when all seems lost and consolation when all is lost. They tell stories of individuals compelled to make fateful decisions when confronted with dire situations; they recount elemental narratives—of love, of war, of the founding city, of oppression and liberation, of promises broken and kept, of courage and cowardice, of fear and longing, of heroes and villains, of fidelity and betrayal. They attempt to explain the nature of God. And they do so in language of such beauty that the words are imprinted not only in the minds of readers and hearers but also in the memory of cultures—as anyone knows who has studied British or American literature. Even ardent atheists ought to be able to honor this view of the Bible or the Koran because over centuries these books have proved both fortifying and enriching in the lived experience of human beings. Awareness of this can, I think, help us be kind to and respectful of students who are grappling with what truth means, even if their faith is something we cannot share.

Most students we categorize as "religious" come from faith traditions wherein the language of the sacred text is read aloud in community. What role do voice and ear and performance play in the valuing of a text? In addition, in the liturgical churches the body is involved: one bows when the Bible is carried into the church by the priest; one stands for the reading of the Gospel. One's identity as a Christian is thus *embodied*, I would argue, drawing on Crowley's analysis of apocalyptic fundamentalism but expanding her notion of the embodiment of identity to include all of us: what we *do* becomes part of who we *are*.[7] The resistance of students to the unfamiliar perspectives they encounter at the university stems from fear of losing identities that seem essential or of having to give up a community that has nurtured them since childhood. As their teachers, we do well to keep this in mind, understanding that even as adults we have identities (and embodied beliefs) that we ourselves might not want challenged and communities we would not want to lose.

But don't literary texts tell similar stories of heroism and finding home and survival and rescue? Yes, of course. But those stories do not typically center on the relationship between God and a people or an individual who represents that group, and, while similar stories are also ancient, they have not been "steeped in prayer" over hundreds or thousands of years. Students from religious backgrounds have been taught that the Bible is not the same as other books. For them, there's a qualitative difference between Genesis and *Paradise Lost*, between the Acts of the Apostles and the *Canterbury Tales*. So the first thing to remember is that no matter how sophisticated we are about hermeneutics and the social construction of texts, our students rarely share that kind of historical or theoretical knowledge. It may be even more important for the professoriate to understand what it means to make a text sacred than it is for our students.

Because questions about language, truth, and the Bible come up almost every time I teach a rhetorical theory class, I have learned to use rhetorical concepts as ways to reply to—and anticipate—those questions. If your students are first-year students or are less theoretically sophisticated, you might want to pick and choose what might be appropriate. While my stance is to be respectful of students' beliefs, my tactic is the typical professorial one of giving more information, often far more, than the students have bargained for. It is not my job to disabuse students of their faith, but it is my job to share my knowledge and to offer tools with which to consider the questions. For example, when the issue of the truth of biblical texts arises, I often remind my rhetoric students of Kenneth Burke's distinction, at the beginning of *Language as Symbolic Action,* between scientistic language and dramatistic language:

> The "scientistic" approach builds the edifice of language with primary stress upon a proposition, such as "It is, or it is *not.*" The "dramatistic" approach puts the primary stress upon such hortatory expression as "thou shalt, or thou shalt not." . . . [T]he scientistic approach culminates in the kinds of speculation we associate with symbolic logic, while the dramatistic culminates in the kinds of speculation that find their handiest material in stories, plays, poems, the rhetoric of oratory and advertising, mythologies, theologies, and philosophies after the classic model.[8]

Perhaps, I suggest, one solution is to see the Bible as a dramatistic text trying to persuade us of the value of its message or to exhort us to behave in this way or that, rather than as a scientistic text naming and defining the physical world. Perhaps one way to understand the truth of the Bible is to see its narratives as teaching a truth different from everyday facts.

Similarly, I invoke Stephen Toulmin's notion of force and criteria.[9] As Toulmin explains, the word "good" may have the same *force* in all fields—a good car, a good poem, a good foreign policy—but the use of the word "good" depends on *criteria* that differ across fields. That is, the standards for claiming a car's "goodness" differ from those for claiming the "goodness" of a poem or of a foreign policy. Perhaps the word "true" is another such word. "True" may have the same *force* when we talk about the results of a criminal investigation or a demographic study or a scriptural passage, but the *criteria* for calling these things true are quite different. Indeed, this is a worthwhile exercise for a class: a discussion of what it means to say that an assertion is "true"; of how circumstances—time, place, technology—might change the criteria we use to make such a statement; of whether factuality is a necessary component of all statements we might call "true"; of whether the status of a fact might also be dependent on the field in which it is seen. While most first-year rhetoric textbooks focus on Toulmin's schema for the structure of argument, the force-criteria notion is just as important. The criteria for value words like "good" or "bad" or "true" are different, though the force may be the same.

Still another strategy is to ask students to consider this question: if the truth of a text were easy to understand, why have people been arguing about the meaning of some texts for thousands of years, as with Plato, or more than two hundred years, as with the United States Constitution? The rhetorician who helps here is Chaim Perelman. In *The New Rhetoric,* Perelman explains that the chief problem with Western epistemology is its insistence on only one right answer.[10] According to Perelman, "Things are very different within a tradition that follows a juridical model, rather than a mathematical model. Thus in the tradition of the Talmud, for example, it is accepted that opposed positions can be equally reasonable; one of them does not have to be right."[11] Perelman illustrates with the story of the Talmud scholars who finally appeal to God to tell them which interpretation of scripture is the correct one. From heaven, God says, "These two theses both express . . . the word of the Living God."[12] Can both the theories of language that students are learning and the Bible be valid at the same time? Does it have to be *either/or*? Can it be *both/and*?

Indeed, in the Talmud the passage of scripture under debate is set in the middle of the page; all around it stand the interpretations of the various rabbis. If students can accept the idea that different interpretations of Hebrew scripture are not only possible but expected and even valued, then they might be willing to learn that some scholars—Ehrman, for example—say that this is what Gospel books of the New Testament do: each gives its own particular interpretation of the life of Jesus, each aiming its story at a particular audience.[13] Because this model, a text with more than one valid interpretation, is how I set up the rhetoric class, with students reading aloud their responses to the assigned class texts, the students know experientially, not just theoretically, that it is possible to hold two or three interpretations in mind at once. What I hope students will learn is that the truth—or reading or interpretation—of the Bible, or of any text for that matter, is by no means one thing. This concept is difficult for many adults, and it surely is for those students who attempt to replace one certainty with another.

RESPONSES FROM CHRISTIAN TRADITION

Another way to deal with the question of the truth of scripture—and all that question implies—is to tell students how the Bible has been read historically. Students who come from religious backgrounds—yes, even those from evangelical or fundamentalist backgrounds—are often unfamiliar with the history of Christianity but interested in learning about it. Typically, they do not know that interpretation and reading have been of concern to Christianity since its inception. How much detail a particular professor might offer particular students is, again, not something I can speak to. But I can recount a brief history of reading in Christianity. At first, as scholars like Elaine Pagels demonstrate, the earliest problem was which of the many documents being passed around the Mediterranean world could be read at all and by whom.[14] The question of what counted as scripture was in great dispute until 367 CE, when Athanasius, Bishop of Alexandria, listed in his Easter letter the "divine books" of both the Old and New Testament.[15] In this same letter, Pagels explains, Athanasius "calls upon Christians . . . to 'cleanse the church of every defilement' and to reject 'the apocryphal books,' which are 'filled with myths, empty, and polluted'—books that, he warns, incite conflict and lead people astray."[16] The idea that the Bible did not spring into culture fully formed is something many Christians do not know but find fascinating when they learn it.

A second problem for early Christianity, according to Pagels, was *how* to read those documents that were circulating among various communities of believers. In the second century, Irenaeus, the Bishop of Lyons, argued that a reader must "discern the obvious meaning" and then be "guided by those passages which seem clear."[17] In the third century, Pagels reports, Origen argued that although John in his Gospel "'does not always tell the truth *literally*, he always tells the truth *spiritually*'—that is, symbolically."[18] In the fourth century, that same Athanasius who was concerned about defining a canon urged Christians, as they read scripture, to turn away from "epinoia," or spiritual intuitions, lest they be deceived by "[their] own preconceptions."[19]

In the early fifth century, Augustine, rhetorician and bishop, showed in the first three books of *On Christian Doctrine* that knowing what to preach—which the preacher finds through reading scripture—is a complicated process.[20] Here Augustine explains that reading is not just calling words but rather engaging in interpretation, which entails recognizing different kinds of signs. For Augustine the starting point is language, with all its complexity and ambiguity, and his standard for judging the correctness of an interpretation is this: if your reading of the Bible fails to encourage charity—that is, the love for God and your fellow human beings—then you've missed the point.[21]

According to literary critic David Richter, Aquinas in *Summa Theologica* codifies two stances toward scripture: historical and spiritual, with spiritual then divided into allegorical, moral, and anagogical: "So far as the things of the Old Law signify the things of the New Law, there is the allegorical sense. . . . So far as the things done in Christ . . . are signs of what we ought to do, there is the moral sense. . . . But so far as they signify what relates to eternal glory, there is the anagogical sense."[22] Literary critics and medievalists are probably more familiar with the levels of reading found in Dante's "Letter to *Can Grande della Scala*."[23] For Dante these levels of reading apply not just to scripture but to literary texts as well: The first "sense" of "a work," Dante says, is the "literal" level; the second sense is "allegorical, or moral, or anagogical."[24] A common example used to explain these levels of interpretation is the story of Abraham and Isaac.[25] Reading literally, or historically, we learn that on God's orders the patriarch Abraham takes his son Isaac up the mountain to sacrifice him to God, but at the last minute God intervenes. Allegorically, this Old Testament story foreshadows the New Testament story of God's sacrifice of his Son Jesus. Morally, it tells us to obey God in everything, even when God asks us to give up something precious. Anagogically, it assures us that, like Isaac, our souls will be saved from death to dwell with the Father in Heaven. Richter says that this sort of "ambiguity and multiplicity of interpretation" disappears with the Renaissance, not to show up again until the twentieth century.[26] Those students who have been taught that scripture means only one thing are often surprised to learn that Christians in previous times read in far more sophisticated ways than some twenty-first century believers.

What replaced these levels of reading scripture, according to conventional wisdom, was Martin Luther's notion of *sola scriptura,* which focuses on the literal, the plain sense of the words. But literary critic Lee Morrissey asserts in *The Constitution of Literature: Literacy, Democracy, and Early English Literary Criticism,* "In reality there is more to Protestant reading than a single sense, . . . more than the *scriptura sola* story usually conveys."[27] In a chapter titled "Radical Literacy and Radical Democracy," Morrissey uses Luther's 1520 "The Pagan Servitude of the Church" and Calvin's 1540 "Three Forms of Exposition" to show two very different Protestant ways of reading the Bible.[28] For Luther, the focus is on the words, but the words are not there alone, Morrissey says: "Like the bread, words not symbols of divinity, but contain divinity itself."[29] Calvin's stance is markedly different: "For Calvin, the words *refer* to meaning, just as the bread *represents* Jesus and the Last Supper."[30] In Calvin's view, as Morrissey explains, "the words are not themselves the meaning, or the meaning is not in the words. . . . [but rather] the meaning is in the reader."[31]

For Milton in the *Areopagitica,* meaning is located in neither the text nor the reader, but rather in the interaction between the two, according to both Morrissey and Stanley Fish. Morrissey says that Milton believes that "[the] relationship between the reader and the book produces a new, third thing, the meaning different from either the reader or the text."[32] In his reading of *Areopagitica,* Fish explains that according to Milton, the virtue or purity or meaning, which seventeenth-century Puritans sought, existed neither in texts nor in the readers themselves.[33] The inability to locate virtue—meaning—in either the text or in the self, Fish says, appears to be an impossible situation until we recall Milton's admonishment that "that which purifies us is triall and triall is by what is contrary."[34] According to Fish, then, "[virtue or meaning] can only be made by sharpening it against the many whetstones provided by the world, by 'what is contrary.'"[35] That is, we discover the meaning of a text by grappling with the text. In other words, the truth is not always easy to discern, found sometimes only with great effort. It has always been my experience that students appreciate being included in these kinds of discussions.

In Morrissey's explanation of Protestant ways of reading, the site of meaning becomes even less securely anchored to the text. Seventeenth-century Puritans, such as pamphleteers Abiezer Coppe and Jacob Bauthumley, locate meaning in the believing reader, who does not in fact have to read the text to possess the message.[36] It is this extreme view—which Morrissey refers to as "radical literacy"—that Hobbes associates in *Leviathan* with the political violence of the of the late 1640s, a time when reading by ordinary people became dangerous, resulting in civil war and regicide.[37] The consequence of this upheaval, Morrissey argues, is that in the eighteenth century, reading is reined in by literary criticism.[38] It seems reasonable to extend this principle to the established religion and to various sects, which became the governors of how the Bible was to be read by their congregations. Thus in our times reading—of both scriptures and other narratives—is regulated by authorities set between the reader and the text. Most students have no conscious idea that their reading of scripture as well as other texts is mired in such contentious theological and political history, but they find intriguing the idea that their own reading has been thus managed by institutions. And sometimes they recognize this control in their own reading experiences.

THE CURRENT PROBLEM

The history of reading sacred texts can help us give some useful direction to students struggling with the question that a rhetoric course might present: if it's all argument, all persuasion, all constructed with words, how do we know that the moral rules we've been taught are right, that the Ten Commandments are valid, that our scripture is true? Here college teachers might turn also to biblical scholar Marcus Borg for information on the current state of Bible reading; indeed, according to Borg, the major division among Christians today is the issue of how to read scripture. In *Reading the Bible Again for the First Time,* Borg describes two contemporary ways of reading scripture: the "literal-factual" way, common to fundamentalists and many conservative evangelical Christians, and the "historical-metaphorical" way, which "has been taught in the seminaries of mainline denominations for the better part of the last century."[39] Borg says that the historical-metaphorical approach to reading the Bible is becoming relatively common in those congregations, but it is not, I submit, being taught in Sunday school classes to the children or adolescents who will shortly inhabit our classrooms.

In Borg's explanation, Bible stories are read at first from the position of "natural literalism," or "precritical naiveté."[40] For persons in this stage a literal (or, to use the medieval term, historical) reading poses no problem. Borg says that children read this way, but it may also be that this is how they are *taught* to think of the Bible stories. Perhaps what Borg may actually mean is that children learn not to express their doubts aloud. (I clearly remember myself as an eight-year-old sitting in a tiny Methodist church in South Georgia thinking, "I'm the only person here who knows that a man can't live inside a whale for three days." I also remember knowing that I could not speak that opinion aloud.) But let's grant Borg his theoretical construct: at first, our stance toward the biblical narratives is precritical naiveté. Problems arise for a natural literal reading of scripture as people become socialized into modernity, Borg says, with its post-Enlightenment, rational worldview; because of its emphasis on "scientific ways of knowing," its "material understanding of reality," and its equation of truth with factuality, the modern world calls scripture into question.[41] Awareness of religious pluralism and of historical and cultural relativity compound the problem.[42] Indeed, this is precisely the situation our students find themselves in when they ask about the truth of the Bible.

One response to the clash of a literal-factual reading of the Bible with modernity is what Borg calls "conscious literalism."[43] This stance accepts modernity's definition of truth as factuality and then aims to make ancient texts square with modern science, thus Borg's term "literal-factual." Conscious literalism is, Borg says, "a modern form of literalism that has become aware of problems posed by a literal reading of the Bible but insists upon it nevertheless. Whereas natural literalism is effortless, conscious literalism is effortful. It requires 'faith,' understood as believing those things that are hard to believe."[44] Another response to the problem of scripture in the modern age is rejection: if God didn't make the world in six twenty-four-hour days, then the hell with it. It's just a fairy tale, anyway. If it isn't scientific, we can dismiss it. This seems to be the stance taken by many of our academic colleagues and by a large part of the culture. Interestingly, this stance also relies on a modernist notion of truth as factuality. It is difficult, however, to sustain this view, especially if one ever has found beauty, joy, acceptance, hope, community, consolation, or meaning in one's faith tradition.

Borg argues that since the problem of the truth of scripture rose out of modernity with its emphasis on facts and rationality, perhaps postmodernity can offer the solution. For example, he points out that postmodernity is marked by "the realization that stories can be true without being literally and factually true."[45] This characteristic, Borg points out, manifests in contemporary theol-

ogy's emphasis on metaphor and metaphorical narratives.[46] The postmodern
way of reading Borg offers is what he calls "postcritical naiveté"—defined as
"the ability to hear the biblical stories once again as true stories, even as one
knows that they may not be factually true and that their truth does not depend
upon their factuality."[47] This makes intuitive sense to those who profess rhetoric: for us, a story is never merely information or plot or artifact but discourse
that can serve any number of functions—to teach, to unite, to bear witness, to
resist, to speak the unspeakable, to argue, to declare identity, to preserve, to
persuade, to create community. For rhetoric, metaphor is not untruth but a way
of expressing the inexpressible—spiritual experience, for instance. As college
teachers we have passed through the critical stages offered by modernity and
have reached postcritical naiveté. It seems to me that one of our tasks is to ease
that transition for students troubled by the purported conflicts between the
academy and faith.

THE EVENT OF READING

In "Cognition, Convention, and Certainty: What We Need to Know about
Writing," Patricia Bizzell argued that demystifying the hidden curriculum is a
crucial step in teaching basic writers but we cannot do this unless we examine
"the historical circumstances" of our methods of teaching and recognize school
as "an agent of cultural hegemony."[48] Although it is true that Bizzell was writing
about different students in a different time, I would argue that we still might
want to contemplate her dire prediction if we fail to see our own role in pass-
ing on certain ideologies: "The result for students who don't share the school's
preferred world views is either failure or deracination."[49] We must not dismiss
those students who grapple with issues of faith, truth, morality, or scripture.
We can use both rhetoric and Christian tradition to guide such students so that
they can see that the solution to the problem does not have to be *either/or*. Both
rhetorical theory and Christian tradition can supply information that can help
them avoid what Ann Berthoff has called a "killer dichotomy" and find instead
a third way.[50] If we are aware that in the greater part of Christian tradition,
reading scripture created multiple interpretations that could exist alongside
one another and that various perspectives on scripture are valued in Judaism,
if we consider the purpose of the scriptural text and the many meanings of the
word "true," then we may be able to help students see that they do not have to
choose between the academy on the one hand and the communities and texts
that have given them identity and sustenance on the other. Perhaps both our
students and we ourselves can be enriched by the knowledge that questions of
reading and arguments about interpretation are in fact part of Christian tradition—that indeed Christian tradition is itself rhetorical.

In "The Order of Discourse," Michel Foucault traces the increasing hold the will to truth—mostly equated with factuality—has over Western thought. In the last paragraph, Foucault asks us to "call into question our will to truth, restore to discourse its character as event, and finally throw off the sovereignty of the signifier."[51] Perhaps rather than demanding that scripture pass some post-Enlightenment true/false test, or trying to pin down the signifier or be pinned down by it, we can suggest to students of rhetoric that what really matters is the *event* of reading—and the event of our discourse *about* reading. After all, for rhetoricians, the event of the discourse is the point—what effect, in its reading or in its hearing or in its performance, the language has upon its audience. For believers, the event of reading scriptural discourse occurs in the worship community, where we seek and sometimes recognize the power of the Word.

Rhetoric in Christian Tradition

—

THE JEWISH CONTEXT OF PAUL'S RHETORIC

Bruce Herzberg

PAUL TELLS HIS readers that he was not only Jewish but a Pharisee: "Circumcised on the eighth day, I was born of the race of Israel, of the tribe of Benjamin, a Hebrew born of Hebrew parents. In the matter of the law, I was a Pharisee" (Philippians 3:5).[1] This statement may sound odd to us, given the generally negative image of the Pharisees in the Gospels, but Paul reveals a pre-Gospel perspective in which the Pharisees are notable for their extensive education and high level of religious observance. The Acts of the Apostles reinforces this view, adding that Paul's teacher was Gamaliel, a prominent Pharisaic leader, frequently cited in the Talmud and other rabbinic writings: "'I am a Jew,' Paul said, 'and was born at Tarsus in Cilicia. . . . It was under Gamaliel that I studied and was taught the exact observance of the law of our ancestors'" (Acts 22:3).[2] Paul does not confirm the Gamaliel connection in his epistles, but whether he studied with Gamaliel or someone else, when he studied "the exact observance of the law of our ancestors," he would have been learning a distinctive form of Jewish biblical interpretation and legal argumentation—and the evidence is in his own writings. There is no question today of Paul's mastery of Greek rhetoric: many critical studies have demonstrated his extensive use of Greco-Roman rhetoric in the epistles.[3] Yet in the vast scholarship on Paul, surprisingly little attention has been paid to his use of Jewish forms of argumentation. Recovering these distinctive forms of argument is an important link to an underappreciated facet of the earliest Christian rhetorical tradition.

JEWISH RHETORICAL PRACTICE

Although there are no surviving writings of Gamaliel or other Pharisees (except, notably, for Paul himself), plenty of other works from the period show a vigorous rhetorical practice aimed at clarifying the meaning of scripture. These include parts of Hebrew scripture itself; works such as Ben Sirach (in the Apocrypha); the Dead Sea Scroll commentaries, pesherim (eschatological interpretations of scripture), and rule codes; interpretive translations of scripture (the Aramaic targumim and the Greek Septuagint); and, finally, the large library of rabbinic works that quote and cite the oral traditions of sages going back to the second century BCE. Pharisees like Paul and Gamaliel were masters and defenders of the "Oral Law" or "Oral Torah," carrying forward a tradition of interpretation—and not, as some may infer from the Gospels, inventing one.[4] The Oral Law was eventually compiled in the second century CE and written down when the rabbis (whom we may think of as a kind of guild of scholars who succeeded the Pharisees as legal interpreters) feared the loss of their ability to maintain the material in oral form alone. The chronology below may be helpful to readers:

SECOND CENTURY BCE: Pharisees and Sadducees arise

FIRST CENTURY BCE: Schools of Hillel and Shammai develop Oral Law
(according to the Talmud)

SECOND CENTURY BCE TO 70 CE: Dead Sea Scrolls written

50–60 CE: Writings of Paul

70 CE: Destruction of the Temple in Jerusalem in the war of 66–73 CE

70–100 CE: Composition of the canonical Gospels

CA. 80 CE: Rabbinic movement begins, succeeding the Pharisees as keepers of
Oral Law

200 CE: Mishnah compiled; other early rabbinic collections in process

400–600 CE: Commentaries on Mishnah compiled as the Talmud in earlier
(Jerusalem) and later (Babylonian) versions

The status of the Oral Law is bolstered by the Mishnah, which attributes to the first-century BCE sage Hillel the idea that Moses received and transmitted both a written Torah ("instruction" or "law" as embodied primarily in the Pentateuch) and an oral Torah, the latter being a set of guidelines for exegesis that produced authoritative interpretations of the former.[5] Pharisees like Paul may well have assumed that rules and interpretations derived by certain forms of textual exegesis were part of the legal tradition handed down from Sinai. Finally, the aim of the Oral Law was to argue for interpretations of biblical law that clarified ambiguities, that insured the continuing observance and relevance of the law, and that made it applicable to contemporary life.

To reiterate, the Pharisees regarded the act of interpretation itself as part of the tradition of which they were heirs. This principle is found in the first chapter of Mishnah Avot: "Moses received Torah at Sinai and handed it on to Joshua, Joshua to the elders, and the elders to the prophets; the prophets handed it on to the men of the great assembly."[6] The passage goes on to list a number of specific members of the great assembly from before the common era, such as Hillel. The Torah that was "handed on" to them was not the written text, which was public and did not need to be handed on, but the oral Torah—the interpretations already given and the methods of further interpretation. The aim of interpretation was, as I have noted, to clarify the laws of the Torah so that they could be carried out correctly. Interpretation was clearly necessary, hence part of the tradition, because so many of the laws were given in general or ambiguous terms. For example, the Sabbath injunction against work does not specify what counts as work. Beyond the obvious prohibition against laboring for pay, it is not clear what activities might be forbidden. Already within scripture there is a recognition that the general rule is vague, so we find what the scholar Michael Fishbane has called "inner biblical exegesis"—later passages that provide some elaborations of a previously stated rule—prohibiting cooking, for example, or lighting a fire.[7] But what about stoking a fire that was already lit? What about rearranging the living room furniture? Carrying a gift to a neighbor? Healing the sick? Surely, the interpreters thought, God would not have given so vague a rule to Moses without telling him the parameters for following the rule. And not only the parameters for specific rules but also—and more important—the principles for further interpretation, because life changes and the Torah must be applicable to new situations.

So to understand Paul as part of this community is to understand him as one who was trained to see the interpretation of Jewish scripture and Jewish tradition as a sacred act, intended to preserve the tradition by making it applicable to real-life situations. Indeed, one of the conflicts between Pharisees and Sadducees seems to have been that the Sadducees scoffed at the Oral Law. Josephus explains: "The Pharisees have delivered to the people a great many observances by succession from their fathers, which are not written in the law of Moses; and for that reason it is that the Sadducees reject them."[8] From the Pharisees' point of view, the Sadducees' conservatism actually put the tradition in danger: if the laws were not relevant to life as it was currently lived, the laws might deteriorate into mere relics.[9]

Rabbinic writings such as midrash (commentary on scripture found in a variety of rabbinic texts), the Mishnah (analysis and elaboration of the rules of Jewish civil law and ritual observance), and the Talmud (a compilation of commentaries on the Mishnah) represent the written form of the Oral Law. These texts employ a very elaborate set of argumentative procedures and do so quite self-consciously, frequently naming an exegetical principle as part of the argument itself. The Talmud attributes the earliest articulation of these argumentative forms to Hillel, whose seven principles are listed below.[10] Talmudic argumentation is dialectical and employs some familiar rhetorical forms, though by no means all of those found in the Greco-Roman style. The Pharisees were presumably bound by the same or very similar methodologies for biblical exegesis and legal exposition as we find in rabbinic writings. Paul clearly studied in both the Jewish and Greco-Roman rhetorical traditions, so where there are similarities we need to be cautious about making definitive judgments about what Paul had in mind.[11]

The Talmud lists the following exegetical principles by Hillel:

1. Lesser to greater (*kal v'khomer*), the commonly used *a minori ad maius*
2. Analogy among known rulings (*gezerah shavah*), an analogy based on identical words or phrases in different parts of scripture
3. A conclusion based on one passage of scripture (*binyan av mikatuv ekhad*)—that is, a "family" of similar texts interpreted according to a "father" (*av*) or guiding passage
4. A conclusion based on two passages of scripture, similar to number 3
5. General and particular and the reverse (*klal u'frat*)—a restriction on a general ruling because of a particular interpretation or the generalization of such a particular
6. Analogy based on scriptural passages (*k'yotzei bo b'makom akher*), a looser form of number 2
7. Proof from context (*davar halameid me'inyano*), where the context is a nearby passage

In addition to these formal principles, we find several very common rhetorical practices and underlying assumptions in rabbinic writings, many of which we find in Paul. Truncated citation is ubiquitous: the scholars, of course, knew the scripture well enough to finish a partial quote and even to know the surrounding verses. The rabbinic texts are extremely telegraphic in other ways as well: perhaps this was a mnemonic aid developed in the oral-transmission period. For example, we find terse antecedent reference, acronyms replacing frequently used phrases and names of sources, and code words indicating such things as the form of an argument or the presumptive authority of sources being quoted. An important underlying assumption is that scripture is never redundant. What appears to be a mere repetition or a form of emphasis is thus available for a different interpretation from the passage it appears to repeat. A corollary is that no verse is superfluous or merely redundant: every verse is subject to a distinctive interpretation. Finally, we can find a variety of common interpretive techniques using puns and other wordplay; basic forms of logic such as consistency and the criticism of fallacies like *reductio*; and practical legal issues such as consideration of whether a derived ruling could actually be followed.[12]

I lack the space to give examples of all the strategies mentioned here, but a small taste of the rabbinic style is instructive. The excerpt I look at deals with the Noahide laws—that is, the laws that Jews believed were given by God to Noah and hence to his offspring for all time—in other words, laws given to all people. These laws are stated or implied in Genesis 9:6, when Noah left the ark. They therefore apply to everybody, including the Jews, who get the additional laws of the Torah later on. Paul deals with this issue in Romans as he considers what laws apply to the Gentiles who have become Christians. The passage is from the Babylonian Talmud, tractate Sanhedrin (pages 59a and 59b). The Talmudic passage is by no means easy to read or understand and may well seem quite obscure to those unfamiliar with Talmudic discourse. It is not, however, an exceptionally difficult passage as an example of Talmudic discourse. It gives us a sense of the heavily coded, telegraphic style of the text and, difficult though it may seem, it shows some strategies that we will also see in Paul. In the text below, the literal translation is in boldface with the "understood" material in roman type and additional clarifications in brackets. It is easy to see the telegraphic and coded style from this example: "**Our Rabbis taught** [in a baraita, explained below]: **seven commandments were given to the sons of Noah**: social **laws**; **'blessing'** [that is, cursing] **the** divine **name** [i.e., blasphemy]; **idol worship; sexual transgressions; spilling blood** [understood as murder]; **theft; and** eating **a limb** torn **from a live** animal" (B. Sanhedrin 56a). A few lines of elaboration follow this statement, and then the question of the source of the law is taken up:

> **What is the source of the ruling** [on the seven laws]? **Rabbi Yochanan said, the verse** [of scripture] **states: "And the Lord God commanded the man saying, of every tree of the garden you may surely eat."** [Genesis 2:16]. "**And he commanded**"—**these are** civil **laws** [i.e., this part of the verse establishes the requirement of having civil laws], **for thus it is written** [in another scriptural verse], "**For I know him, that he will command his children** and his household after him, that they shall keep the way of the Lord, to do righteousness and justice" [Genesis 18:19]. "**The Lord**"—**this** means **blessing** [i.e., cursing] **the Name** of God, for **thus it is written** [in another verse], "**and he who curses the name of the Lord shall surely be put to death**" [Lev. 24:16]. "**God**"—**this**

refs to the injunction against **worshipping the stars** [i.e., idolatry], **for thus it is written, "You shall have no other gods** before Me" [Ex. 20:3]. **"Upon the man"**—this refers to **bloodshed** [murder], **for thus it is written, "Whoever sheds the blood of a man** by man shall his blood be shed" [Genesis 9:6]. **"Saying"**—this refers to **sexual transgressions, for thus it is written, "Saying, if a man sends away his wife, and she goes from him and becomes another man's"** [Jeremiah 3:1]. **"Of every tree of the garden—but not** fruit that was **stolen—you may surely eat"**—[which means] **but not a limb** cut **from a live** animal. (B. Sanhedrin 56b)

To get a feel for the way the Talmud works, try reading the boldface alone. The Talmud text also lacks punctuation of any kind, and there are no capital letters in Hebrew. Thus the text is highly compressed and reveals mnemonic devices that may well go back to the original oral form.

But even with the inserted text and modern punctuation, this passage remains difficult, so let's unpack it further. First, "our Rabbis" refers to authorities from the time of the Pharisees through the first two centuries of the common era. A "baraita" is a legal ruling of considerable weight but secondary to a "mishnah," which is the authoritative ruling. The Talmud often cites *baraitot* (plural of "baraita") as commentaries on a mishnah. So here we have a ruling that nicely summarizes the seven laws of God that are incumbent upon all humans—all the descendants of Noah.

The Talmud then seeks the scriptural source of the Noahide laws as given in the baraita. The obvious place to go would be Genesis 9:1–11, where God makes a covenant with Noah and gives him rules to follow. But the Talmud instead quotes Rabbi Yochanan, who derives the laws from Genesis 2:16, where God tells Adam: "From every tree in the garden you may surely eat." Now this does not seem to say anything about the Noahide laws. Its choice, however, reveals one of the common forms of rabbinic argument mentioned earlier. This verse is regarded as redundant or superfluous, in the sense that it is not necessary for the literal purpose of telling Adam that he can eat from all the trees, which had previously been stated explicitly in Genesis 1:29. Moreover, verse 17, which denies him the Tree of Knowledge, would have been sufficient logically to allow Adam to eat from all the others. It is a principle of midrashic exegesis that a superfluous verse can be used to derive other laws, which Rabbi Yochanan now does, by showing that each word in the superfluous verse is an allusion to *another* verse where the relevant law is stated.

Now we can see that the fragmentary quote (actually a single word in Hebrew), "He commanded," is interpreted to refer to the need for a system of civil laws or courts by reference to Genesis 18:19, where God says about Abraham: "For I know him, that he will command his children and his household after him that they may keep the way of YHWH, to do righteousness and justice." The connection is the word "command" that appears in both verses, an application of the second of Hillel's rules, the *gezerah shavah*. All of the succeeding fragments are enlisted in the same way. "The Lord" (that is, YHWH, the proper name of God) refers to the prohibition against blasphemy by reference to Leviticus 24:16: "If he also pronounces the name YHWH, he shall be put to death." "God" (that is, the generic term for God, *Elohim*) refers to the prohibition against idolatry, from Exodus 20:3: "You shall have no other Gods [*Elohim*] beside me; you shall not make for yourself a sculptured image," and so on. "The man" refers to the prohibition against murder, from Genesis 9:6: "Whoever sheds the blood of man, by man shall his blood be shed" (which line actually comes from the commands to Noah). "Saying" prohibits adultery, from Jeremiah 3:1: "Saying: 'If a man puts away his wife, and she goes from him, and becomes another man's, may he return to her again? Will not that land be greatly polluted?'" (i.e., the answer to the question, "may he return to her again?" is "no"). This connection hardly seems like much to go on (not that the others are so much stronger), but that is not the point: Rabbi Yochanan is following the rules, and being very clever about it. What motives other than cleverness might have been operating here?

The last two laws are derived from inference rather than from allusion to another scriptural text. "Of every tree of the garden" means, by implication, not to eat fruit from somebody else's garden, hence prohibiting theft. "You may surely eat" is interpreted to mean a prohibition against eating a limb torn from a live animal, based on the language of the verse, which can be read as "that which is food, you may eat" and the admittedly circular assumption that live animals are not food.

How should we understand the rhetorical strategies used here? The Talmud cites Rabbi Yochanan who has found a way to midrashically derive the Noahide laws from a command given not to Noah but to Adam. The texts that back up Yochanan's derivation, by the way, are not the only possible choices. In fact, the Talmud goes on to show some alternatives. But Rabbi Yochanan has picked his texts strategically to argue that the Noahide laws were *always* incumbent upon all people, starting from Adam, continuing through Noah, definitely including Abraham and his descendants, continuing into the Torah given to Moses—since the Noahide laws are included in Torah (though this incites a long clarifying discussion in the Talmud) and are even ratified by the prophets. The rabbis liked to derive laws from the earliest parts of the Torah to show that the laws were in a sense "always" there. Thus the rabbis attempted to show, for example, that the patriarchs followed Torah law hundreds of years before the time of Moses.

I have chosen the Talmud passage because it relates to an issue that is also behind Paul's argument in Romans—namely, the status of Gentiles in the early Christian fellowship or Jesus Movement. The issue arises in Galatians as well, where we learn that Peter and James have sent emissaries to tell the Galatians that Paul has misled them into thinking that Gentiles not need become Jewish to join the movement. Some of the Galatians have followed the rule brought from Jerusalem and converted, the men undergoing circumcision. Paul is furious about this and condemns the Galatians who converted as well as Peter and James. The sequel is presented in Acts 15, where Paul comes to Jerusalem to make his case before Peter and James with "no small dissention" (15:2 and 15:7) characterizing the debate. At last, James declares what came to be known as the Apostolic Decree, allowing Gentiles to remain in the movement as Gentiles provided they follow a few rules: not to eat food that has been sacrificed to pagan gods, not to eat blood, not to worship idols, and not to commit adultery. This list of rules is a version of what later would be known as the Noahide Laws—the laws whose origin is interpreted in our Talmud passage. The Apostolic Decree, along with Paul's reflections in Romans, thus represents a remarkable first-century transition from the ancient laws for the "resident alien" articulated in Genesis 9 and Leviticus 17 and 18 to the laws we have looked at in the Talmud, which dates from 200 to 500 CE.[13] This issue concerns Paul deeply, both in Galatians 2 and 3 and in Romans, particularly Romans 9 to 11.[14]

The "resident alien" laws applied to those Gentiles who were in Jewish lands and subject to Jewish laws. The presumptive origin of the laws—either in the Garden of Eden (as our sample text argues) or following the Flood—was God's determination to give minimal rules to all the people on earth by giving these laws to the progenitors of all people, Adam and Noah. Since all the people on earth did not in fact acknowledge the god or the cosmogony of the Jews, the solution was to apply them to resident aliens in places ruled by Jews. This solution also obviated the much more difficult rule of one law for all, which would impose Jewish ritual restrictions on non-Jews.

The acceptance of these Noahide or quasi-Noahide laws by the Gentiles in the Jesus Movement therefore carries with it, presumably, acknowledgment that the movement itself was fundamentally Jewish. Perhaps by imposing Noahide law on their Gentiles, Peter and James (and possibly Paul as well) hoped to guarantee recognition of their leadership or maintain the Jewish provenance of the movement, including the authority of the Torah, whose provisions the Gentiles were now in a limited sense observing. It seems like a reasonable compromise. It also contributes to Paul's determination to find in the Torah some deeper justification for the inclusion of Gentiles. Paul is apparently not entirely satisfied with the notion that following the Noahide Laws or Apostolic Decree justifies the inclusion of Gentiles. Paul, like Rabbi Yochanan in our Talmud passage, is not content to locate these few laws in the story of the Flood. Thus, in precisely the same way and with precisely the same motivation as our Talmud example, Paul seeks to locate the underlying rationale for inclusion of Gentiles in the Torah. Given the background and motivation for Paul's exegesis in Romans, it should not surprise us to find him using techniques of interpretation and argument that had for some time characterized Jewish rhetoric.

To make this case, Paul argues that Abraham was "righteous" before being circumcised. In Romans 4:13, Paul says "the promise to Abraham and his descendants that he should inherit the world was not through the Law but through uprightness [or righteousness] of faith." So, for Paul, those who have faith but have not been circumcised may still regard themselves as the children of Abraham and, though they do not follow Torah law, as righteous before God in the same way that Abraham was before being circumcised and thus beholden to the law. Paul cleverly applies the "pre-Moses" form of argument to Abraham's pre-circumcision faith in God and uses it to say that circumcision and the law are not necessary. (The rabbis would no doubt agree with Paul when he says that circumcision was "a sign and a guarantee that the faith which he [Abraham] had while still uncircumcised was reckoned to him as uprightness" (Romans 4:11). That is, from the rabbinical point of view, Abraham was already observing Torah law and circumcision was "a sign and guarantee.")

Paul argues, in the same vein and at some length (Romans 1:18–32), that the Gentiles "knew God" (1:21) from mere observation of the creation and thus "have no excuse" (1:21) for not worshipping God. Even more: "They are well aware of God's ordinance" (1:32) even though they did not get the laws from Moses. Therefore the Gentiles can't claim not to be sinners, he suggests, simply because they are not Jews. Paul does not specifically mention the laws given to Noah or the Apostolic Decree but does seem to allude to them when describing the bad behavior of Gentiles: they worship images (1:23), they engage in "unnatural" sexual practices (1:24–27), they engage in "all sorts of injustice" (1:29), as well as a long list of nasty practices (1:29–31) (see table 9.1).

The point of this discussion is to show that both Paul and the rabbis were motivated to find the underlying tenets of their positions in pre-Mosaic scriptural texts and then to illustrate them in the prophets using oral-law rhetorical techniques. As we see in Romans 9 to 11, Paul argues by Jewish rhetoric, using scriptural citation and truncated quotation, connecting verses by key words, arguing by definition, by analogy, by context, and by inferential reasoning to show that his principle derives from scripture. In Romans 9, Paul begins with the premise that God has chosen not only Jews but also Gentiles for salvation. He wishes to show that God's promises are given by grace and not merely by

TABLE 9.1

NOAHIDE LAWS (TALMUD)	APOSTOLIC DECREE	ROMANS 1
Civil law	—	Injustices of all sorts
Blasphemy	—	Don't acknowledge God
Idol worship	Idol meat	Idol worship
Sexual transgression	Illicit marriages	Unnatural sex
Murder	—	Murder
Theft	—	—
Eating living flesh	Abstain from blood	—

"physical descent." Here as in the rest of Romans, Paul is particularly concerned about the Jews and their relationship to the revelation of Christ: "They are Israelites; it was they who were adopted as children, the glory was theirs and the covenants; to them were given the law and the worship of God and the promises. To them belong the fathers and out of them, so far as physical descent is concerned, came Christ who is above all, God blessed for ever" (Romans 9:4–5). Paul also wishes to show that "God's promise has not failed" (Romans 9:6), but that "not all born Israelites belong to Israel and not all the descendants of Abraham count as his children" (Romans 9:7). This case he will argue by quoting and interpreting scripture.

Romans 9:7 concludes with the first of a string of citations. To prove that not all of Abraham's descendants "count as his children," Paul says "for 'Isaac is the one through whom your name will be carried on.'" Paul does not explicitly mention Ishmael, yet the sense of the argument requires that the audience know the rest of the story—namely, that Abraham has another son who does not, in some sense, "count" as his child. Like the rabbis and presumably the Pharisees, Paul gives a partial quote and assumes that the context is familiar. In the rest of this argument, Paul strings his citations together with minimal connective commentary. What follows are the quotations or paraphrases with Paul's connections noted (and the original cited text where it may be helpful).

"Isaac is the one through whom your name will be carried on" (Romans 9:7 quoting Genesis 21:12: "It is through Isaac that offspring will be continued for you"). Thus it is not physical descent that determines God's chosen, but the promise, which in the case of Isaac is the following: "I shall come back to you at this season, and Sarah will have a son" (Romans 9:9 quoting Genesis 18:10 and 18:14). An even better example, Paul says, is the promise to Rebekah regarding the twins in her womb: "The elder shall serve the younger" (Romans 9:13 quoting Genesis 25:23). That this means choosing one son and rejecting the other, Paul proves from another quote: "I loved Jacob but hated Esau" (Romans 9:13 quoting Malachi 1:2–3).

God is not being unjust, says Paul, for God says to Moses: "I am gracious to those to whom I am gracious and I take pity on those on whom I take pity" (Romans 9:15 quoting Exodus 33:19). It is not a matter of what someone does, but of God's mercy, as God says to Pharaoh: "I raised you up for this reason, to display my power in you and to have my name talked of throughout the world" (Romans 9:17 quoting Exodus 9:16: "I have spared you for this purpose: in order to show you my power and in order that my fame shall resound throughout the world").

How then, Paul asks rhetorically, can God blame someone he manipulates in such a way? The answer, from scripture, is not to question your maker: "Something that was made, can it say to its maker: why did you make me?" (Romans 9:20, collapsing several verses: "Shall the potter be as the clay, that the thing made should say of him who made it, 'he did not make me'?" [Isaiah 29:16]; "Will the clay say to the one who molds it, 'what are you making?'" [Isaiah 45:9]; and "'O house of Israel, can I not do with you as the potter with his clay?' says the Lord. Behold, as the clay in the hand of the potter, so are you in My hand" [Jeremiah 18:6]).

Here Paul reaches the climax of this part of the argument and gives a longer exposition. What if God "wanted to reveal his retribution" but patiently puts up with those who are "designed to be destroyed" (Romans 9:22), so that he can reveal himself to those he has really chosen—namely, us: "we are that people, called by him not only out of the Jews but out of the Gentiles, too" (Romans 9:24): "Just as he says in the book of Hosea: 'I shall tell those who were not my people, "you are my people," and I shall take pity on those on whom I had no pity.' And in the very place where they were told, 'you are not my people,' they will be told that they are 'children of the living God'" (Romans 9:25 quoting and interpreting Hosea 2:1: "Yet the number of the children of Israel shall be as the sand of the sea, which cannot be numbered; and it shall come to pass that, instead of that which was said to them, 'you are not my people,' it shall be said to them, 'you are the children of the living God'").

Paul goes on in this manner, citing scripture to build his argument, through chapters 9, 10, and 11. Although he is never as telegraphic as the Talmud, we should keep in mind that the Talmud text is the written form of a memorized oral tradition for use by scholars already familiar with the texts and techniques.

It is very possible that the way Paul proceeds with his argument in Romans reveals the way that the Pharisees of his own day would have argued, giving more or less terse connections, citing text in a variety of ways—briefly or fully or paraphrasing or collapsing as it suited their purpose, but still using a full and natural form of exposition. At the same time, it is very easy to imagine Paul's argument turned into a coded text just like the Talmud.

A notable similarity between the passages we are comparing from Paul and Sanhedrin is the sequence of scriptural selections (see table 9.2). In both cases, quotations from the Torah—from the books of Genesis, Exodus, and Leviticus —form the basis of the argument, followed by selections from the prophets— Jeremiah, Isaiah, and so on. While the practice of selecting quotations from Torah first, then from the prophets and writings, is not the inevitable sequence in rabbinic exegesis, this pattern is very common, and for obvious reasons: the Torah simply has more authority than the prophets and writings.[15]

Both Paul and the rabbis in our passages are attempting to ground important principles in legal statements in scripture. Paul begins with the premise that God has chosen not only Jews but also Gentiles for salvation. He wishes to show, from the Torah first and then the prophets, that God's promises are given by grace and not merely by physical descent. The rabbis similarly begin with a statement of the Noahide laws giving seven commandments and then cite Rabbi Yochanan, who provides a scriptural basis that gives the laws the widest possible application by deriving them from a verse about Adam. Both Paul and Rabbi Yochanan start with the earliest possible passage to get the widest possible application for their principles. (Paul is also picking up the thread of an argument he made previously, in Romans 4, regarding Abraham's righteousness before his circumcision.)

Another similarity is that both passages make the assumption that a variety of texts can be pulled together from different scriptural books out of context and that they will nonetheless address the issue at hand.[16] We saw this principle at work in the Sanhedrin passage's use of *gezerah shavah*, which uses word matching among widely disparate texts. In Romans, Paul also links keywords to bring together passages that are similarly out of context. In Romans 4, where the theme of physical descent begins, Paul links his texts with the word "count" (or "reckon"), using it several times in his own exposition as well as emphasizing it in his scriptural selections. In chapter 9, he repeats the word "promise" several times, and he characterizes God's predictions as promises. He also links the quotes from chapters 4 and 9 by the word "seed" (in Hebrew *zerah*, "nations" and "offspring" in most translations).

Blithely ignoring context, both the Talmud and Paul make the assumption that the audience will be able to fill in critical parts of the context of each quoted passage, as it is often the case that the quoted section alone is not clear

TABLE 9.2

Sanhedrin	Paul
Genesis 2:16	Genesis 21:12
Genesis 18:19	Genesis 18:14
Leviticus 24:16	Genesis 25:23
Exodus 20:3	Malachi 1:2–3
Jeremiah 3:1	Exodus 33:19
	Exodus 9:16
	Isaiah 29:16 or 45:9 or Jeremiah 18:6
	Hosea 2:1

by itself. In the Sanhedrin example, this is radically so, for reasons we have already noted, and we see it again in Romans, where, as we saw in the first quoted passage about Isaac, Ishmael is never mentioned. Unless the audience can fill in that information, the mere quotation, "Isaac is the one through whom your name will be carried on," will not make Paul's point about God's choice of Isaac over Ishmael, even though both were Abraham's sons.[17]

In Paul's epistles there are other examples of Pharisaic rhetorical forms. *Kal v'khomer*, or minor to major, appears in Romans 5:15: "If death came to many through the offense of one man, how much greater an effect the grace of God has had" (with a similar statement in 5:17), and in 11:12: "If their fall has proved a great gain to the world . . . how much greater a gain will come when all is restored to them." An instance of general and specific (Hillel's number 5 above, *k'lal ufrat*) is in 13:8–10, where the rule to love one another (quoted from Leviticus 19:18) is used to interpret the negative commandments in the Ten Commandments (Exodus 20:13–15).[18]

THE PLACE OF PAUL'S JEWISH RHETORIC IN CHRISTIAN SCHOLARSHIP

Now, it is possible to claim that Paul could have found many of these techniques in Roman rhetoric. What is so special, after all, about linking keywords or using an argument from lesser to greater? It is certainly the case that Romans as a whole clearly displays the techniques of Greco-Roman rhetoric found throughout Paul's epistles. The letter is widely held to be framed in the Greco-Roman rhetorical genre of the "scholastic diatribe," employing a primarily dialectical form of argumentation, which is to say a thesis-antithesis procedure.[19] The overall argument of the letter is generally identified as "protreptic"—an argument intended to persuade a group to feel unified. Other Greco-Roman rhetorical elements, structural and local, can readily be identified.

But the doubts cast on Paul's use of oral-Torah forms of argument actually derive from another type of objection, one that strikes me as suspect. Some Paul scholars see not rhetoric in this form of argument but mere facility in quoting scripture. Others claim that Paul draws on scripture only because in Romans he is addressing a Jewish audience. Still others reject the idea that Paul could be using Jewish forms of rhetoric because of the conclusions he draws. This sort of objection refuses, in effect, even to engage with the possibility that Paul, a Jew and a Pharisee, deliberately used the rhetorical forms we have been discussing. How can this be?

In 1957, E. Earle Ellis, in *Paul's Use of the Old Testament,* traced the scholarship on "rabbinic" exegetical practices in the New Testament back to the late Reformation, noting a source from 1713 that shows "extensive agreement in methodology between New Testament and rabbinic writers."[20] In his own analysis Ellis also found "distinctively Jewish" procedures in Paul's letters, including "fragmentary quotation with the continuance of the given portion sometimes implied. . . . Midrash, or running commentary; the practice of quoting from the Law, the Prophets, and the Hagiographa; and the employment of Hillel's rules."[21] Yet Ellis declares these practices to be peripheral, noting, for example, that the successive quoting from Torah-prophets-writings is not regular and that use of *kal v'khomer* can be "too greatly stressed."[22] He seems eager to distance these practices from actual interpretation, heaping scorn upon the Talmud and the rabbis: "Their splinterised, purposeless, speculative musings which 'suspend dogmatic mountains on textual hairs' have not the remotest kinship with Paul's theology or hermeneutical principles."[23] Thus Ellis simultaneously locates Jewish rhetoric in Paul and rejects it as irrelevant.

Twenty years later, in 1977, New Testament scholar E. P. Sanders's *Paul and Palestinian Judaism: A Comparison of Patterns of Religion* argued that Paul had been desperately misinterpreted by Christian scholars intent on seeing Paul as a critic and rejecter of Judaism, which, Sanders wrote, he certainly was not. Sanders's work initiated what has come to be called the "new perspective" on Paul, but the new perspective was slow to take hold, particularly with respect to Paul's rhetorical practices.[24] In 1982, for example, W. S. Towner went further than Ellis in claiming to find *no* examples of the use of Hillel's rules anywhere in the New Testament (except the equivocal lesser-to-greater or *kal v'khomer*).[25]

Richard B. Hays, in his 1989 *Echoes of Scripture in the Letters of Paul,* takes much the same line as Ellis (though without the unrestrained scorn). Hays begins with the striking "new perspective" statement that he sees Paul as "a first-century Jewish Christian seeking to come to terms hermeneutically with his Jewish heritage."[26] He goes on to argue, however, that while rabbinic methods can be found in Paul, they are not useful in unpacking Paul's argument. These methods are merely "an inventory of tropes . . . imaginative operations . . . to make the text mean more than it says."[27] For Hays, the results of Paul's exegesis actually reveal his *distance* from rabbinic methods: "The message that Paul finds . . . is the gospel of Jesus Christ . . . a theme hardly central in rabbinic hermeneutics."[28] Yet, despite this disclaimer, much of the book supports the connection between Paul and rabbinic rhetoric.

In their 1995 book, *Judaism in the New Testament*, Bruce Chilton and Jacob Neusner compare the structure of midrash, a typical form of rabbinic commentary on scripture, with Paul's scripturally based argument in Romans 9–11 and conclude that while there is "a certain analogy" between rabbinic midrash and Paul's procedure, it is only an analogy and not a precise match. And, they add, echoing Hays, Paul's "overarching theme, of Jesus Christ's completion of the Torah, the Prophets, and the Writings, could never be described as rabbinic."[29] Despite their caution, Chilton and Neusner point out a considerable number of similarities between Paul's arguments in Romans and the rabbinic methods they find in the Mishnah, so much so that their argument could easily be taken as entirely positive on the question of Paul's use of Pharisaic rhetoric. Just a few years later, though, in 2000, Johann Kim's award-winning dissertation, "God, Israel, and the Gentiles: Rhetoric and Situation in Romans 9–11," makes no mention at all of Jewish rhetoric.[30]

In 2004, Thomas Tobin's big book on Romans, *Paul's Rhetoric in Its Contexts,* somehow fails to mention Paul's training as a Pharisee as one of the contexts, and though it includes a few references to proto-rabbinic arguments that Paul would have known, Tobin rejects the idea that Paul used Jewish rhetoric.[31] As for Paul's use of scriptural quotation, Tobin explains that it is not a form of argument, but that Paul uses it because it is soothing: he quotes to reassure his audience that scripture remains authoritative in his eyes.[32]

Still and all, because of Sanders and scholars following his lead, a sweeping and positive reassessment of the Jewish context of both Jesus and Paul has become prominent in New Testament scholarship, which more and more seems to be grounding Jesus and Paul clearly in Jewish tradition. John Gager, who published *Reinventing Paul* in 2000, reviews the history of the change, before and after Sanders. Still, he notes, it has been difficult to overcome the theological tensions that obscure the view of Paul as a learned Jew who was not rejecting Judaism as a religion of works-righteousness and self-righteousness (as we saw in Ellis's smug contempt for the Talmud). This view, says Gager, "is a beast that will not be slain."[33] For some, it is simply too strange to imagine that Paul invented so much of Christian theology out of the materials of Jewish thought. Paul gave existing Jewish ideas like "grace" or "standing" new meaning.[34] He was inventing in the rhetorical sense of using available means to create a persuasive argument, and he used Jewish forms of argument to argue his case for the fulfillment of the Jewish scriptures and traditions. He was, as the title of this volume puts it, renovating the rhetoric of his culture for his particular message.

Biblical scholar Steven DiMattei drew this conclusion in a 2008 essay: "Without denying the influence that Paul's faith in Christ had on his hermeneutic, I would nevertheless distinguish between Paul's hermeneutical assumptions—those underlying principles that governed his approach to the biblical text—and Paul's Christology, the specific conviction that shaped his interpretation. In other words, although Paul's belief in Christ influences and shapes the content of his hermeneutic, it is not to be confused with the underlying hermeneutical assumption that guides his interpretation."[35] I agree with DiMattei and would go a step further to argue that Paul reveals what might be called an ingrained or assimilated knowledge of Pharisaic argumentation—that is, it comes to him automatically and naturally.

Rabbinic forms of interpretation should be seen as vibrant and creative—and, more important, vital to the project of continuing revelation. Students of the Christian rhetorical tradition may participate in this project by recognizing and understanding the forms of Jewish rhetoric embedded in early Christian texts and by acknowledging (without, we hope, the kinds of discomfort we have reviewed here) that it is only natural that they should be there, since Paul and Jesus would have used rhetorical forms characteristic of their own religion. As for the strangeness of the rhetorical forms we find, it is helpful to remember that, then as now, shared cultural and religious assumptions are expressed in rhetorical forms whose very complexity reinforces the connections between speaker and audience.

10
—

RESISTANCE TO RHETORIC IN CHRISTIAN TRADITION

Thomas Amorose

THE TITLE OF this final chapter may surprise readers, since the preceding chapters of *Renovating Rhetoric* show so many successes for rhetoric at work in Christian tradition. But readers may have noticed that most of the successes documented in these chapters came in the face of resistance by some form of mainstream Christianity. Or they came when classroom instructors developed practices built on a theology espousing opposition to that mainstream status quo. (I am thinking in particular here of Priscilla Perkins and the way her Lonerganian approach to classroom relationships opposes that of her evangelical student, who espouses widely held Christian beliefs.) Bruce Herzberg succeeds in opposing the widely held view that with the birth of Christianity came wholly new ways of expressing faith, new ways of arguing faith. In each of these cases, rhetorical success involved shifting settled views and practices, rigid gender roles, confined homiletics, or narrow constructions of believers' faith. They have in common the renovation of rhetorical materials in Christian tradition to overcome, undercut, or bring about reform, with marginalized rhetors overcoming power structures by shaping those materials for purposes of renewing the tradition, its members, and the rhetors themselves.

But why the resistance to rhetorical practices that, in hindsight, have benefited Christianity so much? This chapter attempts to answer that question, if only in broad terms. My interests here are theoretical rather than historical, though some rhetorical history is involved in my trying to get at an answer. My sad hope is to show that Christian tradition, both early and late, has chosen positions that hamper and limit the possibilities of rhetoric, which explains why the work of renovation has generally fallen to outsiders, like those detailed in preceding chapters. These are figures who have aspired to claim a credible ethos within the tradition, change it, or make the tradition available for transfer to other discursive environments, thereby providing rhetorical flexibility to the likes of Christian students and other newcomers to mature literacies. But why the need for such struggle in the first place?

SOME STARTING POINTS

Anyone familiar with the issue of the roots of Christianity in rhetoric or the influence of rhetoric on Christianity recognizes certain invaluable sources. My intent here is not to replicate, much less try to improve upon (as though I could) the work of such fundamental thinkers in this area as James Kinneavy, Kenneth Burke, or Wayne Booth (on Kenneth Burke)—though I acknowledge their indispensable influence. I also acknowledge the influence of Walter Jost's and Wendy Olmsted's *Rhetorical Invention and Religious Inquiry,* a comprehensive investigation into the relationship of rhetoric and religion as a whole.[1]

All of this fundamental research on rhetoric in Christian tradition speaks of the important theological role played by text and language in Christianity. Christianity is one of the Abrahamic religions, and, as Bruce Herzberg has shown in chapter 9, shares with other faiths in this tradition a firm base in logocentrism. Christianity thus privileges language as the medium for eternal wisdom, that wisdom having been transmitted to humanity through a merging of God and human conceived as the coming of the Word—that is, of wisdom coming as and being shaped by language. But within the Christian tradition, language's role isn't simply transmissive. It's also uniquely identified with the Christian God himself. As the apostle John says, the Word existed from the beginning, was God, and was with God. The Word is simultaneously Christ as one of the persons of a three-personed God *and* God's verbal expression. When observing similarities between the study of language and the study of God, Burke has observed how the relationship between the persons of Father and Son in the triune Christian God shares properties with words as symbols and the things they symbolize. In both instances, says Burke, one of the elements can't exist without the other. Just as the Father relies upon the Son to "symbolize" his power—that is, make it manifest in history—so too, a symbolized "thing" (object, person, property) can't exist, to the mind at least, without a symbol for it.[2] This observation hits on more than some coincidental similarity between how language/text works and how God exists; it explicates as well the profound way, for Christians, that Christ as the Word combines symbol (Word made flesh) and thing symbolized (God himself) into a unity.

But Burke's point here is about the rhetoric of that relationship, not just its linguistics. Christ-as-Word isn't merely communication. It is mediation and persuasion as well. So to examine Christianity's relationship with rhetoric is more than merely a typical study of "rhetoric and . . . [fill in the blank]." This relationship is crucial because Christianity sees as part of its critical function not just the articulation of truth (following through on the divine function of the Word made flesh) but also the teaching of those truths, the motivating of believers to action based on those truths, and the promulgation of those truths to those who haven't yet heard them. All these latter functions necessarily involve rhetoric, and rhetoric has been immensely valued in Christian tradition.

And yet there seem to be resistances in Christian tradition to a wholly unfettered, broadly conceived rhetoric. For our purposes here, I mean the term "rhetoric" as Burke defines it: "the use of language as a symbolic means of inducing cooperation in beings that by nature respond to symbols."[3] Several important things seem implied in this definition. First, the definition implies there must be give-and-take—negotiation—that induces cooperation. Second, this give-and-take must be open and allow free consideration of a range of ideas and options for action. Third, these ideas and options must all be produced and consumed in a public space. (For the record, I am not considering here private or excluding rhetorics, or the purely epideictic.) I see this definition as also assuming that rhetorical negotiation produces shared meaning, that rhetoric involves the interpretation of actions and phenomena for the sake of producing that meaning, and that rhetoric can affect audiences' worldviews. It is precisely this conception of rhetoric—as a meaning-making, interpretive, agency-based, and even transforming activity—that troubles Christian attitudes toward rhetoric, much to Christianity's own detriment (through loss of opportunities for renovating Christian tradition by rhetors like those discussed in this book) and, for that matter, to the detriment of the public sphere. Putting it simplistically, Christianity, from a rhetorical point of view, seems to be a discourse community more concerned with the way that faith gives meaning to human beings than it is with the way human beings give meaning to faith.

The first resistance to rhetoric lies in Christianity's constricting of the role of the rhetor. At the risk of generalizing, I would claim the Christian tradition leans toward conceiving of the ideal Christian rhetor as agent of forces (scripture, spirit, conscience) that work through her and make her something more of a medium for divine meaning and less a human discoverer and shaper of meaning. The rhetor seems conceived of as being less involved in the human, social activity of cooperatively negotiating meanings from evidence than she is in bearing witness to meanings already confirmed through sources either external (e.g., Revelation) or deeply internal (e.g., faith, conscience). In other words, the rhetor is given less agency than would be the case in a broadly conceived rhetoric.

The second resistance comes as a response to the de-centering of authoritative interpretation in the Reformation, the failed attempt at an objective system of Christian hermeneutics in the Enlightenment, and the postmodern critique of supposed hermeneutic objectivity. All three have driven an ongoing crisis, since the Reformation, about who gets to speak with authority in faith matters and who gets to claim objectivity for his or her interpretation of anything and everything from scripture to church history. In a milieu of such concern over the authorizing of interpretation—whether it be at one extreme the deauthorizing of figures ranging from church officials to reformers/heretics (depending on which side of the Reformation one found oneself on) or at the other the overregulating of authorization (as clampdown on those claiming authority for themselves)—rhetoric seems a touchy subject. After all, the number of prophets and false prophets, sects and subsects developing since the Reformation, all claiming some form of authority, continues to threaten Christianity's commonalities. This denial to rhetoric of the full capacity, and freedom, to interpret and argue the meanings of all features in the life-world of believers denies in turn the benefits rhetoric can give the Christian community, notwithstanding the sometimes heroic efforts of rhetorical outsiders like those in this volume or the needs of Christian students wanting to apply their "home rhetoric" to the larger, secular world of discourse.

The final resistance relates to the contemporary Christian attitude toward worldviews. A worldview can be defined as a system of beliefs that exists in the mind prior to a person's critical inquiry into her world or even the development of theories about how her world works. In this way, a worldview operates as the basis for forming those theories and the critical methods necessary for inquiring into the world. It consists of beliefs deeply held and close to the heart, usually identifiable with the person's very being in the world. Moreover, worldviews are shared by any given group. For our discussion two issues emerge. The first is whether contemporary American Christianity is too content with the dominant worldview of its milieu, which some critics would call the worldview of a dying modernism. (These critics even worry that contemporary Christianity is complicit in the propping up of this moribund worldview.) The second issue is whether or not current Christianity assumes that a dominant worldview can even be changed if found objectionable. Here is the relevance of these concerns to our topic: If contemporary Christianity is content with the status quo worldview, then rhetorical negotiation seems *unneeded*. If it does not believe changes in worldviews can occur, then rhetoric as we are defining it here becomes *irrelevant*. Either option proves problematic for the work of rhetoric.

To discover the origins of these three resistances, we can look to (1) the Early Christian construction of human subjectivity and the way that construction seems to linger even today; (2) Post-Reformation Christian views about interpretive authority and the effect of those views on Christian rhetoric ever since; and (3) contemporary Christian attitudes about the nature of worldviews and the possibilities of rhetoric, especially in postmodern times. We can think of these three as, respectively, the anthropology, the hermeneutics, and the epistemology behind Christian tradition's relationship to rhetoric. I would like to discuss each in that order, first providing some description of the three, then proceeding to show how they offer sites of resistance to rhetoric in Christian tradition.

ANTHROPOLOGY: HUMAN SUBJECTIVITY
AND CHRISTIAN RHETORIC'S ORIGINS

A good place to begin describing Christian rhetoric's anthropology is with early Christian writers' appropriation of classical and biblical rhetorics as critical tools for building identity and solidarity within the early church.[4] Broad claims about the compatibility between Western views of language and Western forms of religion are a common feature of twentieth-century scholarship on rhetoric and religion. Burke, for example, explicates the Western habit of describing language and Christian theology in similar ways, an inheritance from both Greek and biblical sources. Kinneavy goes so far as to say that early constructs of Christian faith have their roots in Greek rhetoric. And Geoffrey Galt Harpham states that "the Christian God is modeled on language."[5] So it comes as no surprise to anyone aware of the discursive history of the early Christian church that its leaders borrowed heavily from Greek theories and techniques of rhetoric.[6] But even before the assimilation of classical learning occurred, according to Averil Cameron, "early Christians were already preoccupied with the question of the nature of Christian discourse."[7] This preoccupation stemmed from the foundations of Christian language and texts, early Christianity's centering itself on and in texts, and then, later, the rich multiplication of discourses in the early centuries of Christianity.

We should pause here to note that, from the beginning, Christian discourse has valued emotion as well as solely rational comprehension in the communicating and comprehending of truth. The result is an expansive conception of human beings, one that emphasizes the faculty of understanding more than that of mere cognition and producing a more inclusive idea of personhood.

This anthropology values rhetoric highly because it is seen as a way to reach the "fuller" person in two areas of utmost importance to early Christian leaders: the teaching and promulgating of the new faith.

Early Christian rhetoric found bases for this idea of an expansive person-hood and a rhetoric suitable to it in biblical resources. Kennedy notes that the typical rhetorical strategy of Old Testament authors is not dialectic, which would appeal to the cognitive faculty of readers, but rather proclamation, based in revelation and signs, prophetically set forth in language designed to move readers into action.[8] This same aversion (if it is that) to logical appeal is seen in Jesus's sermons, says Kennedy, where rational proof is in fact purposely con-founded by the use of paradox and metaphor, both of which seek to cultivate deep understanding, not mere intellectual knowing.[9] As they read scripture, early Christian rhetorical theorists come to believe that God as author of Old and New Testaments is intent on persuading human readers not by appeals to their cognitive capacities but to their emotions—by the pathos evoked either by the memory of the people's suffering or the hope of salvation to come. They be-gin to develop a rhetoric in which the author of sermon or exigesis is instructed not to persuade listeners or readers with proofs but instead to proclaim the truth in such a way that it speaks to a fuller personhood of author and reader, both redefined by grace into knowing God's truth through feeling it and envi-sioning it imaginatively.

In a way that is difficult to imagine in a world like ours, saturated by secu-lar, post-Enlightenment ideas of author and text, the assumption in this earlier rhetoric seems to be that the speaker or writer who hopes to bear God's truth to an audience is not fully the controlling agent of textual meaning, marshalling arguments and engineering their effect upon the listener or reader. Instead, as Kennedy says, these theorists feel that "truth must be apprehended by the listener" or reader, and "not proved by the speaker," and that such apprehension comes when discourse opens the entire personhood of a listener to a profound moving by the Spirit.[10]

But as wonderful as this expansiveness and grace-inspired insight may seem, from a rhetorical point of view it offers at least one problem for Christianity: constriction of the speaker/writer's agency. Spending time with Augustine of Hippo, perhaps the supreme theoretician of this early Christian conception of rhetoric, will help us understand this constricting of rhetorical agency in early Christianity.[11] My point will be that this constriction seems to cling to Chris-tian attitudes toward rhetoric down through the ages, even unto today, and shows up as one of the resistances I described at the beginning of this chapter. Perhaps it is responsible, along the way, for limiting the possibilities of agency for those seeking to renovate Christian tradition.

Augustine exhorts Christian rhetors to de-emphasize their own rhetorical agency and focus instead on the emotional content of messages, and a good place to see the roles of emotion and agency in Augustine's rhetoric is in the area of eloquence. (This discussion will take a few paragraphs before its relevance to the matter of constricted rhetorical agency becomes apparent.) Augustine notes classical eloquence's capacity for moving listeners to feel. Nonetheless, he finds that Ciceronian eloquence draws too much attention to and admiration for the rhetor himself, not the subject matter. So Augustine sought to exhort the use of classical eloquence in Christian preaching and teaching but also to discard eloquence's function of drawing attention to the author/speaker. Eloquence would serve instead to help listeners access the "emotional truths" of Christianity as complement to their intellectual comprehension of the rhetor's message. Again, the emphasis is on accessing the audience's full personhood, on feeling, not just thought, as a doorway into understanding.

In fact, one can evince from statements Augustine makes in the *Confessions* and Book IV of *On Christian Doctrine* that, for Augustine, the texts that result from rightly deployed eloquence, if truly inspired, transfer truth from God to the reader/listener at the same time as they move the reader/listener toward accepting God's truth. One could say that, whether Augustine is urging the Christian rhetor to use the simple style when teaching or the grand style when audience members need to be moved to action, his objective is the same: to connect God's message and the full person, envisioned not merely as a thinking creature but as a feeling being. The early-church scholar Debora K. Shuger has described how, in this anthropology, Augustine and his later followers develop the theory that all thought and feeling rely ultimately on the imagination to turn them into rhetorically forceful elements. Shuger also describes how feelings especially can be turned into rhetorical tools because they prompt desire, conceived as a yearning for connection—to God, to one another, and (in its most ignoble form) to things. This desire, in turn, is *the* motivator of action in human beings, action being the most important component of human behavior.[12] To summarize, in Augustine's anthropology, the central feature of human life seems to be the action of the imagination on the faculty of feeling, creating desire that leads to action.

So we can see why rhetoric, and especially the grand style, are of such great importance to Augustine as a Christian. In Shuger's words, rhetoric for Augustine "appeals to the imagination and is therefore able to move and transform the desires of the heart."[13] Rhetoric's important function here is to make the imagination stir feelings that shape action. The emphasis lies on how rhetoric can *transform* desire—that is, transform the motivator of human action (and thus human action). The grand style is the best style, says Augustine, when motivating is the goal of the rhetor because it has such a pull on the imagination and its affective response to grand discourse.

But herein lies a paradox in this early Christian rhetorical theory—a paradox relevant to our concern about restricted rhetorical agency. While the speaker's enactment of his full personhood is considered vital to rhetorical success, the speaker's exertion of too much control of either the message or its effect seems undesirable. Instead, emotion, with its remarkable, stand-alone rhetorical power, seems to be able to serve as direct connection between subject (for example, God or the idea of Christian community) and audience, with the power to transform that audience. The rhetor in the middle of this "transmission," so to speak, seems less agentive than we, in the post-Enlightenment, might expect or like him to be: less the interpreter of the subject matter, giver-of-meaning to the subject matter, or actor engaged in the public negotiation of meanings associated with the subject matter. In other words, given how profoundly communicative emotion turns out to be for Augustine, it seems capable of operating with less human agency than we in the modern world would feel is possible (or desirable?) in rhetoric.

This same attitude toward human agency may explain Augustine's ambivalence about the function and nature of eloquence, made clear in his *Confessions* and identifiable there as a reaction to the Second Sophistic and Augustine's conversion to Christianity. As noted earlier, a rhetoric emphasizing the power of eloquent emotion enables the rhetor to mediate the interaction between God and audience. But, on the other hand, the use of emotional appeal to call attention to the rhetor himself actually interferes with the interaction. So Augustine must confine the role of rhetor so that God's transforming love and the transforming, emotional force it exerts on human nature avoid corruption. Perhaps this very concern for "interruption" of God's message lies behind the resistance to women preachers and their renovative rhetoric described in Vicki Tolar Burton's chapter in this volume on the Methodist figure Mary Bosanquet Fletcher.

In any case, Augustine's view that rhetoric is indispensable to Christianity *but* that the role of rhetor needs to be limited may have served as source for a simultaneous trust/distrust of rhetoric that, I am suggesting, constitutes one of the points of resistance to rhetoric in Christian tradition. To put it bluntly, did this de-emphasizing of agency tacitly encourage in Christian tradition a certain resistance to the cooperative shaping of meaning and encourage the role of proclaimer of meaning? If the answer to this question is "yes," that answer has important consequences. With respect to the rhetor, the role of proclaimer might seem at first noble and steadfast, and could even be mistaken for the prophetic, but it could in fact lead to a faith that is untested, and therefore unshaped, by a rhetorical community—in other words, an idiosyncratic faith undesirable in any religion.

With respect to rhetoric, this role might tempt the rhetor to excuse herself from the responsibility for being effective. She might feel that either audience members are filled with the spirit and moved, or they are not; rhetorical effectiveness becomes not a matter of the rhetor's skill but instead a matter of whether or not an audience is capable of receiving God's truth. As outlandish as this may sound, it is not an uncommon sentiment in Christian tradition. Indeed, we see this sentiment at work on the evangelical Christian "Tina" featured in Priscilla Perkins's chapter in this book. "Tina's" refusal to enter into negotiations about the meanings of her faith effectively cuts her off not only from her classroom community but also from the means for her own faith exploration. Such are the limits that the Christian framework could be placing on rhetorical agency. How can rhetoric flourish within a tradition that is so fearful of human agency's power that it seems to resist granting much of it to rhetors?

HERMENEUTICS: RHETORIC AND CHRISTIAN AUTHORIZING

Related to this anxiety about the overintrusion of human agency into the act of producing texts is another anxiety, one about the act of interpreting texts. We saw in Augustine's views on rhetoric an implied concern over the rightful role of authoring, and therefore of human "author-ity." We might identify a similar concern elsewhere in Christian tradition over rightful interpreting—the producing or discovering of meaning out of the raw materials of facts—and the ancillary issue of the methods by which authoritative meanings of important phenomena or texts get determined. These seem to be significant issues because all religions, including Christianity, depend upon hermeneutics: given the intangibility of their ultimate subject matters and sources of meaning, they must engage in interpretation to discover meaning and assert truths. If we want to maintain, as I am in this chapter, that the role of rhetor in a fully conceived rhetoric must be broader than only that of transmitter of teachings or exhorter to action based on preestablished truths, then that role should allow for interpretation as part of the rhetorical act. Otherwise, when we talk about rhetoric that is distinctly Christian, we are talking about a rhetoric of nondiscovery within a fixed system of already established meanings and values. This situation seems so limiting to the possibilities for renovating any discourse community (as many figures in this book have desired to do) through marshaling new arguments and negotiating new meanings cooperatively that rhetoric would have limited opportunities. One wonders what meaningful function it could serve at all. What seems, then, to be a second resistance to rhetoric in Christian tradition lies in the limiting of hermeneutic freedoms.

In this area, rhetorical effectiveness would seem especially problematic for Christianity beginning with the Reformation and intensifying in this, the postmodern era. The great disruptions to Christianity caused by the Reformation involved strenuous debate on hermeneutics, and hermeneutic procedures multiplied—ranging from the purely idiosyncratic (for example, the "church of one" position taken by the English poet and apologist John Milton late in life) to the reactionary, when authorities attempted to stanch the flood of hermeneutic practices unleashed by religious freedom. Attitudes toward the authorizing of interpretation have now become even more unsettled by postmodernism. Whereas some Christians may have embraced a postmodern hermeneutics of suspicion, most, it seems fair to say, have only increased their suspicion of hermeneutics. As the philosopher Roger Lundin and others have explained it, the unsettling of interpretation that began in the disintegration of the church's monolithic authority in areas of interpretation only increased in the Enlightenment, when biblical scholars and others attempted to establish objective methods and systems of interpretation.[14] Such methodology ignored, says Lundin, the value of tradition in the development of interpretive approaches and results, attempting to deprive believers of that tradition but also individual innovation granted—albeit contentiously and uneasily—during the Reformation.[15] Postmodernism, in turn, has called into question the possibility of such Cartesian objectivity that could lead to such methodologies, only increasing the unsettling. Roger Lundin, Clarence Walhout, and Anthony C. Thiselton, stating the postmodern perspective, explain that even if we wanted to, we can never "transform any of our actions—including those of interpreting—into timeless activities that neither bear the stamp of history nor share its responsibilities and promise."[16] Nevertheless, at least as far as some American Christian groups are concerned, it would seem that the impulse to impose and maintain strict interpretive regulation has grown beyond even twentieth-century fundamentalism in response to the anxiety over the de-authorizing of interpretation in everything from science to the Bible. (The intelligent design movement comes to mind here.) Developments in the modern and postmodern world have made hermeneutics a touchy area in many strands of Christianity.

It is important to distinguish this (I would argue) unnecessary anxiety from genuine concern over the authority of any and every kind of interpretive strategy imagined. After all, authorizing of hermeneutic methods and the interpretation of significant texts and events is among the principal functions of religion. All I am arguing here is that hermeneutic overregulation in reaction to the expanding role of individual faith in modern times, and then the questioning of interpretive bias in postmodern times, can both squelch the hermeneutical activities necessary to a healthy, full-spectrumed rhetoric of the sort imagined in this volume.

The effects of this hermeneutical unsettledness on rhetoric's relation to Christian tradition can be summed up neatly, if not very profoundly. Simply put, resistance to hermeneutical variety places a drag on rhetoric's potential to serve as method for exploration of new ways *to* faith, new ways *of* faith, new ways *to express* faith—that is, to serve as a method for renovating a faith tradition. As we have seen throughout this book, the forces behind this resistance include the wariness and risks associated with finding fresh perception or even fresh language, lest that freshness alter the approved understanding of a text, alienate the community of belief, or disrupt that community. Stale discourse inevitably encourages stale thinking about Christian faith, however, and that staleness can lead to a stagnation of faith among believers. Not unimportantly, non-Christians quickly point to this stagnation as a hallmark of Christianity, seeing it as a sign that Christianity is out of touch with the world or (perhaps worse) merely the vaguely perceived structure behind a quaintly sentimental set of practices.

Some will respond that to call this phenomenon "stagnation" or to say that it results from resistance is to miss out on an important role that rhetoric plays *within* the belief community. They would concede that the apparent staleness in Christian rhetoric comes from the repetition of stock discourse, of stock perceptions in Christian discourse. But, in their minds perhaps, these "stock items" exist to serve legitimate rhetorical purposes *within* the believing community. Rather than intended as supple instrument of faith investigation or articulation, rhetoric, some will say, serves a function more resembling ritual than exploration: repetition of familiar ideas in familiar language, to the end of comforting believers and demonstrating solidarity within the fellowship of belief. I acknowledge that this ritual function of rhetoric is, of course, crucial as a form of epideictic activity. But at times it does seem to allow the People of the Word to run the risk of engaging in logomancy, resisting the nonritualized functions of a language of faith—fresh ways to provide meaning to Christian faith through language. I would add that this restricting activity may also lead to Christian rhetoric being an insider's practice; those outside the faith are encouraged to join the discourse community but not necessarily encouraged, through their bringing of fresh interpretive moves, to change or broaden it. As was said at the beginning of this chapter, at times contemporary Christianity seems more interested in a rhetoric that explores how faith gives meaning to its followers' lives than it is in how its followers give meaning to faith.

To the extent that such a rhetoric discourages the use of persuasive discourse to negotiate meaning among believers or persuade others cooperatively in the marketplace of ideas, it may maintain the faith. But it may also cease to be an effective tool for renewing or developing faith. Again, the question remains whether or not this ritual, epideictic function is all that Christianity needs from rhetoric. Can it not be possible, as Anne Ruggles Gere has shown in this book in the context of Mormonism, that rhetoric can both remain "devout" and at the same time press Christianity to explore new ways of understanding? Is it not possible, as Karen K. Seat similarly shows in her chapter on women's mission work, that believers can simultaneously uphold cherished values and show how those values inevitably lead to change (e.g., the emancipation of women everywhere)?

EPISTEMOLOGY: RHETORIC AND THE CHRISTIAN DEBATE OVER BELIEF STRUCTURES

A similar question awaits us when we examine a possible third area of resistance to rhetoric in Christian tradition: Christianity's response to belief structures, or worldviews. (For the sake of this chapter, I am using the two terms to mean the same thing.) The question is whether or not Christianity in America today (to narrow the focus) finds itself merely supporting society's dominant worldview or is capable, if necessary, of critiquing that worldview. If Christianity sees critique as its fundamental worldview-work, then rhetoric as defined at the beginning of this chapter certainly has a role to play in contemporary Christianity. But if, on the other hand, Christians feel their religion merely ought to sustain the dominant worldview, then the possibilities for Christian rhetoric will be limited to the mere role of supporting that worldview—hardly the idea of rhetoric described in the opening of this chapter. The choice between these two options will determine whether contemporary Christianity seems to embrace or resist rhetoric. To determine which of these two options—worldview critique or support—seems to be operating in American Christianity today, we need first to examine briefly the nature of worldviews and the more important question of whether or not a person's worldview can be changed—by rhetoric or anything else. The issues at hand can be neatly examined by juxtaposing two theories about worldviews, each offering an opposite answer to that question.

Representing one theory are Brian J. Walsh and J. Richard Middleton, who, writing separately and together, accomplish three things in their theory of worldviews: a delineation of the functioning of a worldview, an explication of the inadequacies of modernism's worldview from a Christian standpoint, and a call for, as Walsh states, a "radically comprehensive cultural vision," based in biblical precept, that must supplant modernism's worldview if the West is to survive.[17] According to Walsh, all worldviews, including the Christian one, have their source in faith, which provides "ultimate answers to ultimate questions." Worldviews also have in common the fact that they "are pre-theoretical in character."[18] That is, worldviews, if they are to function sufficiently, must serve as a culture's entire basis for theorizing its reality, rather than a product of such theorizing: they must be a bedrock "more likely argued from than argued to."[19] But despite their source in faith and their status as pre-theoretical, the validity of worldviews is open to challenge, principally through lived experience and the "way of life" that grows out of a worldview. If the constructed reality fails to explain, to give meaning to experience, then the worldview fails. Such is the case, say Walsh and Middleton writing together, with modernism's worldview, which places enormous importance on "human autonomy" over a nature and society that remain "out there," away from the "autonomous self."[20] Indeed, both Walsh and Middleton re-envision culture via a critique of modernity's dualism, which has separated reality into the two entities of self as controlling will and the world as object to be controlled.

According to Walsh, the dangers that flow from this dualism include promoting "individualistic rights" over "a normed world"; and hanging on to "worn-out Enlightenment ideals of human progress" that are really forms of self-idolatry, not the means of forming a viable society.[21] But, according to Walsh, the current Christian (and especially evangelical) response to the collapse of the modernist worldview has hardly been to work toward replacing modernism with a biblically based Christian worldview. In fact, it has been the exact opposite: much of Christianity has taken up a "stance of entrenchment," "defending the status quo" and "privatizing Christian faith" because Christianity "has *de facto* been taken captive by the dominant secular worldview and is, therefore, as much a part of the problem in the present crisis as it is part of the solution."[22] What is needed, Walsh stipulates, is a prophetic Christianity to provide "the basis for a prophetic critique of the dominant worldview's idolatry." Once such a critique is finished, we must then also "go beyond critique . . . to embrace new ways of living and to embody an alternative reality" to that of modernity.[23] Walsh's view seems to be shared by Lizabeth Rand's Seventh-day Adventists in Rand's chapter in this volume on Adventists' outsider opposition to Sunday-keeping Christians. It also seems shared by Aesha Adams-Roberts, Rosalyn Collings Eves, and Liz Rohan's figures who embody an "apostolic rhetoric" that renovates from within the Christian community.

So we can see in these and many other cases rhetoric functioning to alter radically the dominant worldview of modernist culture. Indeed, this role for rhetoric is enacted in the classrooms of Elizabeth Vander Lei and Beth Daniell, both of whose chapters describe rhetorical practices based in contemporary theologians' critique of this worldview. The question is whether the contemporary Christian community is really interested in such renovating change or wants to resist it, along with the rhetoric that makes change possible. Walsh makes the claim that evangelical Christians are not very interested and do resist, and it may be that his claim applies to a larger cross-section of the Christian world as well.

While Walsh may be right that complicity with the prevailing worldview lies behind this lack of interest in prophetic change, it seems to me that the inverse of complicity might equally explain this resistance to engage—namely, the assumption that it is impossible to change anyone's or any society's worldview. To explain what such a position might look like, we can turn to a theorist who is perhaps the unlikeliest thinker to be discussing "ultimate answers": the antifoundationalist critic Stanley Fish. (I should add quickly that Fish is profoundly interested in religion, seeing it as the successor to theory as the topic of most concern among cultural scholars.) According to Gary A. Olson and Fish himself, Fish's antifoundationalism does not preclude at all the existence of foundations for belief, provided they are pre-theoretical. The foundations he opposes with his "anti-" are those that lie in theory, since Fish opposes the false promise of total explanatory power that comes along with accepting any theory, since a theory must explain fully the phenomenon it seeks to explain or it fails completely. (After all, such is the nature and purpose of a theory.) Given the limits of human nature, says Fish, our theories can never stand as reliable foundations for understanding.[24]

But for Fish there does exist a pre-theoretical bedrock constituted of "heartfelt" belief—to use a word that, as Olson notes, Fish is fond of using. Fish, the antifoundationalist antitheorist, believes apparently in something very much like a worldview as defined above. For the nature of these heartfelt beliefs, says Fish, precludes their being altered by the exertion of rhetorical argument. In our deepest convictions, according to his thinking in this area, we are unswayable. The function of rhetoric, then, is to help us justify these beliefs for ourselves; it has no role in renovating belief or constructing new belief through, say, evangelism.[25] In this framework rhetoric can compete in the public sphere (for example, the courts) using arguments put forth by rhetors, but its only hope for success lies not in changing the beliefs of the audience with arguments but in aligning those arguments with society's heartfelt beliefs. The argument that the audience judges to be most in line with those beliefs is the one that likely prevails.[26] And since theory is an unreliable guide to anything, including rhetoric, it cannot provide guidelines for how these arguments are to be constructed. Instead, says Fish, rhetorical practices must be shaped only by the restraints of the rhetorical situation; rhetoric is particularist, pragmatic, and localized in all true instances of its use.[27]

To which of these seemingly mutually exclusive worldview theories—Walsh/Middleton's or Fish's—does contemporary American Christianity subscribe, and what effect does either theory have on the nature of a Christian rhetoric? It might be possible that both theories can be seen at work in Christians in America today, with individuals or groups choosing one or the other. Based on their discourse and behavior, many contemporary Christian figures and groups seem to believe in complicity with the status quo on matters of nationalism, foreign policy, domestic human rights, education, and so on. But other contemporary Christians seem to enact Fish's theory, this theory manifesting in one of two ways. The first is advocacy for withdrawal from the contest of worldviews altogether, a withdrawal into a separate self-protecting realm. Since, in this way of thinking, worldviews are beyond alteration, withdrawing from engagement helps conserve and consolidate the Christian community. The second manifestation of this theory would impose on others, unwillingly, a worldview quite different from the dominant one—what advocates would call rather simplistically a "Christian" worldview.

Whichever option is chosen—whether it be complicit participation in the prevailing worldview (as explained by the Walsh/Middleton theory) or (as explained by Fish's theory) either withdrawal from the world or involuntary imposition of a different worldview upon it—a robust, engaged rhetoric seems unwanted or, in the minds of advocates of these various "Christian" worldviews, unnecessary. This is why I perceive there being a resistance to genuine rhetoric in contemporary American Christianity. And perhaps this explains why the kind of discourse on display in the contemporary Christian scene can seem so limited and so unattractive from a rhetorical point of view. Consider the options for genuine rhetorical functioning in the activities associated with any of the three worldview theories described in this chapter. If Christians subscribing to the first of these worldviews want only to work to show Christianity's consonance with and relevance to dominant social structures and ideologies, then the rhetoric they would desire seems impossibly narrow. If those subscribing to the second seek withdrawal from mainstream society, then the rhetoric they might use seems dysfunctional, no longer a tool for engaging the marketplace of ideas. Finally, those Christians whose worldview has them working to forcefully impose their worldview on others might wish for a rhetoric of ultimatums, which is no rhetoric at all. All of these options are a far cry from the prophetic role for rhetoric imagined by Middleton and Walsh, or Augustine for that matter, all of whom want nothing less than the transformation of the human heart—a transformation that would in turn renovate society.

So that *Renovating Rhetoric* does not end on such a melancholy note, we should remind ourselves of the rhetorical successes, demonstrated throughout this book, that Christians have had and continue to have (in classrooms as elsewhere) in overcoming all the resistances discussed in this chapter. We should take comfort in the way oppositional views *do* get mainstreamed, thanks to the rhetorical intelligence of the figures described throughout *Renovating Rhetoric*. My hope is that, through the work of this book's authors, resistance to rhetoric will diminish and oppositional rhetoric will be less needed for the maintenance of a healthy, self-renewing Christianity. I am heartened by the belief that Christianity, like all religions, is the organized human response to encounters with the divine, that it is shaped by humans, and that the organizing and shaping of Christianity results (at least from a rhetorical point of view) from cooperation among human beings. And human beings, including Christians, do show the capacity to cooperate in making change occur.

NOTES

INTRODUCTION

1. Patricia Bizzell, "Rationality as Rhetorical Strategy at the Barcelona Disputation, 1263: A Cautionary Tale," *College Composition and Communication* 58, no. 1 (2006): 12–29.

2. Ibid., 16.

3. Ibid., 21.

4. Ibid., 17.

5. Ibid., 28.

6. Ibid., 15.

7. Shannon Carter, "Living inside the Bible (Belt)," *College English* 69, no. 6 (2007): 582.

8. Sharon Crowley, *Toward Civil Discourse: Rhetoric and Fundamentalism* (Pittsburgh: University of Pittsburgh Press, 2006), 4. Scholars like Crowley invoke the restricting image of religious orthodoxy in the context of Christian fundamentalism and sometimes extend that description to Christianity and even religion in general. For a more extended analysis of Crowley's argument, see Beth Daniell, "Whetstones Provided by the World: Trying to Deal with Difference in a Pluralistic Society," *College English* 70, no. 1 (2007): 79–88.

9. Crowley, *Toward a Civil Discourse*, 4.

10. Lisa J. Shaver, *Beyond the Pulpit: Women's Rhetorical Roles in the Antebellum Religious Press* (Pittsburgh: University of Pittsburgh Press, 2012), 3, 9.

11. Shaver, *Beyond the Pulpit*, 7.

12. Ibid., 129, 130.

13. Ibid., 127–33.

14. Ibid., 131.

15. Rebecca S. Nowacek, *Agents of Integration: Understanding Transfer as a Rhetorical Act* (Carbondale: Southern Illinois University Press, 2011), 12.

16. The scholar Jeffrey Ringer demonstrates how religious faith can be altered when rhetors put it to use for argumentative purposes. See Jeffrey M. Ringer, "The

Consequences of Integrating Faith into Academic Writing: Casuistic Stretching and Biblical Citation," *College English* 75, no. 3 (2013): 270–97.

17. See "I Have a Dream," in *A Call to Conscience: The Landmark Speeches of Dr. Martin Luther King, Jr.*, ed. Clayborne Carson and Kris Shepard (New York: Warner Books, 2001).

18. For the full text of Carey's speech, see Archibald Carey, "Address to the Republican National Convention," in *Rhetoric of Black Revolt*, ed. Roy Hill (Denver, CO: Golden Bell, 1964).

19. Nowacek, *Agents of Integration*, 39.

20. For example, the scholar Chris Anderson considers an instructor's outrage at the academic writing of a student who uses genres associated with Christian fundamentalism. He describes the student's academic writing by referring to genres associated with Christian fundamentalism and evangelicalism: "the language is that of the fundamentalist, of the testimonial, of *Guideposts* magazine, and Sunday morning television." Chris Anderson, "The Description of an Embarrassment: When Students Write about Religion," *ADE Bulletin* 94 (1989): 12–15, 12. See also Amy Goodburn, "It's a Question of Faith: Discourses of Fundamentalism and Critical Pedagogy in the Writing Classroom," *JAC: Journal of Composition Theory* 18 (2003): 333–53; Priscilla Perkins, "'A Radical Conversion of the Mind'": Fundamentalism, Hermeneutics, and Metanoic Classroom," *College English* 63, no. 5 (2001): 585–611; and Doug Downs, "True Believers, Real Scholars, and Real True Believers: Discourses of Inquiry and Affirmation in the Composition Classroom," in *Negotiating Religious Faith in the Writing Classroom*, ed. Elizabeth Vander Lei and bonnie kyburz (Portsmouth, NH: Boynton/Cook, 2005).

21. See, for example, the scholar Michael-John DePalma's argument for "a pragmatic view of discourse that acknowledges the fluctuating nature of language and casts religious discourse as a resource for writing in academic contexts" in his "Re-envisioning Religious Discourses as Rhetorical Resources in Composition Teaching: A Pragmatic Response to the Challenge of Belief," *College Composition and Communication* 63, no. 2 (2011): 219–43, 221. See also Priscilla Perkins's argument for using the theology of Reformed Christianity as a bridge between fundamentalist students and the demands of academic writing, in her "A Radical Conversion of the Mind," 598–99.

22. See, for example, the conclusion of Susan Jarrett et al. that "very little can be carried forward from first-year writing" to subsequent academic writing, in "Pedagogical Memory: Writing, Mapping, Translating," *WPA Journal* 33, nos. 1–2 (2009): 46–73, 46.

23. Nowacek, *Agents of Integration*, 39.

24. Ibid., 32.

25. Stanley Fish, "One University under God," *Chronicle of Higher Education*, January 7, 2005, C1, C4.

1. Susa Young Gates and Lucy Bigelow Young, quoted in Carolyn W. D. Person, "Susa Young Gates," in *Mormon Sisters: Women in Early Utah*, ed. Claudia Bushman (Cambridge, MA: Emmeline Press Ltd., 1976).

2. Elizabeth Barnes makes a related point for the antebellum period by arguing that American preoccupation with familial feelings as the foundation for sympathy, and sympathy as the basis of a democratic republic, leads to a confounding of familial and social bonds. Priscilla Wald, *Constituting Americans: Cultural Anxiety and Narrative Form* (Durham: Duke University Press, 1995), 245.

3. Sarah Barringer Gordon, "Our National Hearthstone: Anti-Polygamy Fiction and the Sentimental against Moral Diversity in Antebellum America," *Yale Journal of Law and the Humanities* 8 (1996): 345.

4. Nancy Bentley, *Sex and Citizens: Bigamy, Polygamy, and Southern Concubinage in Late-Nineteenth-Century Fiction* (Washington, DC: MLA, 1996).

5. Gordon explores the sentimental vision of the largely female authors of anti-polygamy fiction in "Our National Hearthstone."

6. Jane Tompkins, *Sensational Designs: The Cultural Work of American Fiction, 1790–1860* (New York: Oxford University Press, 1985), 141.

7. Coauthors Leonard Arrington and John Haupt list fifty anti-Mormon novels, of which twenty-nine appear to have been written by women. The number of female authors may actually be slightly higher since several authors use pseudonyms. See Arrington and Haupt's "Intolerable Zion: The Image of Mormonism in Nineteenth Century American Literature," *Western Humanities Review* 22 (1968): 243–60.

8. Sandra Gunning, *Race, Rape, and Lynching: The Red Record of American Literature, 1890–1912* (New York: Oxford University Press, 1996). Gunning makes a related point about the "neglected, absented, evacuated, expelled, and displaced" (9–10) figure of the black woman in the lynching ritual. Gunning goes on to suggest that black women were "profoundly present in the dimension of the symbolic" as victims of white sexual excess. I believe that the devout Mormon woman was similarly present in late-nineteenth-century anti-Mormon discourses.

9. Thomas G. Alexander, "An Experiment in Progressive Legislation: The Granting of Woman Suffrage in Utah in 1870," *Utah Historical Quarterly* 38, no. 1 (1970): 20–30.

10. Lola Van Wagenen, "In Their Own Behalf: The Politicization of Mormon Women and the 1870 Franchise," in *Battle for the Ballot: Essays on Woman Suffrage in Utah, 1870–1896*, ed. Carol Cornwell Madsen (Logan: Utah State University Press, 1997), 60–75.

11. Jill Mulvay Derr, "Eliza R. Snow and the Woman Question," in *Battle for the Ballot: Essays on Woman Suffrage in Utah, 1870–1896*, ed. Carol Cornwell Madsen (Logan: Utah State University Press, 1997), 72.

12. Howard Lamar, "Statehood for Utah: A Different Path," in *Mormonism and American Culture*, ed. Marvin S. Hill and James B. Allen (New York: Harper and Row, 1972), 134.

13. Ibid., 140.

14. "Woman Journalism in Utah," *Woman's Exponent*, September 21, 1893, 28.

15. Quoted in Leonard J. Arrington, "The Economic Role of Pioneer Mormon Women," *Western Humanities Review* 9 (1955): 162.

16. Jan Shipps, *Mormonism: The Story of a New Religious Tradition* (Chicago: University of Illinois Press, 1987), 32.

17. The historian Grant Underwood argued that since only a minority of Mormons practiced polygamy and communal economic systems were short-lived, statehood did not require significant accommodations on the part of Mormons. Grant Underwood, "Mormonism as a Historical Concept," quoted in Carol Cornwall Madsen, "Schism in the Sisterhood: Mormon Women and Partisan Politics, 1890–1900," in *New Views of Mormon History: A Collection of Essays in Honor of Leonard J. Arrington*, ed. Davis Bitton and Maureen Ursenbach Beecher (Salt Lake City: University of Utah Press, 1987), 235.

18. Karen Blair's *The Clubwoman as Feminist: True Womanhood Redefined, 1868–1914* (New York: Holmes and Meier, 1980) and *The Torchbearers: Women and Their Amateur Arts Associations in America, 1890–1930* (Bloomington: University of Indiana Press, 1994); Theodora Penny Martin's *The Sound of Their Own Voices: Women's Study Clubs, 1860–1910* (Boston: Beacon Press, 1987); and Sandra Haarsager's *Organized Womanhood Cultural Politics in the Pacific Northwest, 1840–1920* (Norman: University of Oklahoma Press, 1997) all focus on white middle-class groups. Anne Firor Scott's *Natural Allies: Women's Associations in American History* (Urbana: University of Illinois Press, 1991) includes a wider range of populations but gives most attention to black and white women's groups. To be sure, some studies of women's clubs among other populations have emerged: Joanne Reitano's "Working Girls Unite," *American Quarterly* 36 (1984): 112–34, traces the history of the League of Working Women as does Priscilla Murolo, *The Common Ground of Womanhood: Class, Gender, and Working Girls' Clubs, 1884–1928* (Urbana: University of Illinois Press, 1999). Paula Giddings's *When and Where I Enter: The Impact of Black Women on Race and Sex in America* (New York: Bantam, 1984) includes some information on African American clubwomen as does Evelyn Brooks Higginbotham's *Righteous Discontent: The Women's Movement in the Black Baptist Church, 1880–1920* (Cambridge, MA: Harvard University Press, 1993), and more specialized studies are offered by Anne Meis Knupfer's *Toward a Tenderer Humanity and a Nobler Womanhood: African American Women's Clubs in Turn-of-the-Century Chicago* (New York: New York University Press, 1996), Elizabeth Lindsay Davis's *The Story of the Illinois Federation of Colored Women's Clubs* (New York: G. K. Hall, 1997), and Wanda A. Hendricks's *Gender, Race, and Politics in the Midwest: Black*

Club Women in Illinois (Bloomington: Indiana University Press, 1998). Paula M. Kane, in *Separatism and Subculture Boston Catholicism, 1900–1920* (Chapel Hill: University of North Carolina Press, 1994), deals with Catholic women's clubs and the 1920 formation of the National Council of Catholic Women; Nancy A. Hewitt's "Varieties of Voluntarism: Class, Ethnicity, and Women's Activism in Tampa," in *Women, Politics, and Change*, ed. Louise A. Tilly and Patricia Gurin (New York: Russell Sage Foundation, 1990), 63–86, considers Hispanic groups; Daiva Markelis's "Union Halls and Church Pews: Language and Literacy among Early Chicago Lithuanians" (PhD diss., University of Illinois at Chicago, forthcoming) deals with a Slavic population; Faith Rogow's *Gone to Another Meeting: The National Council of Jewish Women* (Tuscaloosa: University of Alabama Press, 1993) focuses on Jewish clubwomen; Anne Ruggles Gere's *Intimate Practices: Literacy and Cultural Work in U.S. Women's Clubs 1880–1920* (Urbana: University of Illinois Press, 1997) considers Jewish, African American, working-class, and Mormon clubwomen in addition to white middle-class Protestant groups; Nikki Brown's *Private Politics and Public Voices: Black Women's Activism from World War I to the New Deal* (Bloomington: University of Indiana Press, 2006) and Kate Dossett's *Bridging Race Divides: Black Nationalisms, Feminism, and Integration in the United States, 1896–1935* (Gainesville: University Press of Florida, 2009) consider how black clubwomen contributed to social reform, but the dominant image of clubwomen still adheres to the white middle-class model, and Mormon clubwomen have received very little attention.

19. Tolstoy is reported to have told Andrew Dickson White, the first president of Cornell University, "the Mormon people teach the American religion." Quoted in Harold Bloom, *The American Religion* (New York: Simon and Schuster, 1993), 116.

20. Mary Church Terrell, "1904 Presidential Address to National Association of Colored Women," in *Righteous Discontent: The Women's Movement in the Black Baptist Church, 1880–1920*, ed. Evelyn Brooks Higginbotham (Cambridge, MA: Harvard University Press, 1993), 207.

21. Rogow, *Gone to Another Meeting*, 134.

22. Mary Louise Pratt, "Arts of the Contact Zone," *Profession* 91 (1991): 34.

23. Cartoons, public statements, satirical articles, and an ongoing negative campaign by the club-hating Edward Bok, editor of the best-selling *Ladies Home Journal* from 1889 to 1919, continued from 1868 through the 1920s to denigrate women's clubs. One culmination of this unfavorable response occurred when the General Federation of Women's Clubs was included in the famous Spider-Web chart developed by Brigadier General Amos A. Fries of the Chemical Warfare Service and circulated, between 1923 and 1924, among governmental agencies including J. Edgar Hoover's FBI and hyperpatriotic groups such as the American Defense Society. Henry Ford's reactionary *Dearborn Independent* published the chart along with an article titled "Are Women's Clubs 'Used by Bolshevists?'" in 1924. See Gere, *Intimate Practices*, 256–69, for a more detailed account. Although I have found similar

instances of criticism among other populations, I have not seen negative statements about clubwomen from Mormon men.

24. "An Important Event," *Woman's Exponent,* June 3, 1905.

25. Jennie June Croly, *The History of the Woman's Club Movement in America* (New York: Henry G. Allen Press, 1898), 1117.

26. "Social Purity" is quoted in "Utah Federation of Woman's Clubs," *Woman's Exponent,* June 1, 1896, 10.

27. "Utah Woman's Press Club: First Decade of Its Organization," *Woman's Exponent,* February 1902, 88. Although published in 1902, this quotation refers to a meeting that occurred in the early 1890s.

28. "Editorial," *Woman's Exponent,* July 1, 1893, 188.

29. Clubwomen were not the only Mormons represented at the Chicago Exposition, as the scholar Jan Shipps explains in *Marketing Mormonism: The LDS Church's Use of Public Relations and Advertising Techniques to Represent Themselves and Sell Their Message to the World* (Atlanta: American Society of Church History, 1996). Shipps notes that the Mormon church launched its first large-scale public relations effort by building an "elaborate exhibition building to display 'Mormon achievements' and performances of the Mormon Tabernacle choir to 'affirm the normality and morality of the Saints'" (79).

30. Jean Bickmore White's "Woman's Place Is in the Constitution: The Struggle for Equal Rights in Utah in 1895," *Utah Historical Quarterly* 42 (1974) details the final constitutional convention's battle over woman suffrage, and it was this debate to which clubwomen responded.

31. "World's Congress of Women," *Woman's Exponent,* June 1, 1893, 172.

32. "UWPC," *Woman's Exponent,* February 1 and February 15, 1895, 253.

33. Quoted in Carol Cornwall Madsen, "Decade of Détente: The Mormon-Gentile Female Relationship in Nineteenth Century Utah," *Utah Historical Quarterly* 63 no. 4 (1995): 309.

34. "Utah Federation of Woman's Clubs," *Woman's Exponent,* June 15, 1896, 157.

35. "Current Literature," *Woman's Exponent,* June 15, 1894, 149.

36. "Our Girls," *Young Woman's Journal,* April 1, 1890, 225.

37. "An Important Event," 4.

38. "Current Literature," 149.

39. Derr, "Eliza R. Snow and the Woman Question," 86.

40. George Marsden, *The Soul of the American University: From Protestant Establishment to Established Nonbelief* (New York: Oxford University Press, 1994), 6.

41. T. J. Jackson Lears, *No Place of Grace: Antimodernism and the Transformation of American Culture, 1880–1920* (Chicago: University of Chicago Press, 1981), 192. See also James Turner, "Secularization and Sacralization: Speculations on Some Religious Origins of the Secular Humanities Curriculum, 1850–1900," in *The*

Secularization of the Academy, ed. George M. Marsden and Bradley J. Longfield (New York: Oxford University Press, 1992), 74–106.

42. Stephen Carter, *The Culture of Disbelief* (New York: Anchor, 1994).

43. Mark Hulsether's "It's the End of the World As We Know It," *American Quarterly* 48, no. 2 (1996): 381, makes this point in his review of Paul Boyer's *When Time Shall Be No More: Prophecy Belief in Modern American Culture*.

44. Scott Keeter, "How the Public Perceives Romney, Mormons," *Pew Forum on Religion and Public Life*, December 4, 2007. Available online at http://www.pewforum.org/Politics-and-Elections/How-the-Public-Perceives-Romney-Mormons.aspx.

45. Ralph Waldo Emerson, "Divinity School Address," 1838. Available online at http://www.age-of-thesage.org/transcendentalism/emerson/divinity_school_address.html.

CHAPTER 2. A RHETORIC OF OPPOSITION: THE SEVENTH-DAY ADVENTIST CHURCH AND THE SABBATH TRADITION

1. Raymond F. Cottrell, "The Sabbath in the New World," in *The Sabbath in Scripture and History*, ed. Kenneth A. Strand (Washington, DC: Review and Herald, 1982), 251.

2. Stephen M. Feldman, *Please Don't Wish Me a Merry Christmas: A Critical History of the Separation of Church and State* (New York: New York University Press, 1997), 5.

3. Ibid., 23.

4. Ibid., 20.

5. Ibid., 15.

6. Kenneth A. Strand, "The Sabbath and Sunday from the Second through Fifth Centuries," in *The Sabbath in Scripture and History*, ed. Kenneth A. Strand (Washington, DC: Review and Herald, 1982), 323.

7. Ibid., 326.

8. Samuele Bacchiocchi, "The Rise of Sunday Observance in Early Christianity," in *The Sabbath in Scripture and History*, ed. Kenneth A. Strand (Washington, DC: Review and Herald, 1982), 139–41.

9. Ibid., 141; emphasis in the original.

10. Strand, "The Sabbath and Sunday," 329.

11. Daniel Augsburger, "The Sabbath and Lord's Day during the Middle Ages," in *The Sabbath in Scripture and History*, ed. Kenneth A. Strand (Washington, DC: Review and Herald, 1982), 192. Augsburger was a professor of historical theology at Andrews University.

12. Craig Harline, *Sunday: A History of the First Day from Babylonia to the Super Bowl* (New York: Doubleday, 2007), 12.

13. Lesley Lawrence-Hammer, "Red, White, but Mostly Blue: The Validity of

Modern Sunday Closing Laws under the Establishment Clause," *Vanderbilt Law Review* 60 (2007): 1274.

14. Lawrence-Hammer, "Red, White, but Mostly Blue," 1276.

15. Ken McFarland, "Sunday Laws in America," *Liberty* (July–August 2008). Available online at http://www.libertymagazine.org/article/sunday-laws-in-america.

16. Lawrence-Hammer, "Red, White, but Mostly Blue," 1277.

17. Malcolm Bull and Keith Lockhart, *Seeking a Sanctuary: Seventh-day Adventism and the American Dream* (San Francisco: Harper & Row, 1989), ix.

18. Ibid., ix.

19. Ellen White, *The Great Controversy* (Nampa, ID: Pacific Press, 1950).

20. Bull and Lockhart, *Seeking a Sanctuary,* 164.

21. White, *Great Controversy,* 143.

22. Ibid., 592.

23. Ibid., 516.

24. Ibid., 530.

25. Bull and Lockhart, *Seeking a Sanctuary,* 140–41.

26. Eric Syme, *A History of SDA Church-State Relations in the United States* (Mountain View, CA: Pacific Press, 1973), 20.

27. Ibid., 30.

28. Harline, *Sunday,* 313.

29. Ibid., 314.

30. Feldman, *Please Don't Wish Me a Merry Christmas,* 263.

31. Ibid., 263.

32. Bull and Lockhart, *Seeking a Sanctuary,* 171.

33. Ibid., 244.

34. Ibid., 253, 255.

35. Stephen Carter, *Civility* (New York: Harper Collins, 1998), 258.

36. Landon Schnabel, "Former Head of National Council of Churches Speaks at Andrews Seminary Symposium—Part II," *Spectrum,* February 2, 2012. Available online at http://spectrummagazine.org/blog/2012/02/02/former-head-national -council-churches-speaks-andrews-seminary-symposium.

37. Denis Fortin, "Briefing," *Andrews University,* January 31, 2012. Available online at http://www.andrews.edu/news/2012/01/symposium.html.

38. Nicholas Miller, "Adventists and Ecumenism: The Good and the Bad," *Memory, Meaning, and Faith,* February 3, 2012. Available online at http://www .memorymeaningfaith.org/blog/2012/02/adventists-and-ecumenism-the-good -and-the-bad.html.

39. Schnabel, "Former Head of National Council of Churches."

40. John Schilb, *Rhetorical Refusals* (Carbondale: Southern Illinois University Press, 2007), 3.

41. Ibid., 10.

42. Ibid., 18.

43. Ibid., 12.

CHAPTER 3. PREACHING FROM THE PULPIT STEPS: MARY BOSANQUET FLETCHER AND WOMEN'S PREACHING IN EARLY METHODISM

1. Mary Fletcher, *The Life of Mrs. Mary Fletcher, Consort and Relict of the Rev. John Fletcher, Vicar of Madeley, Salop,* ed. Henry Moore (London: Wesleyan-Methodist Book Room, n.d.), 102.

2. For more on early women preachers, see Phyllis Mack, *Visionary Women: Ecstatic Prophecy in Seventeenth-Century England* (Berkeley: University of California Press, 1992).

3. Kathleen Hall Jamieson and Karlyn Kohrs Campbell, "Rhetorical Hybrids: Fusions of Generic Elements," *Quarterly Journal of Speech* 68 (1982): 146.

4. Vicki Tolar Burton, *Spiritual Literacy in John Wesley's Methodism: Reading, Writing, and Speaking to Believe* (Waco, TX: Baylor University Press, 2008), 15–19, and chapter 4, "Speaking to Believe: Literacy and Rhetorical Practices of Traveling Preachers."

5. Earl Kent Brown, *Women of Mr. Wesley's Methodism* (New York: Edwin Mellen Press, 1983), 20–22.

6. Richard P. Heitzenrater, *Wesley and the People Called Methodists* (Nashville TN: Abingdon Press, 1995), 118–19.

7. Brown, *Women of Mr. Wesley's Methodism,* 19–25.

8. For definitions of "exhortation" and of "exhorter," see entries under those terms in *The Encyclopedia of World Methodism,* ed. Nolan B. Harmon, vol. 1 (Nashville, TN: United Methodist Publishing House, 1974), 821–22; for a definition of "Testimony," see *Encyclopedia of World Methodism,* vol. 2, 327. For distinctions between British and American female exhorters, see Tolar Burton, *Spiritual Literacy,* 160. Phyllis Mack discusses women's preaching during the British Enlightenment in *Heart Religion in the British Enlightenment: Gender and Emotion in Early Methodism* (Cambridge: Cambridge University Press, 2008), 291–301. See also Deborah M. Valenze, *Prophetic Sons and Daughters: Female Preaching and Popular Religion in Industrial England* (Princeton, NJ: Princeton University Press, 1985). For discussions and examples of women exhorters and preachers in America, see Jane Donawerth, *Conversational Rhetoric: The Rise and Fall of a Women's Tradition, 1600–1900* (Carbondale: Southern Illinois University Press, 2012), especially chapter 3; see also Catherine A. Brekus, *Strangers and Pilgrims: Female Preaching in America, 1740–1845* (Chapel Hill: University of North Carolina Press, 1998); and John H. Wigger, *Taking Heaven by Storm: Methodism and the Rise of Popular Christianity in America* (New York: Oxford University Press, 1998).

9. Wigger, *Taking Heaven by Storm*, 152.

10. Lisa J. Shaver, *Beyond the Pulpit: Women's Rhetorical Roles in the Antebellum Religious Press* (Pittsburgh: Pittsburgh University Press, 2012), 37–52.

11. Brown, *Women of Mr. Wesley's Methodism*, 23–24.

12. Donawerth, *Conversational Rhetoric*, xi.

13. A fuller discussion of women's preaching in early British Methodism appears in chapter 5 of Tolar Burton's *Spiritual Literacy*.

14. D. R. Wilson, "'Thou Shal[t] Walk with me in White': Afterlife and Vocation in the Ministry of Mary Bosanquet Fletcher," *Wesley and Methodist Studies* 1 (2009): 76–77.

15. Fletcher, *Life of Mrs. Mary Fletcher*, 1–101; and Brown, *Women of Mr. Wesley's Methodism*, 125–54.

16. Fletcher, *Life of Mrs. Mary Fletcher*, 46.

17. Ibid., 83.

18. Unless stated otherwise, references to Mary Bosanquet's letter to John Wesley are cited from "Appendix D: A Mary Bosanquet Letter to John Wesley, June 1771," which can be found in Paul Wesley Chilcote, *John Wesley and the Women Preachers of Early Methodism* (Metuchen, NJ: American Theological Library Association and Scarecrow Press, 1991), 299–304. The letter also appears in Sarah Crosby, MS Letterbook, Duke University Archives. The location of the original letter is not known. It was first published in Zachariah Taft, *Scripture Doctrine of Women's Preaching* (High Ousgate, UK: N.p., 1820), 19–21. The full manuscript is also in Rupert E. Davies, A. Raymond George, E. Gordon Rupp, *A History of the Methodist Church in Great Britain* (Epworth, UK: Epworth Press, 1988).

19. Chilcote, *John Wesley*, 299–300.

20. Ibid.

21. Ibid., 300–301.

22. Ibid., 303.

23. Tolar Burton, *Spiritual Literacy*, 78–80.

24. Chilcote, *John Wesley*, 302.

25. Ibid.

26. Ibid., 143.

27. Heitzenrater, *Wesley and the People Called Methodists*, 176.

28. Cited in Chilcote, *John Wesley*, 128.

29. Donawerth, *Conversational Rhetoric*, 73–104.

30. Zachariah Taft, *Biographical Sketches of the Lives and Public Ministry of Various Holy Women*, vol. 1 (London: Kershaw, 1825), 84.

31. Taft, *Scripture Doctrine of Women's Preaching*, 19–20.

32. Fletcher, MS Journal, October 19, 1775.

33. Mack, *Heart Religion*, 9.

34. Brett C. McInelly, "Mothers in Christ: Mary Fletcher and the Women of

Early Methodism," in *Religion, Gender, and Industry: Exploring Church and Methodism in a Local Setting*, ed. Geordan Hammond and Peter S. Forsaith (Eugene, OR: Pickwick, 2011), 131.

35. Fletcher, MS Journal, October 6, 1777.

36. Fletcher, *Life of Mrs. Mary Fletcher*, 77–80.

37. Wilson, "Afterlife and Vocation," 82.

38. Fletcher, *Life of Mrs. Mary Fletcher*, 187.

39. Brown, *Women of Mr. Wesley's Methodism*, 146–47.

40. Chilcote, *John Wesley*, 236.

CHAPTER 4. "WITH THE TONGUE OF [WO]MEN AND ANGELS":
APOSTOLIC RHETORICAL PRACTICES AMONG RELIGIOUS WOMEN

1. The full text of Anne Hart Gilbert's history can be found in Moira Ferguson, ed., *The Hart Sisters: Early African Caribbean Writers, Evangelicals, and Radicals* (Lincoln: University of Nebraska Press, 1993).

2. Elisabeth Ceppi, "In the Apostle's Words: Elizabeth Ashbridge's Epistle to the Goshen Monthly Meeting," *Legacy* 21, no. 2 (2004): 141–55.

3. Sandra Hack Polaski, *Paul and the Discourse of Power* (Sheffield, England: Sheffield Academic Press, 1999).

4. Ceppi, "In the Apostle's Words"; Polaski, *Paul and the Discourse of Power*; and Ceppi, "In the Apostle's Words."

5. Moira Ferguson, *Colonialism and Gender from Mary Wollenstonecraft to Jamaica Kincaid* (New York: Columbia University Press, 1993), 36.

6. Ferguson, *Hart Sisters*.

7. Ibid., 57.

8. Ibid., 18.

9. Ferguson, *Colonialism and Gender*, 43.

10. Ferguson, *Hart Sisters*, 65–66.

11. Polaski, *Paul and the Discourse of Power*, 27.

12. Ferguson, *Hart Sisters*, 67.

13. Ibid., 70.

14. Ibid., 71.

15. 2 Timothy 2:1–3, King James Version: "You therefore, my son, be strong in the grace that is in Christ Jesus. And the things that you have heard from me among many witnesses, commit these to the faithful men who will be able to teach others also. You therefore must endure hardship as a good soldier of Jesus Christ."

16. Ferguson, *Hart Sisters*, 63.

17. Ibid., 28

18. Anne Hart does not explicitly state if Mary Alley is a member of the free colored society or a slave. However, her attention to complexion differences between the women is significant: "Increasing fairness of complexion through miscegenous

relations was an almost guaranteed way of moving up the social ladder. . . . This vigorous system of racial disparity meant that the most poverty-stricken and subjugated group consisted of black slaves." Ferguson, *Colonialism and Gender,* 4.

19. Ferguson, *Hart Sisters,* 75.

20. Ferguson, *Colonialism and Gender.*

21. Judith Weisenfeld, "Introduction: We Have Been Believers: Patterns of African-American Women's Religiosity," in *This Far By Faith: Readings in African-American Religious Biography,* ed. Judith Weisenfeld and Richard Newman (New York: Routledge, 1996), 1–18.

22. Ceppi, "In the Apostle's Words."

23. Joycelyn Moody, *Sentimental Confessions: Spiritual Narratives of Nineteenth Century African American Women* (Athens: University of Georgia Press, 2001), 17.

24. Sylvia R. Frey, *Come Shouting to Zion: African American Protestantism in the American South and British Caribbean to 1830* (Chapel Hill: University of North Carolina Press, 1998).

25. From Charles Thwaites's journal: "Tuesday 20th. Took my wife to town and attended her to Court House. She did not approve of the questions [about her antislavery activities], nor with the design apparently with which they were asked, and therefore declined replying." Ferguson, *Hart Sisters,* 135.

26. Ibid., 135.

27. See, for example, John Salliant, "Antiguan Methodism and Antislavery Activity: Anne and Elizabeth Hart in the Eighteenth-Century Black Atlantic," *Church History* 69, no. 1 (2000): 86–115.

28. Ferguson, *Colonialism and Gender.*

29. Ferguson, *Hart Sisters,* 92.

30. Ibid., 93–94.

31. Ibid., 98–99.

32. Polaski, *Paul and the Discourse of Power.*

33. Ferguson, *Hart Sisters,* 73.

34. The Reverend John Baxter's "Letter to a Fellow Methodist in London" summarizes the "problem" of black families in Antigua: "And with regard to the rising generation, although we have a pleasing prospect concerning many that bid fair for leading virtuous lives; yet I fear not a few will fall prey to a vice, so prevalent in this country. And many that have been baptised in an infant state with us, when they grow-up, will not take husbands & wives properly. As for living a single life properly and chastely there is no such thing known among the Blacks after they are eighteen years old I believe. I believe few of the females at sixteen, and their coming together improperly without affection, young women taking old men and young men old women is the cause of constant jealousy and separating from each other in which case we exclude the guilty person and never receive." Baxter's comments demonstrate white religious leaders' inability to recognize the systems that

disrupted the families of slave persons. Instead of attacking the oppressive systems, they punish the people for violating religious and social norms. In Ferguson, *Hart Sisters*, 159.

35. Cheryl Townsend Gilkes, "The Roles of Church and Community Mothers: Ambivalent American Sexism or Fragmented African Familyhood?" *Journal of Feminist Studies in Religion* 2, no. 1 (1986): 41–60.

36. Bernard Semmel, *The Methodist Revolution* (New York: Basic Books, 1973).

37. Ferguson, *Hart Sisters*, 112.

38. Ibid., 113.

39. Ibid., 160.

40. Jill Mulvay Derr, "The Significance of 'O My Father' in the Personal Journey of Eliza R. Snow," *BYU Studies* 36, no. 1 (1996–97): 85–126.

41. Following Smith's murder in 1844 and their forcible exile from Missouri, the Mormons moved west to Utah, where they sought both refuge and the chance to build a "kingdom of God." Thomas F. O'Dea, *The Mormons* (Chicago: University of Chicago Press, 1957). Maureen Ursenbach Beecher, "Priestess among the Patriarchs: Eliza R. Snow and the Mormon Relief Society, 1842–1887," in *Religion and Society in the American West: Historical Essays*, ed. Carl Guarneri and David Alvarez (Lanham, MD: University Press of America, 1969), 153. Maureen Ursenbach Beecher, "The Eliza Enigma: The Life and Legend of Eliza R. Snow," in *Essays in the American West, 1974–1975*, ed. Thomas G. Alexander (Provo, UT: Brigham Young University Press, 1976), 29–46.

42. It should be noted, however, that Mormon women "distinguished subjugation to man's 'absolute tyranny' to submission to the priesthood" and "did not consider themselves slaves; they were stewards" whose work, like that of their male counterparts, was indispensable to kingdom building. Jill Mulvay Derr, "Eliza R. Snow and the Woman Question," *BYU Studies* 16, no. 2 (1976): 250–64, 251, 263.

43. Julie Roy Jeffrey, *Frontier Women: "Civilizing" the West? 1840–1880*, rev. ed. (New York: Hill and Wang, 1998), 181.

44. Anne Ruggles Gere, *Intimate Practices: Literacy and Cultural Work in U.S. Women's Clubs, 1880–1920* (Urbana: University of Illinois Press, 1997).

45. Studying Snow's rhetoric is important not only because of the paucity of studies of Mormon women's rhetorical practices, but because her rhetorical practices help scholars understand how Mormon women found meaningful places for themselves in a religious tradition whose public institutional structure was (and continues to be) dominated by men.

46. Derr, "Significance of 'O My Father,'" 103.

47. Eliza R. Snow, "An Address," *Woman's Exponent*, September 15, 1873, 62–63.

48. Kenneth Burke, *A Grammar of Motives* (Berkeley: University of California Press, 1969), 54.

49. Snow, "An Address," 63.

50. Ibid.

51. Eliza R. Snow, "To Every Branch of the Relief Society in Zion," *Woman's Exponent*, April 1, 1875, 164–65.

52. Snow, "An Address," 63.

53. Eliza R. Snow, "Position and Duties," *Woman's Exponent*, July 15, 1874, 28.

54. Snow, "An Address," 63.

55. Much of this background for Janette Miller comes from primary research by Liz Rohan in the Janette Miller Papers, Box 1, Bentley Historical Collection, University of Michigan, Ann Arbor. See also Liz Rohan, "A Woman's Guide to Wholeness: The Diaries of Janette Miller, 1879–1969," *WILLA (Women in Literature and Life Assembly)* 8 (Fall 1999): 21–36.

56. Lawrence Henderson, *Angola: Five Centuries of Conflict* (Ithaca: Cornell University Press, 1979), 154.

57. Ibid.

58. Gerhard Grohs and Godehard Czernick, *State and the Church in Angola, 1450–1980* (Geneva: Institut Universitaire de Hautes Etudes Internationales, 1983), 35.

59. Ceppi, "In the Apostle's Words."

60. Janette Miller, "First Impressions," in "Miscellaneous Missionary Materials," Janette Miller Papers, Box 1, Bentley Historical Collection, University of Michigan, Ann Arbor.

61. Moody, *Sentimental Confessions*.

62. Ibid., 165.

63. Ibid., 174; emphasis in the original.

CHAPTER 5. RHETORICAL STRATEGIES IN PROTESTANT WOMEN'S MISSIONS: APPROPRIATING AND SUBVERTING GENDER IDEALS

1. Between 1868 and 1900, Protestant women organized nearly forty denominational women's foreign mission societies in North America. By the 1930s nearly all of these societies—and their considerable resources—were required by denominational governing bodies to merge with male-controlled general mission boards. See Dana Robert, *American Women in Mission: A Social History of Their Thought and Practice* (Macon, GA: Mercer University Press, 1996), 302–7.

2. Frances J. Baker, *The Story of the Woman's Foreign Missionary Society of the Methodist Episcopal Church, 1869–1895* (Cincinnati, OH: Curts and Jennings; New York: Hunt & Eaton, 1896; reprint, New York: Garland Publishing, Inc., 1987), 16.

3. Baker, *Story of the Woman's Foreign Missionary Society*, 73–74.

4. "The Duty of the Women of the Methodist Episcopal Church," *Heathen Woman's Friend* 5, no. 6 (December 1873): 589.

5. For more on foreign missionaries' influence on their home denominations, see Dana Robert, "The Influence of American Missionary Women on the World Back Home," *Religion and American Culture: A Journal of Interpretation* 12, no. 1

(2002): 59–89; Daniel H. Bays and Grant Wacker, eds., *The Foreign Missionary Enterprise at Home: Explorations in North American Cultural History* (Tuscaloosa: University of Alabama Press, 2003); and Karen K. Seat, *"Providence Has Freed Our Hands": Women's Missions and the American Encounter with Japan* (Syracuse, NY: Syracuse University Press, 2008).

6. Barbara Welter, "The Cult of True Womanhood, 1820–1860," *American Quarterly* 18, no. 2, part 1 (Summer 1966): 151–74.

7. James Monroe Buckley, *"Because They Are Women" and Other Editorials from "The Christian Advocate" on the Admission of Women to the General Conference* (Hunt & Eaton, 1891; reprinted in *The Debate in the Methodist Episcopal Church over Laity Rights for Women,* ed. Carolyn De Swarte Gifford [New York: Garland Publishing, Inc., 1987]), 11.

8. Ibid., 11, 17.

9. Ibid., 26, 14.

10. "Their Sacred Book and Ours," *Heathen Woman's Friend* 6, no. 5 (November 1874): 749.

11. Catharine E. Beecher, *A Treatise on Domestic Economy* (Boston: Marsh, Capen, Lyon, and Webb, 1841), 13.

12. *Woman's Work for Woman and Our Mission Field* (Philadelphia: Woman's Foreign Missionary Society of the Presbyterian Church, 1886), 6.

13. "Fourth Annual Report of the Woman's Board of Missions," *Light and Life for Heathen Women* (1872): 8–9.

14. *Heathen Woman's Friend* 1, no. 2 (July 1869): 11.

15. Quoted in Clementina Butler, *Mrs. William Butler: Two Empires and the Kingdom* (New York: The Methodist Book Concern, 1929), 110.

16. Baker, *Story of the Woman's Foreign Missionary Society,* 29.

17. Quoted in Butler, *Mrs. William Butler,* 110.

18. Josiah C. Nott, *Two Lectures; on the Connection between the Biblical and Physical History of Man* (New York: Bartlett and Welford, 1849; reprinted, New York: Negro Universities Press, 1969), 17–18.

19. Montaville Flowers, *The Japanese Conquest of American Opinion* (New York: George H. Doran Co., 1917), 165, 201.

20. See Robert, "Influence of American Missionary Women," 76; Nancy A. Hardesty, "The Scientific Study of Missions: Textbooks of the Central Committee on the United Study of Foreign Missions," in *The Foreign Missionary Enterprise at Home: Explorations in North American Cultural History,* ed. Daniel H. Bays and Grant Wacker (Tuscaloosa: University of Alabama Press, 2003), 106–22; and Seat, *"Providence Has Freed Our Hands,"* chapter 6.

21. E. J. Humphrey, "Gems of India," *Heathen Woman's Friend* 6, no. 10 (April 1875): 839.

22. *Heathen Woman's Friend* 1, no. 1 (May 1869): 7.

23. Mary Isham, *Valorous Ventures: A Record of Sixty and Six Years of the Woman's Foreign Missionary Society, Methodist Episcopal Church* (Boston: Woman's Foreign Missionary Society, Methodist Episcopal Church, 1936), 11–12.

24. Robert, *American Women in Mission*, 128.

25. *Heathen Woman's Friend* 1, no. 2 (July 1869): 9, 10; emphasis in the original.

26. *Heathen Woman's Friend* 1, no. 4 (September 1869): 30.

27. "The Master-Coin," *Heathen Woman's Friend* 4, no. 11 (May 1873): 461.

28. See Lori D. Ginzberg, *Women in Antebellum Reform* (Wheeling, IL: Harlan Davidson, 2000).

29. "Fourth Annual Report of the Woman's Board of Missions," 8.

30. Frances J. Baker, "Waymarks in the History of the Woman's Foreign Missionary Society in China," *Woman's Missionary Friend* 39, no. 4 (April 1907): 115–17.

31. "The Emancipation of the Women of the East," *Woman's Missionary Friend* 50, no. 11 (November 1918).

32. Baker, *Story of the Woman's Foreign Missionary Society*, 400, 418.

33. Helen Barrett Montgomery, *Western Women in Eastern Lands* (New York: MacMillan Company, 1910), 3.

34. Ibid., 9–10; emphasis in the original.

35. Ibid., 45.

36. Ibid.

37. Ibid., 69.

38. "There is neither Jew nor Greek, there is neither bond nor free, there is neither male nor female: for ye are all one in Christ Jesus" (King James Version). Montgomery, *Western Women in Eastern Lands*, 72.

39. Montgomery, *Western Women in Eastern Lands*, 72–73.

CHAPTER 6. "ATTENTIVE, INTELLIGENT, REASONABLE, AND RESPONSIBLE": TEACHING COMPOSITION WITH BERNARD LONERGAN

Epigraph: Kenneth Melchin, *Living with Other People: An Introduction to Christian Ethics Based on Bernard Lonergan* (Ottawa: Novalis, 1998), 125.

1. James Paul Gee, *Social Linguistics and Literacies: Ideology in Discourse* (New York: Taylor and Francis, 1996), 191.

2. John Elias, "Whatever Happened to Catholic Philosophy of Education?" *Religious Education* 94 (1999): 106.

3. Priscilla Perkins, "'A Radical Conversion of the Mind': Fundamentalism, Hermeneutics, and the Metanoic Classroom," *College English* 63, no. 5 (May 2001): 585–611.

4. Andrea Lunsford and John Ruskiewicz, *Everything's an Argument*, 3rd ed. (Boston: Bedford/St. Martin's, 2003), 72; emphasis in the original.

5. Ibid., 69.

6. John C. Haughey, "Responsibility for Human Rights: Contributions from Bernard Lonergan," *Theological Studies* 63 (2002): 770.

7. Michael-John DePalma, Jeffrey Ringer, and Jim Webber, "Re-envisioning Religious Discourses as Rhetorical Resources in Composition Teaching: A Pragmatic Response to the Challenge of Belief," *College Composition and Communication* 63, no. 2 (December 2011): 220.

8. Jeffrey M. Ringer, "The Consequences of Integrating Faith into Academic Writing: Casuistic Stretching and Biblical Citation," *College English* 75, no. 3 (January 2013): 282.

9. Neil Postman, *Building a Bridge to the Eighteenth Century: How the Past Can Improve Our Future* (New York: Vintage, 2000).

10. Gee, *Social Linguistics and Literacies*, 147.

11. Priscilla Perkins, note on "Tina's" "Essay 1," February 2002.

12. Andrea Fishman, "Becoming Literate: A Lesson from the Amish," in *Literacies: Reading, Writing, Interpretation,* 2nd ed., edited by Terence Brunk, Suzanne Diamond, Priscilla Perkins, and Ken Smith, 237–48; Jeffrey Weeks, "Values in an Age of Uncertainty," in *Literacies,* edited by Brunk et al., 709–24; Frank Black Elk, "Observations on Marxism and Lakota Tradition," in *Literacies*, edited by Brunk et al., 90–104; Jennifer Cobb, "Cybergrace: The Search for God in the Digital World," in *Literacies,* edited by Brunk et al., 155–66; Nawal el-Saadawi, "Love and Sex in the Life of the Arab," in *Literacies,* edited by Brunk et al., 515–36; and Renato Rosaldo, "Grief and a Headhunter's Rage," in *Literacies,* edited by Brunk et al., 469–87.

13. Elizabeth Vander Lei and Lauren Fitzgerald, "What in God's Name? Administering the Conflicts of Religious Belief in Writing Programs," *WPA: Writing Program Administration* 31, no. 1–2 (2007): 187.

14. Mark Morelli and Elizabeth Morelli, introduction to *The Lonergan Reader,* ed. Mark Morelli and Elizabeth Morelli (Toronto: University of Toronto Press, 1997).

15. John C. Haughey, "Church-ianity and Christ-ianity," *America,* May 24–31, 2004, 8.

16. "Tina," "John 3:16": 1.

17. For excellent arguments against this code, see Kristine Hansen, "Religious Freedom in the Public Square and the Composition Classroom," in *Negotiating Religious Faith in the Composition Classroom,* ed. Elizabeth Vander Lei and bonnie l. kyburz, 24–38 (Portsmouth, NH: Heinemann, 2005); and Vander Lei and Fitzgerald, "What in God's Name?"

18. Melchin, *Living with Other People,* 5.

19. Bernard J. F. Lonergan, *Insight: A Study of Human Understanding,* vol. 3 of *Collected Works of Bernard Lonergan,* 5th ed., ed. Frederick E. Crowe and Robert M. Doran (Toronto: University of Toronto Press, 1992), 101–2. Note that Lonergan's "common sense" differs from everyday usage of this phrase. Our "common sense"

is what the *Oxford English Dictionary* calls "the plain wisdom which is everyone's inheritance" (e.g., "Common sense tells us to wear coats in cold weather"). Lonergan's, on the other hand, refers specifically to unspoken guidelines for daily life that are developed and revised through our interactions with each other.

20. Melchin, *Living with Other People*, 11.

21. Ibid., 11; emphasis in the original.

22. Hans-Georg Gadamer, "On the Scope and Function of Hermeneutical Reflection," in *Philosophical Hermeneutics*, 2nd ed., ed. and trans. David E. Linge (Berkeley: University of California Press, 2008), 20–21.

23. Peter Ashworth, "Understanding as the Transformation of What Is Already Known," *Teaching in Higher Education* 9, no. 2 (2004): 155.

24. "Sara," "Essay 4," draft 1: 2.

25. Tom Strong, "Getting Curious about Meaning-Making in Counselling," *British Journal of Guidance and Counselling* 31, no. 3 (2003): 268.

26. "Sara," "Essay 4," draft 2: 6; emphasis in the original.

27. Ibid., 6.

28. Perkins, "'Radical Conversion of the Mind,'" 593.

29. "Sara," "Essay 4," draft 2: 7.

30. Bernard J. F. Lonergan, *A Third Collection: Papers*, ed. Frederick E. Crowe (Mahwah, NJ: Paulist Press, 1985), n.p., quoted in Morelli and Morelli, introduction to *The Lonergan Reader*, 25.

31. Melchin, *Living with Other People*, 14; emphasis in the original.

32. See Perkins, "'Radical Conversion of the Mind.'"

33. Michael J. Himes, "Catholicism as Integral Humanism: Christian Participation in Pluralistic Moral Education," in *The Challenge of Pluralism: Moral Education in a Pluralistic Society* (Notre Dame, IN: University of Notre Dame Press, 1992), 125, 130.

34. "Tina," "Essay 4," draft 1: 1.

35. Ibid., 9.

36. The brackets are original in Tina's text.

37. "Tina, "Essay 4," draft 1: 4.

38. Peter Augustine Lawler, "Liberal Education? It Can Happen Here," *American Spectator* 38, no. 3 (April 2005): 47.

39. Ashworth, "Understanding as the Transformation," 156.

40. Melchin, *Living with Other People*, 28.

41. Bernard J. F. Lonergan, *Method in Theology* (New York: Seabury, 1971), 273.

CHAPTER 7. "AIN'T WE GOT FUN?":
TEACHING WRITING IN A VIOLENT WORLD

Epigraphs: Stanley Hauerwas, *The Peaceable Kingdom: A Primer in Christian Ethics* (Notre Dame, IN: Notre Dame Press, 1983), 49; and Thomas Darwin, "Pathos,

Pedagogy, and the Familiar: Cultivating Rhetorical Intelligence," in *The Realms of Rhetoric: The Prospects for Rhetoric Education*, ed. Joseph Petraglia and Deepika Bahri (Albany: State University of New York Press, 2005), 23.

1. T. R. Johnson summarizes Scarry's argument in his article "School Sucks," *College Composition and Communication* 52, no. 4 (2001): 632.

2. Paul Lynch, "Bruno Latour and Composition's Apocalyptic Turn," *College English* 74, no. 5 (2012): 460.

3. Mary Rose O'Reilley, *The Peaceable Classroom* (Portsmouth, NH: Boynton/ Cook Heinemann, 1993), 9.

4. Lynch, "Bruno Latour," 479.

5. Lynn Worsham, "Going Postal: Pedagogic Violence and the Schooling of Emotion," *Journal of Advanced Composition* 18, no. 2 (1998): 219.

6. Ibid., 221.

7. Ibid., 216.

8. See Lynch, "Bruno Latour," 462.

9. Sharon Crowley, *Toward a Civil Discourse: Rhetoric and Fundamentalism* (Pittsburgh: University of Pittsburgh Press, 2006), 1.

10. Ibid., 2.

11. O'Reilley, *Peaceable Classroom*, 12.

12. George Lakoff and Mark Johnson, *Metaphors We Live By* (Chicago: University of Chicago Press, 1980), 3.

13. Johnson, "School Sucks," 632.

14. Doug Downs, "True Believers, Real Scholars, and Real True Believing Scholars: Discourses of Inquiry and Affirmation in the Writing Classroom," in *Negotiating Religious Faith in the Writing Classroom*, ed. Elizabeth Vander Lei and bonnie l. kyburz (Portsmouth, NH: Boynton/Cook Heinemann, 2005), 39–40.

15. Ibid., 41.

16. Lizabeth Rand, "Enacting Faith: Evangelical Discourse and the Discipline of Composition Studies," *College Composition and Communication* 52, no. 3 (2001): 350.

17. Crowley, *Toward a Civil Discourse*, 70, 72.

18. Ibid., 72.

19. Ibid.

20. Ibid., 73.

21. Beth Daniell, "Whetstones Provided by the World: Trying to Deal with Difference in a Pluralistic Society," *College English* 70, no. 1 (2007): 81.

22. Crowley, *Toward a Civil Discourse*, 133. For a similar critique, see Michael-John DePalma, Jeffrey Ringer, and Jim Webber, "(Re)Charting the (Dis) Courses of Faith and Politics, or Rhetoric and Democracy in the Burkean Barnyard," *Rhetoric Society Quarterly* 38, no. 3 (2008): 311–34.

23. Jacqueline Jones Royster, "When the First Voice You Hear Is Not Your Own," *College English* 47, no. 1 (1996): 29–40.

24. Crowley, *Toward a Civil Discourse*, x.

25. Shari Stenberg, "Liberation Theology and Liberatory Pedagogies: Renewing the Dialogue," *College English* 68, no. 3 (2006): 288.

26. O'Reilley, *Peaceable Classroom*, 59.

27. Ibid., 60.

28. Hauerwas, *Peaceable Kingdom*, 114.

29. Ibid., 113.

30. Ibid., 26.

31. Ibid., 27.

32. See Christian Smith, *Souls in Transition: The Religious and Spiritual Lives of Emerging Adults* (New York: Oxford University Press, 2009).

33. O'Reilley, *Peaceable Classroom*, 60–61.

34. T. J. Geiger, "Unpredictable Encounters: Religious Discourse, Sexuality, and the Free Exercise of Rhetoric," *College English* 75, no. 3 (2013): 251.

35. Worsham, "Going Postal," 223.

36. O'Reilley, *Peaceable Classroom*, 86.

37. Wendell Berry, "Peaceableness toward Enemies," in *Sex, Economy, Freedom, and Community* (New York: Pantheon Books, 1993), 84.

38. Kristine Hansen, "Religious Freedom in the Public Square and in the Composition Classroom," in *Negotiating Religious Faith in the Writing Classroom*, ed. Elizabeth Vander Lei and bonnie l. kyburz (Portsmouth, NH: Heinemann, 2005), 27–28.

39. Stephen L. Carter, *The Culture of Disbelief: How American Law and Politics Trivialize Religious Devotion* (New York: Basic Books, 1993), 21.

40. Miroslav Volf, "Forgiveness, Reconciliation, and Justice: A Christian Contribution to a More Peaceful Social Environment," in *Forgiveness and Reconciliation: Religion, Public Policy, and Conflict Transformation*, ed. Raymond G. Helmick SJ and Rodney L. Peterson (Philadelphia: Templeton Foundation Press, 2001), 28.

41. Ibid., 29.

42. Miroslav Volf, "Indefensible War," *Christian Century*, September 25, 2002, 35.

43. Ibid.

44. Religious Leaders for Sensible Priorities, "President Bush, Jesus Changed Your Heart. Now Let Him Change Your Mind," advertisement, *New York Times*, December 4, 2002.

45. Diane Mutz, *Hearing the Other Side: Deliberative versus Participatory Democracy* (New York: Cambridge University Press, 2006), 149–50.

46. This approach is consistent with Geiger's in "Unpredictable Encounters."

47. Volf, "Forgiveness, Reconciliation, and Justice," 33.

48. Ibid., 42.

49. Ibid., 44.

50. Ibid., 45.

51. Mutz, *Hearing the Other Side*, 65.

52. Ibid., 84.

53. Danielle Allen, *Talking to Strangers: Anxieties of Citizenship since Brown v. Board of Education* (Chicago: University of Chicago Press, 2004), 182–83.

54. Carter, *Culture of Disbelief*, 587.

55. Jeffrey M. Ringer, "The Consequences of Integrating Faith into Academic Writing: Casuistic Stretching and Biblical Citation," *College English* 75, no. 3 (2013): 270–97.

56. Mutz, *Hearing the Other Side*, 3.

57. Ibid., 125.

58. Ibid., 128.

59. Ibid., 150.

60. Virginia Chappell, "Teaching—and Living—in the Meantime," in *The Academy and the Possibility of Belief: Essays on Intellectual and Spiritual Life*, ed. Mary-Louise Buley-Meissner, Mary McCaslin Thompson, and Elizabeth Bachrach Tan (Cresskill, NJ: Hampton Press, 2000), 49.

61. Ibid., 50.

CHAPTER 8. A QUESTION OF TRUTH: READING THE BIBLE, RHETORIC, AND CHRISTIAN TRADITION

1. Flannery O'Connor, *Mystery and Manners: Occasional Prose,* ed. Sally Fitzgerald (New York: Farrar, Straus, and Giroux, 1969), 44. The sentence reads: "I think it is safe to say that while the South is hardly Christ-centered, it is most certainly Christ-haunted."

2. Sharon Crowley, *Toward a Civil Discourse: Rhetoric and Fundamentalism* (Pittsburgh: University of Pittsburgh Press, 2006); and Nancy Grimm, *Good Intentions: Writing Center Work for Postmodern Times* (Portsmouth, NH: Boynton/ Cook Heinemann, 1999). Other work in composition that sees the religious students as problematic includes Douglass Downs, "True Believers, Real Scholars, and Real True Believing Scholars: Discourses of Inquiry and Affirmation in the Composition Classroom," in *Negotiating Religious Faith in the Writing Classroom,* ed. Elizabeth Vander Lei and bonnie lenore kyburz (Portsmouth, NH: Boynton/Cook Heinemann, 2005), 39–55; Chris Anderson, "The Description of an Embarrassment: When Students Write about Religion," *ADE Bulletin* 94 (1989): 12–15; Shannon Carter, "Living inside the Bible (Belt)," *College English* 69, no. 6 (2007): 572–95; Amy Goodburn, "It's a Question of Faith: Discourses of Fundamentalism and Critical Pedagogy in the Writing Classroom," *JAC: Journal of Composition Theory* 18, no. 2 (1998): 333–53; and Priscilla Perkins, "'A Radical Conversion of the Mind': Funda-

mentalism, Hermeneutics, and the Metanoic Classroom," *College English* 63, no. 5 (2001): 585–611.

3. Alfred Tennyson. *In Memoriam, A. H. H.,* in *The Norton Anthology of English Literature,* vol. 2, ed. M. H. Abrams et al. (New York: W. W. Norton, 1962), lines 11–12, p. 764.

4. Marcus Borg, *Reading the Bible Again for the First Time: Taking the Bible Seriously but Not Literally* (San Francisco: HarperSanFrancisco, 2001), 4.

5. Bart D. Ehrman, *Misquoting Jesus: The Story Behind Who Changed the Bible and Why* (San Francisco: HarperSanFrancisco 2005), 19.

6. Ibid.

7. Crowley, *Toward a Civil Discourse,* 69, but see chapter 3, "Belief and Passionate Commitment" in its entirety.

8. Kenneth Burke, from *Language as Symbolic Action,* in *The Rhetorical Tradition: Readings from Classical Times to the Present,* 2nd ed., ed. Patricia Bizzell and Bruce Herzberg (Boston: Bedford/St. Martin, 2001), 1340.

9. Stephen Toulmin, from *The Uses of Argument,* in *Rhetorical Tradition,* ed. Bizzell and Herzberg, 1414–16.

10. Chaim Perelman, from *The New Rhetoric: A Theory of Practical Reasoning,* in *Rhetorical Tradition,* ed. Bizzell and Herzberg, 1392.

11. Ibid.

12. Ibid.

13. Ehrman, *Misquoting Jesus,* 212–15. The rhetorical approach is the way many New Testament scholars read the Gospel books; see, for example, John Dominic Crossan, *The Power of the Parable: How Fiction by Jesus Became Fiction about Jesus* (New York: Harper Collins, 2012). Richard Elliott Friedman does much the same with the Hebrew Testament in *Who Wrote the Bible* (New York: Harper Collins, 1997), arguing that its sources, J, E, D, and P and their redactions were composed for particular groups in particular situations.

14. I rely here on Elaine Pagels's study of the gnostic gospels in *Beyond Belief: The Secret Gospel of Thomas* (New York: Random House, 2003). See also Bart D. Ehrman, *Lost Scriptures: Books That Did Not Make It into the New Testament* (New York: Oxford University Press, 2003).

15. Pagels, *Beyond Belief,* 176–77.

16. Ibid., 177.

17. Ibid., 117.

18. Ibid., 118.

19. Ibid., 177.

20. Augustine of Hippo, *On Christian Doctrine,* trans. D. W. Robertson Jr. (Upper Saddle River, NJ: Prentice Hall, 1997).

21. Patricia Bizzell and Bruce Herzberg, "Synopsis of Books I–IV," in *Rhetorical Tradition,* ed. Bizzell and Herzberg, 453.

22. Quoted in David Richter, *The Critical Tradition: Classic Texts and Contemporary Trends,* 2nd ed. (Boston: Bedford, 1998), 119. The ellipses are Richter's.

23. Dante Alighieri, from "Letter to *Can Grande della Scala,*" in David Richter, *Critical Tradition,* 120–22.

24. Ibid., 120.

25. See also Dante's Exodus example in Richter, *Critical Tradition,* 121. The story of Abraham's sacrifice can be found in Gen. 22: 1–19.

26. Richter, *Critical Tradition,* 120.

27. Lee Morrissey, *The Constitution of Literature: Literacy, Democracy, and Early English Literary Criticism* (Stanford, CA: Stanford University Press, 2008), 34.

28. Ibid., 25–60.

29. Ibid., 37.

30. Ibid., 38; my emphasis.

31. Ibid.

32. Ibid., 41.

33. Stanley Fish, "Driving from the Letter: Truth and Indeterminacy in Milton's *Areopagitica,*" in *Remembering Milton: Essays on the Texts and Traditions,* ed. Mary Nyquist and Margaret W. Ferguson (New York: Methuen, 1987), 241.

34. Quoted in ibid., 241.

35. Ibid.

36. Morrissey, *Constitution of Literature,* 45–47.

37. Ibid., 50–52.

38. As Morrissey (ibid., ix) puts it, "what we now know as literary criticism attempts to organize what was then seen as one particularly troubling aspect of print culture: democratized reading."

39. Borg, *Reading the Bible Again for the First Time,* ix.

40. Borg says that in a state of natural literalism "the Bible is read and accepted literally without effort. Because someone in this state has no reason to think differently, a literal reading of the Bible poses no problems" (ibid., 8). Borg defines precritical naiveté as "an early childhood state in which we take it for granted that whatever the significant authority figures in our lives tell us to be true is indeed true" (ibid., 49). At this stage children "hear the stories of the Bible as true stories" (ibid.).

41. Ibid., 13–16.

42. Ibid., 14.

43. Ibid., 8–9.

44. Ibid.

45. Ibid., 17.

46. Ibid.

47. Ibid., 50.

48. Patricia Bizzell, "Cognition, Convention, and Certainty: What We Need to

Know about Writing," in *Academic Discourse and Critical Consciousness*, ed. Patricia Bizzell (Pittsburgh: University of Pittsburgh Press, 1992), 99.

49. Ibid.

50. Ann E. Berthoff, "Problem-Dissolving by Triadic Means," *College English* 58, no. 1 (1996): 10.

51. Michel Foucault, from "The Order of Discourse," in *Rhetorical Tradition*, ed. Bizzell and Herzberg, 1470.

CHAPTER 9. THE JEWISH CONTEXT OF PAUL'S RHETORIC

1. See also Rom. 4:1, 11:1; Gal. 1:13, 2:15; and I Cor. 9:20. Acts is also amply clear about Paul's Jewishness. All biblical quotations are from *The New Testament of the New Jerusalem Bible* (New York: Doubleday, 1986).

2. See also Acts 5:34–39, discussing Gamaliel.

3. See Thomas H. Tobin SJ, *Paul's Rhetoric in Its Contexts: The Argument of Romans* (Peabody, MA: Hendrickson, 2004), which provides an extensive bibliography.

4. See Michael Fishbane, "Inner Biblical Exegesis: Types and Strategies of Interpretation in Ancient Israel," in *Midrash and Literature*, ed. Geoffrey H. Hartman and Sanford Burdick (New Haven, CT: Yale University Press, 1986), 20. His entire essay is relevant to this point. Also see, in the same volume, the essay by James Kugel, "Two Introductions to Midrash," especially pages 80–84. Kugel argues that midrash is "not a genre of interpretation, but an interpretive stance" that can also be found in the targumim, apocrypha, sermons, prayers, and so on. Texts other than those I mention are discussed in a useful summary by Hermann Lichtenberger in "The Understanding of the Torah in the Judaism of Paul's Day," in *Paul and the Mosaic Law*, ed. James D. G. Dunn (Grand Rapids, MI: Eerdmans, 1996).

5. The scholar David Daube argues that Hillel was looking for post facto justification in scripture of Pharisaic rulings. Daube makes some very interesting points about Hillel's work, his sources, and the possible influence of Greek rhetoric on his ideas: "Rabbinic Methods of Interpretation and Hellenistic Rhetoric," *Hebrew Union College Annual* 22 (1949): 239–64.

6. The Mishnah divides the laws into sixty-three chapters organized in six larger divisions. Avot (Fathers) is one of the middle chapters.

7. Fishbane, "Inner Biblical Exegesis," 26–28.

8. Flavius Josephus, *Antiquities*, 13.10.6. The translation is from *The New Complete Works of Josephus*, trans. William Whiston (Grand Rapids, MI: Kregel Publications, 1999), 441.

9. Jesus may not have been a Pharisee like Paul, but the similarities between Jesus and the Pharisees have become increasingly evident to scholars. In addition to sharing beliefs about the apocalypse and the messianic age (in opposition to the Sadducees), Jesus and the Pharisees agree on the need for the relevance of Torah

law to daily life. The Gospels show Jesus engaged in debates with the Pharisees that suggest they are on different sides of the issues that arise, like Sabbath laws and cleanliness. But all of the debate topics in the Gospels can be found in rabbinic texts that show rabbis arguing both sides of the issue, and in most cases the position Jesus takes matches the position that prevails among the rabbis. In *Jesus the Pharisee* (London: SCM, 2003), the scholar Hyam Maccoby overargues his position that Jesus was actually a Pharisee, but in the process he reviews every debate and explains the complexities that are elided in the Gospel accounts. See also E. P. Sanders, *Jesus and Judaism* (Philadelphia: Fortress, 1985); Bruce Chilton, *Rabbi Jesus* (New York: Doubleday, 2000); Harvey Falk, *Jesus the Pharisee: A New Look at the Jewishness of Jesus* (Eugene, OR: Wipf and Stock, 2003); Geza Vermes, *Jesus the Jew* (1973; reprint, Minneapolis: Fortress Press, 1981); and Phillip Segal, *The Halakhah of Jesus of Nazareth According to the Gospel of Matthew* (Atlanta: Society of Biblical Literature, 2007).

10. A thirteen-rule elaboration of this list by the second-century Rabbi Ishmael is still recited as part of the Jewish daily morning prayer service, a testament to the sacredness accorded to these hermeneutic rules.

11. W. D. Davies in 1948, for example, concluded that despite Hellenistic elements, Paul's thought was best understood in rabbinic terms. See Davies, *Paul and Rabbinic Judaism: Some Rabbinic Elements in Pauline Theology* (London: SPCK, 1948, 1955), 1. The question of whether Paul uses rabbinic or proto-rabbinic methods is a subtopic of the Society of Biblical Literature's Symposium on Paul's Use of Scripture. The symposium's 2008 book identifies several contexts in which such questions should be investigated: theological, historical, literary, and rhetorical. The symposium reinforces the caution about trying to determine what Paul had in mind, finding questions in all four contexts. See Stanley E. Porter and Christopher D. Stanley, *As It Is Written: Studying Paul's Use of Scripture* (Atlanta: Society of Biblical Literature, 2008).

12. Scholar James Kugel helpfully identifies four basic assumptions of ancient biblical interpretation: that the text is fundamentally cryptic and requires interpretation; that the Bible is a book of lessons addressed to the reader; that there are no contradictions in the Bible; and that the Bible is divinely given. See his *How to Read the Bible* (New York: Free Press, 2007), 14–16.

13. See Davies, *Paul and Rabbinic Judaism*, 115, 117–18.

14. See Mark D. Nanos, *The Mystery of Romans: The Jewish Context of Paul's Letter* (Minneapolis: Fortress Press, 1996), 166, 169: "The Jerusalem Council, according to Luke's account in Acts 15, decided that gentiles were to be admitted as equals into the new community of Christian Jews through faith in Jesus Christ without needing to become Jews. Yet they were not to be admitted to this new faction of Judaism as pagans, for they were to respect the halakhah of the 'righteous gentile' operative in Judaism at the time"; the apostolic decree thus "represents a first-

century development that stands somewhere between the ancient Mosaic model for governing the behavioral requirements for the 'stranger within your gates,' that is, of the non-Jew living in the land of Israel (Lev. 17–18), and the later rabbinic model of the Noahide Commandments."

15. See Bruce Chilton and Jacob Neusner, *Judaism in the New Testament: Practices and Beliefs* (London: Routledge, 1995), 62–69, which gives a similar (but by no means identical) analysis of Romans 9–11. Chilton and Neusner speak of the Torah-Prophets connection on page 64.

16. Ibid., 65.

17. New Testament scholar Christopher Stanley has argued that Paul could not have expected his audiences to know the context of quotations, as they often don't actually support his argument. Indeed, in some cases, Stanley points out, the quotation is a non sequitur. He concludes that "Paul did not expect his actual addressees in Galatia to be capable of checking his references" and that Paul's constructed audience "was incapable of consulting the original context of most of his biblical references." Christopher Stanley, "Paul's 'Use' of Scripture: Why the Audience Matters," in *As It Is Written: Studying Paul's Use of Scripture,* ed. Stanley E. Porter and Christopher D. Stanley (Atlanta: Society of Biblical Literature, 2008), 152, 155.

18. See Arne Jarrod Hobbel, "Hermeneutics in Talmud, Midrash, and the New Testament," *Immanuel* 24–25 (1990): 132–46.

19. See David Daube, *The New Testament and Rabbinic Judaism* (London: Athlone Press, 1956). See also William Richard Stegner, "Romans 9.6–29: A Midrash," *Journal for the Study of the New Testament* 22 (1984): 37–52, where, on page 42, Stegner finds that the rabbis borrowed the diatribe. See also Thomas H. Tobin SJ, *Paul's Rhetoric in Its Contexts,* particularly page 84, and Stanley K. Stowers, *The Diatribe and Paul's Letter to the Romans* (Chico, CA: Scholar's Press, 1981), on the diatribe.

20. E. Earle Ellis, *Paul's Use of the Old Testament* (Grand Rapids, MI: Eerdmans, 1957), 3.

21. Ibid., 46.

22. Ibid.

23. Ibid., 54, 75. The internal quote is from F. W. Farrar, *The Life and Work of St. Paul,* vol. 1 (New York: E. P. Dutton, 1879), 49.

24. E. P. Sanders, *Paul and Palestinian Judaism: A Comparison of Patterns of Religion* (Philadelphia: Fortress Press, 1977).

25. W. S. Towner, "Hermeneutical Systems of Hillel and the Tannaim: A Fresh Look," *Hebrew Union College Annual* 53 (1982): 133–34.

26. Richard B. Hays, *Echoes of Scripture in the Letters of Paul* (New Haven, CT: Yale University Press, 1989), xii.

27. Ibid., 12. A similar view is in James W. Aageson, "Scripture and Structure in the Development of the Argument in Romans 9–11," *Catholic Biblical Quarterly* 48 (1986): 273: "In Paul's method of argumentation, Scripture has functioned as a

stimulus" rather than in any kind of identifiable, rabbinic, persuasive, or interpretive method.

28. Hays, *Echoes of Scripture*, 13. I confess that I do not understand the distinction Hays is drawing here: does an interpretive technique always produce the same ideological result? It seems to me, rather, that Paul and the rabbis are trying to find authentic meaning in scripture, according, of course, to their presumptions about what meanings are to be found. Steven DiMattei comments on this problem in his essay "Biblical Narratives" that appears in *As It Is Written: Studying Paul's Use of Scripture*, ed. Stanley E. Porter and Christopher D. Stanley (Atlanta: Society of Biblical Literature, 2008), 59–93.

29. Chilton and Neusner, *Judaism in the New Testament*, 69.

30. Johann D. Kim, "God, Israel, and the Gentiles: Rhetoric and Situation in Romans 9–11," PhD diss., Union Theological Seminary, 1999.

31. Tobin, *Paul's Rhetoric in Its Contexts*, 58. This book, published in paperback by a major press, is a throwback to an older view of Paul's relationship not only to Pharisaic discourse, but to Torah law itself. In the course of four pages of argument, Tobin reaches the conclusion that for Paul, "it was the whole law as such that no longer needed to be observed by believers, whether they were Jewish or Gentile." Compare Martin Hengel's argument on page 29 of his essay "The Attitude of Paul to the Law in the Unknown Years between Damascus and Antioch" that "we should not speak of a preaching that was free from the law, as I myself used to do. At root there never was such a thing in early Christianity in any strict sense, not even in Paul." This essay can be found in Dunn, *Paul and the Mosaic*, 29.

32. Tobin, *Paul's Rhetoric in Its Contexts*, 7. Tobin speculates that the Romans to whom Paul writes may have been familiar with the letter to the Galatians, which casts doubt on Paul's attachment to Jewish scripture.

33. John Gager, *Reinventing Paul* (New York: Oxford University Press, 2000), 32.

34. In the purely Jewish context, "standing" means the physical act, as in standing before God. Paul means it in a moral sense—one's right standing, in an evaluative sense, before God.

35. DiMattei, "Biblical Narratives," 77.

CHAPTER 10. RESISTANCE TO RHETORIC IN CHRISTIAN TRADITION

1. See James Kinneavy, *Greek Rhetorical Origins of Christian Faith: An Inquiry* (New York: Oxford University Press, 1987); Kenneth Burke, *A Rhetoric of Motives* (Berkeley: University of California Press, 1969); Wayne C. Booth, "Kenneth Burke's Religious Rhetoric: 'God-Terms' and the Ontological Proof," in *Rhetorical Invention and Religious Inquiry: New Perspectives*, ed. Walter Jost and Wendy Olmsted (New Haven, CT: Yale University Press, 2000), 25–46; Jost and Olmsted, *Rhetorical Invention and Religious Inquiry: New Perspectives* (New Haven, CT: Yale University Press, 2000).

2. Burke, *Rhetoric of Motives.*

3. Ibid., 43.

4. George A. Kennedy, "'Truth' and 'Rhetoric' in the Pauline Epistles," in *The Bible as Rhetoric: Studies in Biblical Persuasion and Credibility,* ed. Martin Warner (New York: Routledge, 1990), 196.

5. Geoffrey Galt Harpham, *The Ascetic Imperative in Culture and Criticism* (Chicago: University of Chicago Press, 1987), 11.

6. George A. Kennedy, *Classical Rhetoric and Its Christian and Secular Tradition from Ancient to Modern Times* (Chapel Hill: University of North Carolina Press, 1980).

7. Averil Cameron, *Christianity and the Rhetoric of Empire: The Development of Christian Discourse* (Berkeley: University of California Press, 1991), 5.

8. Kennedy, *Classical Rhetoric,* 121–23.

9. Ibid., 127–28.

10. Ibid., 125.

11. See Augustine of Hippo, *On Christian Doctrine,* trans. D. W. Robertson Jr. (Upper Saddle River, NJ: Prentice Hall, 1958), and *Confession,* trans. F. J. Sheed (Indianapolis, IN: Hackett, 2006).

12. See Debora K. Shuger, *Sacred Rhetoric: The Christian Grand Style in the English Renaissance* (Princeton, NJ: Princeton University Press, 1988).

13. Ibid., 8.

14. See Roger Lundin, *Disciplining Hermeneutics: Interpretation in Christian Perspective* (Grand Rapids, MI: Eerdmans, 1997); and Roger Lundin, Clarence Walhout, and Anthony C. Thiselton, *The Promise of Hermeneutics* (Grand Rapids, MI: Eerdmans, 1999).

15. Lundin, *Disciplining Hermeneutics,* 5.

16. Lundin, Walhout, and Thiselton, *Promise of Hermeneutics,* 4.

17. Brian J. Walsh, "Worldviews, Modernity, and the Task of Christian College Education," *Faculty Dialogue* 18 (Fall 1992): 13–35, 25.

18. Ibid., 20, 16.

19. Ibid., 16, 19.

20. Brian J. Walsh and J. Richard Middleton, *The Transforming Vision: Shaping a Christian World View* (Downers Grove, IL: InterVarsity Press, 1984), 119.

21. Walsh, "Worldviews, Modernity, and the Task," 26, 28, 27.

22. Ibid., 25, 26, 26.

23. Ibid., 27, 27.

24. See Stanley E. Fish, *Doing What Comes Naturally: Change, Rhetoric, and the Practice of Theory in Literary and Legal Studies* (Durham, NC: Duke University Press, 1989); Stanley E. Fish, "Driving from the Letter: Truth and Indeterminacy in Milton's *Areopagitica,*" in *How Milton Works,* ed. Stanley E. Fish (Cambridge, MA: Harvard University Press, 2001), 187–214; Stanley E. Fish, "One University under

God?" *Chronicle of Higher Education,* January 7, 2005, C1–C4; and Gary A. Olson, *Justifying Belief: Stanley Fish and the Work of Rhetoric* (Albany: State University of New York Press, 2002).

25. Olson, *Justifying Belief,* 77; and Fish, "Driving from the Letter," 192.

26. Olson, *Justifying Belief,* 63; see also Fish, *Doing What Comes Naturally.*

27. Olson, *Justifying Belief,* 63.

BIBLIOGRAPHY

—

Aageson, James W. "Scripture and Structure in the Development of the Argument in Romans 9–11." *Catholic Biblical Quarterly* 48 (1986): 265–89.

Alexander, Thomas G. "An Experiment in Progressive Legislation: The Granting of Woman Suffrage in Utah in 1870." *Utah Historical Quarterly* 38, no. 1 (1970): 20–30.

Alighieri, Dante. From "Letter to *Can Grande della Scala*." In *The Critical Tradition: Classic Texts and Contemporary Trends*, edited by David Richter, 119–22. 2nd ed. Boston: Bedford, 1998.

Allen, Danielle S. *Talking to Strangers: Anxieties of Citizenship since Brown v. Board of Education*. Chicago: University of Chicago Press, 2004.

Anderson, Chris. "The Description of an Embarrassment: When Students Write about Religion." *ADE Bulletin* 94 (1989): 12–15.

Arrington, Leonard J. "The Economic Role of Pioneer Mormon Women." *Western Humanities Review* 9 (1955): 145–64.

Arrington, Leonard, and Jon Haupt. "Intolerable Zion: The Image of Mormonism in Nineteenth Century American Literature." *Western Humanities Review* 22 (1968): 243–60.

Ashworth, Peter. "Understanding as the Transformation of What Is Already Known." *Teaching in Higher Education* 9, no. 2 (2004): 147–58.

Augsburger, Daniel. "The Sabbath and Lord's Day during the Middle Ages." In *The Sabbath in Scripture and History*, edited by Kenneth A. Strand, 192. Washington, DC: Review and Herald, 1982.

Augustine of Hippo. *Confessions*. Translated by F. J. Sheed. Indianapolis, IN: Hackett, 2006.

———. *On Christian Doctrine*. Translated by D. W. Robertson Jr. Upper Saddle River, NJ: Prentice Hall, 1997.

Bacchiocchi, Samuele. "The Rise of Sunday Observance in Early Christianity." In *The Sabbath in Scripture and History*, edited by Kenneth A. Strand, 132–50. Washington, D.C.: Review and Herald, 1982.

Baker, Frances J. *The Story of the Woman's Foreign Mission Society of the Method-*

ist Episcopal Church, 1869–1895. New York: Hunt and Eaton, 1896; reprint, New York and London: Garland Publishing, Inc., 1987.

———. "Waymarks in the History of the Woman's Foreign Missionary Society in China." *Woman's Missionary Friend* 39, no. 4 (April 1907): 115–17.

Barnes, Elizabeth. *States of Sympathy: Seduction and Democracy in the American Novel.* New York: Columbia University Press, 1997.

Bays, Daniel H., and Grant Wacker, eds. *The Foreign Missionary Enterprise at Home: Explorations in North American Cultural History.* Tuscaloosa: University of Alabama Press, 2003.

Beecher, Catharine E. *A Treatise on Domestic Economy.* Boston: Marsh, Capen, Lyon, and Webb, 1841.

Beecher, Maureen Ursenbach. "The Eliza Enigma: The Life and Legend of Eliza R. Snow." In *Essays in the American West 1974–1975,* edited by Thomas G. Alexander, 29–46. Charles Redd Monographs in Western History. No. 6. Provo, UT: Brigham Young University Press, 1976.

———. "Eliza R Snow." In *Mormon Sisters: Women in Early Utah,* edited by Claudia L. Bushman, 25–42. Salt Lake City, UT: Olympus Publishing, 1976.

———. "Priestess among the Patriarchs: Eliza R. Snow and the Mormon Female Relief Society, 1842–1887." In *Religion and Society in the American West: Historical Essays,* edited by Carl Guarneri and David Alvarez, 153–70. Lanham, MD: University Press of America, 1987.

Bentley, Nancy. *Sex and Citizens: Bigamy, Polygamy, and Southern Concubinage in Late-Nineteenth-Century Fiction.* Washington, D.C.: MLA, 1996.

Berry, Wendell. "Peaceableness toward Enemies." In *Sex, Economy, Freedom, and Community,* by Wendell Berry, 69–92. New York: Pantheon Books, 1992–93.

Berthoff, Ann E. "Problem-Dissolving by Triadic Means." *College English* 58, no. 1 (1996): 9–21.

Bizzell, Patricia. "Cognition, Convention, and Certainty: What We Need to Know about Writing." In *Academic Discourse and Critical Consciousness,* edited by Patricia Bizzell and Bruce Herzberg, 75–104. Pittsburgh: University of Pittsburgh Press, 1992. Reprinted from *Pre-Text* 3 (1982): 213–43.

———. "Rationality as Rhetorical Strategy at the Barcelona Disputation, 1263: A Cautionary Tale." *College Composition and Communication* 58, no. 1 (2006): 12–29.

Bizzell, Patricia, and Bruce Herzberg, eds. *The Rhetorical Tradition: Readings from Classical Times to the Present,* 2nd ed. Boston: Bedford/St. Martins, 2001.

Black Elk, Frank. "Observations on Marxism and Lakota Tradition." In *Literacies: Reading, Writing, Interpretation,* 2nd ed., edited by Terence Brunk, Suzanne Diamond, Priscilla Perkins, and Ken Smith, 90–104. New York: Norton, 2000.

Blair, Karen. *The Clubwoman as Feminist: True Womanhood Redefined, 1868–1914.* New York: Holmes and Meier, 1980.

————. *The Torchbearers: Women and Their Amateur Arts Associations in America, 1890–1930*. Bloomington: University of Indiana Press, 1994.

Bloom, Harold. *The American Religion*. New York: Simon and Schuster, 1993.

Booth, Wayne C. "Kenneth Burke's Religious Rhetoric: 'God-Terms' and the Ontological Proof." In *Rhetorical Invention and Religious Inquiry*, edited by Walter Jost and Wendy Olmsted, 25–46. New Haven, CT: Yale University Press, 2000.

Borg, Marcus. *Reading the Bible Again for the First Time: Taking the Bible Seriously but Not Literally*. San Francisco: HarperSanFrancisco, 2001.

Bosanquet Fletcher, Mary. "*Watchwords*: Names of Christ." Edited by David Frudd. *Asbury Journal* 61, no. 2 (Fall 2006): 13–96.

Bowie, Fiona, Deborah Kirkwood, and Shirley Ardener. *Women and Missions: Past and Present: Anthropological and Historical Perceptions*. Providence, RI: Berg, 1993.

Brekus, Catherine A. *Strangers and Pilgrims: Female Preaching in America, 1740–1845*. Chapel Hill: University of North Carolina Press, 1998.

Brown, Earl Kent. *Women of Mr. Wesley's Methodism*. New York: Edwin Mellen Press, 1983.

Brown, Nikki. *Private Politics and Public Voices: Black Women's Activism from World War I to the New Deal*. Bloomington: University of Indiana Press, 2006.

Brunk, Terence, Suzanne Diamond, Priscilla Perkins, and Ken Smith, eds. *Literacies: Reading, Writing, Interpretation*. 2nd ed. New York: Norton, 2000.

Buckley, James Monroe. *"Because They Are Women" and Other Editorials from "The Christian Advocate" on the Admission of Women to the General Conference*. Hunt and Eaton, 1891. Reprinted in *The Debate in the Methodist Episcopal Church over Laity Rights for Women*, edited by Carolyn De Swarte Gifford. New York: Garland Publishing, Inc., 1987.

Bull, Malcolm, and Keith Lockhart. *Seeking a Sanctuary: Seventh-day Adventism and the American Dream*. San Francisco: Harper and Row, 1989.

Burke, Kenneth. *A Grammar of Motives*. Berkeley: University of California Press, 1969.

————. *A Rhetoric of Motives*. Berkeley: University of California Press, 1969.

————. From *Language as Symbolic Action*. In *The Rhetorical Tradition: Readings from Classical Times to the Present*, 2nd ed., edited by Patricia Bizzell and Bruce Herzberg, 1340–47. Boston: Bedford/St. Martins, 2001.

Butler, Clementina. *Mrs. William Butler: Two Empires and the Kingdom*. New York: The Methodist Book Concern, 1929.

Cameron, Averil. *Christianity and the Rhetoric of Empire: The Development of Christian Discourse*. Berkeley: University of California Press, 1991.

Carey, Archibald. "Address to the Republican National Convention." In *Rhetoric of Black Revolt*, edited by Roy Hill, 149–54. Denver, CO: Golden Bell, 1964.

Carey, Hilary M., ed. *Empires of Religion*. New York: Palgrave Macmillan, 2008.

Carter, Shannon. "Living inside the Bible (Belt)." *College English* 69, no. 6 (2007): 572–95.

Carter, Stephen. *Civility*. New York: Harper Collins, 1998.

———. *The Culture of Disbelief: How American Law and Politics Trivialize Religious Devotion*. New York: Basic Books, 1993.

Ceppi, Elisabeth. "In the Apostle's Words: Elizabeth Ashbridge's Epistle to the Goshen Monthly Meeting." *Legacy* 21, no. 2 (2004): 141–55.

Chappell, Virginia. "Teaching—and Living—in the Meantime." In *The Academy and the Possibility of Belief: Essays on Intellectual and Spiritual Life,* edited by Mary-Louise Buley-Meissner, Mary McCaslin Thompson, and Elizabeth Bachrach Tan, 39–53. Cresskill, NJ: Hampton Press, 2000.

Chilcote, Paul Wesley. *John Wesley and the Women Preachers of Early Methodism*. Metuchen, NJ: American Theological Library Association and Scarecrow Press, 1991.

Chilton, Bruce. *Rabbi Jesus*. New York: Doubleday, 2000.

Chilton, Bruce, and Jacob Neusner. *Judaism in the New Testament: Practices and Beliefs*. London: Routledge, 1995.

Choi, Hyaeweol. *Gender and Mission Encounters in Korea: New Women, Old Ways*. Berkeley: University of California Press, 2009.

Cobb, Jennifer J. "Cybergrace: The Search for God in the Digital World." In *Literacies: Reading, Writing, Interpretation,* 2nd ed., edited by Terence Brunk, Suzanne Diamond, Priscilla Perkins, and Ken Smith, 155–66. New York: Norton, 2000.

Cottrell, Raymond F. "The Sabbath in the New World." In *The Sabbath in Scripture and History,* edited by Kenneth A. Strand, 244–63. Washington, D.C.: Review and Herald, 1982.

Croly, Jennie June. *The History of the Woman's Club Movement in America*. New York: Henry G. Allen Press, 1898.

Crosby, Sarah. MS Letterbook. Frank Baker Collection. Duke University Archives. Durham, NC.

Crossan, John Dominic. *The Power of Parable: How Fiction by Jesus Became Fiction about Jesus*. New York: Harper Collins, 2012.

Crowley, Sharon. *Toward a Civil Discourse: Rhetoric and Fundamentalism*. Pittsburgh: University of Pittsburgh Press, 2006.

Daniell, Beth. "Whetstones Provided by the World: Trying to Deal with Difference in a Pluralistic Society." *College English* 70, no. 1 (2007): 79–88.

Darwin, Thomas. "Pathos, Pedagogy, and the Familiar: Cultivating Rhetorical Intelligence." In *The Realms of Rhetoric: The Prospects for Rhetoric Education,* edited by Joseph Petraglia and Deepika Bahri, 23–37. Albany: State University of New York Press, 2003.

Daube, David. *The New Testament and Rabbinic Judaism*. London: Athlone Press, 1956.

———. "Rabbinic Methods of Interpretation and Hellenistic Rhetoric." *Hebrew Union College Annual* 22 (1949): 239–64.

Davies, Rupert E., A. Raymond George, E. Gordon Rupp. *A History of the Methodist Church in Great Britain*. Epworth, UK: Epworth Press, 1988.

Davies, W. D. *Paul and Rabbinic Judaism: Some Rabbinic Elements in Pauline Theology*. London: SPCK, 1948, 1955.

Davis, Elizabeth Lindsay. *The Story of the Illinois Federation of Colored Women's Clubs*. New York: G. K. Hall, 1997.

DePalma, Michael-John. "Re-envisioning Religious Discourses as Rhetorical Resources in Composition Teaching: A Pragmatic Response to the Challenge of Belief." *College Composition and Communication* 63, no. 2 (December 2011): 219–43.

DePalma, Michael-John, Jeffrey M. Ringer, and Jim Webber. "(Re)Charting the (Dis)Courses of Faith and Politics, or Rhetoric and Democracy in the Burkean Barnyard." *Rhetoric Society Quarterly* 38, no. 3 (2008): 311–34.

Derr, Jill Mulvay. "Eliza R. Snow and the Woman Question." *BYU Studies* 16, no. 2 (1976): 250–64.

———. "Eliza R. Snow and the Woman Question." In *Battle for the Ballot: Essays on Woman Suffrage in Utah, 1870–1896*, edited by Carol Cornwell Madsen, 68–82. Logan: Utah State University Press, 1997.

———. "The Significance of 'O My Father' in the Personal Journey of Eliza R. Snow." *BYU Studies* 36, no. 1 (1996–97): 85–126.

DiMattei, Steven. "Biblical Narratives." In *As It Is Written: Studying Paul's Use of Scripture*, edited by Stanley E. Porter and Christopher D. Stanley, 59–93. Atlanta, GA: Society of Biblical Literature, 2008.

Donawerth, Jane. *Conversational Rhetoric: The Rise and Fall of a Women's Tradition, 1600–1900*. Carbondale: Southern Illinois University Press, 2012.

Dossett, Kate. *Bridging Race Divides: Black Nationalisms, Feminism, and Integration in the United States, 1896–1935*. Gainesville: University Press of Florida, 2009.

Downs, Doug. "True Believers, Real Scholars, and Real True Believing Scholars: Discourses of Inquiry and Affirmation in the Composition Classroom." In *Negotiating Religious Faith in the Writing Classroom*, edited by Elizabeth Vander Lei and bonnie kyburz, 39–55. Portsmouth, NH: Boynton/Cook, 2005.

Dunn, James D. G. *Paul and the Mosaic Law*. Grand Rapids, MI: Eerdmans, 1996.

Ehrman, Bart D. *Lost Scriptures: Books That Did Not Make It into the New Testament*. New York: Oxford University Press, 2003.

———. *Misquoting Jesus: The Story Behind Who Changed the Bible and Why*. San Francisco: HarperSanFrancisco, 2005.

Elias, John. "Whatever Happened to Catholic Philosophy of Education?" *Religious Education* 94, no. 1 (1999): 92–110.

Ellis, E. Earle. *Paul's Use of the Old Testament.* Grand Rapids, MI: Eerdmans, 1957.

el-Saadawi, Nawal. "Love and Sex in the Life of the Arab." In *Literacies: Reading, Writing, Interpretation,* 2nd ed., edited by Terence Brunk, Suzanne Diamond, Priscilla Perkins, and Ken Smith, 515–36. New York: Norton, 2000.

Emerson, Ralph Waldo. "Divinity School Address." 1838. Available online at http://www.age-of-thesage.org/transcendentalism/emerson/divinity_school _address.html.

Falk, Harvey. *Jesus the Pharisee: A New Look at the Jewishness of Jesus.* Eugene, OR: Wipf and Stock, 2003.

Farrar, F. W. *The Life and Work of St. Paul.* Vol. 1. New York: E. P. Dutton, 1879.

Feldman, Stephen M. *Please Don't Wish Me a Merry Christmas: A Critical History of the Separation of Church and State.* New York: New York University Press, 1997.

Ferguson, Moira. *Colonialism and Gender from Mary Wollenstonecraft to Jamaica Kincaid.* New York: Columbia University Press, 1993.

Ferguson, Moira, ed. *The Hart Sisters: Early African Caribbean Writers, Evangelicals, and Radicals.* Lincoln: University of Nebraska Press, 1993.

Fish, Stanley E. *Doing What Comes Naturally: Change, Rhetoric, and the Practice of Theory in Literary and Legal Studies.* Durham, NC: Duke University Press, 1989.

———. "Driving from the Letter: Truth and Indeterminacy in Milton's *Areopagitica.*" In *How Milton Works,* edited by Stanley E. Fish, 187–214. Cambridge, MA: Harvard University Press, 2001.

———. "Driving from the Letter: Truth and Indeterminacy in Milton's *Areopagitica.*" In *Remembering Milton: Essays on the Texts and Traditions,* edited by Mary Nyquist and Margaret Ferguson, 234–54. New York: Methuen, 1987.

———. "One University under God?" *Chronicle of Higher Education,* January 7, 2005, C1, C4.

Fishbane, Michael. *The Garments of Torah: Essays in Biblical Hermeneutics.* Bloomington: Indiana University Press, 1989.

———. "Inner Biblical Exegesis: Types and Strategies of Interpretation in Ancient Israel." In *Midrash and Literature,* edited by Geoffrey H. Hartman and Sanford Burdick, 29–37. New Haven, CT: Yale University Press, 1986.

Fishman, Andrea. "Becoming Literate: A Lesson from the Amish." In *Literacies: Reading, Writing, Interpretation,* 2nd ed., edited by Terence Brunk, Suzanne Diamond, Priscilla Perkins, and Ken Smith, 237–48. New York: Norton, 2000.

Fletcher, Mary. *The Life of Mrs. Mary Fletcher, Consort and Relict of the Rev. John Fletcher, Vicar of Madeley, Salop,* edited by Henry Moore. London: Wesleyan-Methodist Book Room, n.d.

———. *Ms. Journal.* Methodist Archives and Research Center. John Rylands University Library, Manchester, Fletcher-Tooth Collection.

Flowers, Montaville. *The Japanese Conquest of American Opinion.* New York: George H. Doran Co., 1917.

Fortin, Denis. "Briefing." *Andrews University.* January 31, 2012. Available online at http://www.andrews.edu/news/2012/01/symposium.html.

Foucault, Michel. From "The Order of Discourse." In *The Rhetorical Tradition: Readings from Classical Times to the Present,* edited by Patricia Bizzell and Bruce Herzberg, 2nd ed., 1460–70. Boston: Bedford/St. Martins, 2001.

Frey, Sylvia R. *Come Shouting to Zion: African American Protestantism in the American South and British Caribbean to 1830.* Chapel Hill: University of North Carolina Press, 1998.

Friedman, Richard Elliott. *Who Wrote the Bible?* New York: Harper Collins, 1997.

Gadamer, Hans-Georg. "On the Scope and Function of Hermeneutical Reflection." In *Philosophical Hermeneutics,* 2nd ed., edited and translated by David E. Linge. Berkeley: University of California Press, 2008.

Gager, John. *Reinventing Paul.* New York: Oxford University Press, 2000.

Gee, James Paul. *Social Linguistics and Literacies: Ideology in Discourse.* New York: Taylor and Francis, 1996.

Geiger, T. J., II. "Unpredictable Encounters: Religious Discourse, Sexuality, and the Free Exercise of Rhetoric." *College English* 75, no. 3 (2013): 250–71.

Gere, Anne Ruggles. *Intimate Practices: Literacy and Cultural Work in U.S. Women's Clubs 1880–1920.* Urbana: University of Illinois Press, 1997.

Giddings, Paula. *When and Where I Enter: The Impact of Black Women on Race and Sex in America.* New York: Bantam, 1984.

Gilkes, Cheryl Townsend. "The Roles of Church and Community Mothers: Ambivalent American Sexism or Fragmented African Familyhood?" *Journal of Feminist Studies in Religion* 2, no. 1 (1986): 41–60.

Ginzberg, Lori D. *Women in Antebellum Reform.* Wheeling, IL: Harlan Davidson, 2000.

Goodburn, Amy. "It's a Question of Faith: Discourses of Fundamentalism and Critical Pedagogy in the Writing Classroom." *JAC: Journal of Composition Theory* 18 (1998): 333–53.

Gordon, Sarah Barringer. "Our National Hearthstone: Anti-Polygamy Fiction and the Sentimental against Moral Diversity in Antebellum America." *Yale Journal of Law and the Humanities* 8 (1996): 295–350.

Grimm, Nancy. *Good Intentions: Writing Center Work for Postmodern Times.* Portsmouth, NH: Boynton/Cook Heinemann, 1999.

Grohs, Gerhard, and Godehard Czernick. *State and the Church in Angola, 1450–1980.* Geneva: Institut Universitaire de Hautes Etudes Internationales, 1983.

Gunning, Sandra. *Race, Rape, and Lynching: The Red Record of American Literature, 1890–1912.* New York: Oxford University Press, 1996.

Haarsager, Sandra. *Organized Womanhood Cultural Politics in the Pacific Northwest, 1840–1920.* Norman: University of Oklahoma Press, 1997.

Hansen, Kristine. "Religious Freedom in the Public Square and the Composition Classroom." In *Negotiating Religious Faith in the Composition Classroom,* edited by Elizabeth Vander Lei and bonnie l. kyburz, 24–38. Portsmouth, NH: Heinemann, 2005.

Hardesty, Nancy A. "The Scientific Study of Missions: Textbooks of the Central Committee on the United Study of Foreign Missions." In *The Foreign Missionary Enterprise at Home: Explorations in North American Cultural History,* edited by Daniel H. Bays and Grant Wacker, 106–22. Tuscaloosa: University of Alabama Press, 2003.

Harline, Craig. *Sunday: A History of the First Day from Babylonia to the Super Bowl.* New York: Doubleday, 2007.

Harpham, Geoffrey Galt. *The Ascetic Imperative in Culture and Criticism.* Chicago: University of Chicago Press, 1987.

Hartman, Geoffrey H., and Sanford Burdick, eds. *Midrash and Literature.* New Haven, CT: Yale University Press, 1986.

Hauerwas, Stanley. *The Peaceable Kingdom: A Primer in Christian Ethics.* Notre Dame, IN: University of Notre Dame Press, 1983.

Haughey, John C. "Church-ianity and Christ-ianity." *America,* May 24–31, 2004, 8–9.

———. "Responsibility for Human Rights: Contributions from Bernard Lonergan." *Theological Studies* 63 (2002): 764–85.

Hays, Richard B. *Echoes of Scripture in the Letters of Paul.* New Haven, CT: Yale University Press, 1989.

Heathen Woman's Friend. Boston: Woman's Foreign Missionary Society of the Methodist Episcopal Church, 1869–1895. Accessed through the United Methodist Archives, Drew University, Madison, NJ.

Heitzenrater, Richard P. *Wesley and the People Called Methodists.* Nashville, TN: Abingdon Press, 1995.

Henderson, Lawrence. *Angola: Five Centuries of Conflict.* Ithaca, NY: Cornell University, 1980.

Hendricks, Wanda A. *Gender, Race, and Politics in the Midwest: Black Club Women in Illinois.* Bloomington: Indiana University Press, 1998.

Hengel, Martin. "The Attitude of Paul to the Law in the Unknown Years between Damascus and Antioch." In *Paul and the Mosaic Law,* edited by James D. G. Dunn, 25–52. Grand Rapids, MI: Eerdmans, 1996.

Hewitt, Nancy A. "Varieties of Voluntarism: Class, Ethnicity, and Women's Activism in Tampa." In *Women, Politics, and Change,* edited by Louise A. Tilly and Patricia Gurin, 63–86. New York: Russell Sage Foundation, 1990.

Higginbotham, Evelyn Brooks. *Righteous Discontent: The Women's Movement in the Black Baptist Church, 1880–1920.* Cambridge, MA: Harvard University Press, 1993.

Hill, Marvin S., and James B. Allen, eds. *Mormonism and American Culture.* New York: Harper and Row, 1972.

Hill, Patricia R. *The World Their Household: The American Woman's Foreign Mission Movement and Cultural Transformation, 1870–1920.* Ann Arbor: University of Michigan Press, 1984.

Himes, Michael J. "Catholicism as Integral Humanism: Christian Participation in Pluralistic Moral Education." In *The Challenge of Pluralism: Moral Education in a Pluralistic Society,* edited by F. Clark Power and Daniel K. Lapsley, 117–39. Notre Dame, IN: University of Notre Dame Press, 1992.

Hobbel, Arne Jarrod. "Hermeneutics in Talmud, Midrash, and the New Testament." *Immanuel* 24–25 (1990): 132–46.

Hulsether, Mark. "It's the End of the World As We Know It." *American Quarterly* 48, no. 2 (1996): 375–84.

Humphrey, E. J. "Gems of India." *Heathen Woman's Friend* 6, no. 10 (April 1875): 839.

Hunter, Jane. *The Gospel of Gentility: American Women Missionaries in Turn-of-the-Century China.* New Haven, CT: Yale University Press, 1984.

Isham, Mary. *Valorous Ventures: A Record of Sixty and Six Years of the Woman's Foreign Missionary Society, Methodist Episcopal Church.* Boston: Woman's Foreign Missionary Society, Methodist Episcopal Church, 1936.

Jamieson, Kathleen Hall, and Karlyn Kohrs Campbell. "Rhetorical Hybrids: Fusions of Generic Elements." *Quarterly Journal of Speech* 68, no. 2 (1982): 146–57.

Jarrett, Susan, Katherine Mack, Alexandra Sartor, and Shevaun Watson. "Pedagogical Memory: Writing, Mapping, Translating." *WPA Journal* 33, nos. 1–2 (2009): 46–73.

Jeffrey, Julie Roy. *Frontier Women: "Civilizing" the West? 1840–1880.* Rev. ed. New York: Hill and Wang, 1998.

Johnson, T. R. "School Sucks." *College Composition and Communication* 52, no. 4 (2001): 620–50.

Josephus, Flavius. *Antiquities.* In *The New Complete Works of Josephus,* translated by William Whiston. Grand Rapids, MI: Kregel Publications, 1999.

Jost, Walter, and Wendy Olmsted. *Rhetorical Invention and Religious Inquiry: New Perspectives.* New Haven, CT: Yale University Press, 2000.

Kane, Paula M. *Separatism and Subculture: Boston Catholicism, 1900–1920.* Chapel Hill: University of North Carolina Press, 1994.

Keeter, Scott. "How the Public Perceives Romney, Mormons." *Pew Forum on Religion and Public Life.* December 4, 2007. Available online at http://www .pewforum.org/Politics-and-Elections/How-the-Public-Perceives-Romney -Mormons.aspx.

Kennedy, George A. *Classical Rhetoric and Its Christian and Secular Tradition from Ancient to Modern Times.* Chapel Hill: University of North Carolina Press, 1980.

———. "'Truth' and 'Rhetoric' in the Pauline Epistles." In *The Bible as Rhetoric: Studies in Biblical Persuasion and Credibility,* edited by Martin Warner, 195–202. New York: Routledge, 1990.

Kim, Johann D. "God, Israel, and the Gentiles: Rhetoric and Situation in Romans 9–11." PhD dissertation, Union Theological Seminary, 1999.

King, Martin Luther, Jr. "I Have a Dream." In *A Call to Conscience: The Landmark Speeches of Dr. Martin Luther King, Jr.,* edited by Clayborne Carson and Kris Shepard, 81–87. New York: Warner Books, 2001.

Kinneavy, James. *Greek Rhetorical Origins of Christian Faith: An Inquiry.* New York: Oxford University Press, 1987.

Knupfer, Anne Meis. *Toward a Tenderer Humanity and a Nobler Womanhood: African American Women's Clubs in Turn-of-the-Century Chicago.* New York: New York University Press, 1996.

Kugel, James. *How to Read the Bible.* New York: Free Press, 2007.

———. "Two Introductions to Midrash." In *Midrash and Literature,* edited by Geoffrey H. Hartman and Sanford Burdick, 77–103. New Haven, CT: Yale University Press, 1986.

Lakoff, George, and Mark Johnson. *Metaphors We Live By.* Chicago: University of Chicago Press, 1980.

Lamar, Howard. "Statehood for Utah: A Different Path." In *Mormonism and American Culture,* edited by Marvin S. Hill and James B. Allen, 140–41. New York: Harper and Row, 1972.

Lasch, Christopher. *The New Radicalism in America, 1889–1963: The Intellectual as a Social Type.* New York: Random House, 1965.

Lawler, Peter Augustine. "Liberal Education? It Can Happen Here." *American Spectator* 38, no. 3 (April 2005): 46–47.

Lawrence-Hammer, Lesley. "Red, White, but Mostly Blue: The Validity of Modern Sunday Closing Laws under the Establishment Clause." *Vanderbilt Law Review* 60 (2007): 1273–1306.

Lears, T. J. Jackson. *No Place of Grace: Antimodernism and the Transformation of American Culture, 1880–1920.* Chicago: University of Chicago Press, 1981.

Lichtenberger, Hermann. "The Understanding of the Torah in the Judaism of Paul's Day." In *Paul and the Mosaic Law,* edited by James D. G. Dunn, 7–23. Grand Rapids, MI: Eerdmans, 1996.

Lonergan, Bernard J. F. *Insight: A Study of Human Understanding.* Vol. 3 of *Col-*

lected Works of Bernard Lonergan, 5th ed., edited by Frederick E. Crowe and Robert M. Doran. Toronto: University of Toronto Press, 1992.

———. *The Lonergan Reader,* edited by Mark Morelli and Elizabeth Morelli. Toronto: University of Toronto Press, 1997.

———. *Method in Theology.* New York: Seabury, 1971.

———. *A Third Collection: Papers,* edited by Frederick E. Crowe. New York: Paulist Press, 1985.

Lundin, Roger. *Disciplining Hermeneutics: Interpretation in Christian Perspective.* Grand Rapids, MI: Eerdmans, 1987.

Lundin, Roger, Clarence Walhout, and Anthony C. Thiselton. *The Promise of Hermeneutics.* Grand Rapids, MI: Eerdmans, 1991.

Lunsford, Andrea, and John Ruszkiewicz. *Everything's an Argument,* 3rd ed. Boston: Bedford/St. Martin's, 2003.

Lynch, Paul. "Bruno Latour and Composition's Apocalyptic Turn." *College English* 74, no. 5 (2012): 458–76.

Maccoby, Hyam. *Jesus the Pharisee.* London: SCM, 2003.

Mack, Phyllis. *Heart Religion in the British Enlightenment: Gender and Emotion in Early Methodism.* Cambridge: Cambridge University Press, 2008.

———. *Visionary Women: Ecstatic Prophecy in Seventeenth-Century England.* Berkeley: University of California Press, 1992.

Madsen, Carol Cornwell. "Decade of Détente: The Mormon-Gentile Female Relationship in Nineteenth Century Utah." *Utah Historical Quarterly* 63, no. 4 (1995): 298–319.

———. "Schism in the Sisterhood: Mormon Woman and Partisan Politics, 1890–1900." In *Battle for the Ballot: Essays on Woman Suffrage in Utah, 1870–1896,* edited by Carol Cornwell Madsen, 245–72. Logan: Utah State University Press, 1997.

———. "Schism in the Sisterhood: Mormon Women and Partisan Politics, 1890–1900." In *New Views of Mormon History: A Collection of Essays in Honor of Leonard J. Arrington,* edited by Davis Bitton and Maureen Ursenback Beecher. Salt Lake City: University of Utah Press, 1987.

Madsen, Carol Cornwell, ed. *Battle for the Ballot: Essays on Woman Suffrage in Utah, 1870–1896.* Logan: Utah State University Press, 1997.

Markelis, Daiva. "Union Halls and Church Pews: Language and Literacy among Early Chicago Lithuanians." PhD dissertation, University of Illinois at Chicago, forthcoming.

Marsden, George. *The Soul of the American University: From Protestant Establishment to Established Nonbelief.* New York: Oxford University Press, 1994.

Marsden, George M., and Bradley J. Longfield, eds. *The Secularization of the Academy.* New York: Oxford University Press, 1992.

Martin, Theodora Penny. *The Sound of Their Own Voices: Women's Study Clubs, 1860–1910.* Boston: Beacon Press, 1987.

Marzlouf, Philip. "Religion in U.S. Writing Classes: Challenging the Conflict Narrative." *Journal of Writing Research* 2 (2011): 265–97.

McFague, Sallie. *Metaphorical Theology: Models of God in Religious Language.* Philadelphia: Fortress Press, 1982.

McFarland, Ken. "Sunday Laws in America." *Liberty* (July–August 2008). Available online at http://www.libertymagazine.org/index.

McInelly, Brett C. "Mothers in Christ: Mary Fletcher and the Women of Early Methodism." In *Religion, Gender, and Industry: Exploring Church and Methodism in a Local Setting,* edited by Geordan Hammond and Peter S. Forsaith, 123–36. Eugene, OR: Pickwick, 2011.

Melchin, Kenneth. *Living with Other People: An Introduction to Christian Ethics Based on Bernard Lonergan.* Ottawa: Novalis, 1998.

Miller, Janette. "A Letter from Miss Janette E. Miller, Ochileso, West Central Africa, to Personal Friends." *Mission Studies* 29, no. 8 (1911): 243–45.

———. "Miscellaneous Missionary Materials." Janette Miller Papers, Box 1, Bentley Historical Collection, University of Michigan–Dearborn.

Miller, Nicholas. "Adventists and Ecumenism: The Good and the Bad." *Memory, Meaning, and Faith,* February 3, 2012. Available online at http://www.memorymeaningfaith.org/blog/2012/02/adventists-and-ecumenism-the-good-and-the-bad.html.

Milton, John. *Areopagitica.* In *Complete Poems and Major Prose,* edited by Merritt Y. Hughes, 716–49. New York: Bobbs-Merrill, 1957.

Montgomery, Helen Barrett. *Western Women in Eastern Lands.* New York: MacMillan Company, 1910.

Moody, Joycelyn. *Sentimental Confessions: Spiritual Narratives of Nineteenth-Century African American Women.* Athens: University of Georgia Press, 2001.

Morelli, Mark, and Elizabeth Morelli. Introduction to *The Lonergan Reader,* edited by Mark Morelli and Elizabeth Morelli, 3–28. Toronto: University of Toronto Press, 1997.

Morrissey, Lee. *The Constitution of Literature: Literacy, Democracy, and Early English Literary Criticism.* Stanford, CA: Stanford University Press, 2008.

Murolo, Priscilla. *The Common Ground of Womanhood: Class, Gender, and Working Girls' Clubs, 1884–1928.* Urbana: University of Illinois Press, 1999.

Mutz, Diane C. *Hearing the Other Side: Deliberative versus Participatory Democracy.* New York: Cambridge University Press, 2006.

Nanos, Mark D. *The Mystery of Romans: The Jewish Context of Paul's Letter.* Minneapolis, MN: Fortress Press, 1996.

The New Testament of the New Jerusalem Bible. New York: Doubleday, 1986.

Nott, Josiah C. *Two Lectures; on the Connection between the Biblical and Physical History of Man.* New York: Bartlett and Welford, 1849; reprint, New York: Negro Universities Press, 1969.

Nowacek, Rebecca S. *Agents of Integration: Understanding Transfer as a Rhetorical Act*. Carbondale: Southern Illinois University Press, 2011.

Nupur, Chaudhuri, and Margaret Strobel, eds. *Western Women and Imperialism: Complicity and Resistance*. Bloomington: Indiana University Press, 1992.

O'Dea, Thomas F. *The Mormons*. Chicago: University of Chicago Press, 1957.

Olson, Gary A. *Justifying Belief: Stanley Fish and the Work of Rhetoric*. Albany: State University of New York Press, 2002.

O'Reilley, Mary Rose. *The Peaceable Classroom*. Portsmouth, NH: Boynton/Cook Heinemann, 1993.

Pagels, Elaine. *Beyond Belief: The Secret Gospel of Thomas*. New York: Random House, 2003.

Perelman, Chaim. From *The New Rhetoric: A Theory of Practical Reasoning*. In *The Rhetorical Tradition: Readings from Classical Times to the Present*, edited by Patricia Bizzell and Bruce Herzberg, 2nd ed., 1384–1409. Boston: Bedford/St. Martins, 2001.

Perkins, Priscilla. "'A Radical Conversion of the Mind': Fundamentalism, Hermeneutics, and the Metanoic Classroom." *College English* 63, no. 5 (2001): 585–611.

Person, Carolyn W. D. "Susa Young Gates." In *Mormon Sisters: Women in Early Utah*, edited by Claudia Bushman, 199–224. Salt Lake City, UT: Olympus Publishing, 1976.

Polaski, Sandra Hack. *Paul and the Discourse of Power*. Sheffield, England: Sheffield Academic Press, 1999.

Porter, Stanley E., and Christopher D. Stanley, eds. *As It Is Written: Studying Paul's Use of Scripture*. Atlanta, GA: Society of Biblical Literature, 2008.

Postman, Neil. *Building a Bridge to the Eighteenth Century: How the Past Can Improve Our Future*. New York: Vintage, 2000.

Pratt, Mary Louise. "Arts of the Contact Zone." *Profession* 91 (1991): 33–40.

Pruitt, Lisa Joy. *A Looking-Glass for Ladies: American Protestant Women and the Orient in the Nineteenth Century*. Macon, GA: Mercer University Press, 2005.

Rand, Lizabeth. "Enacting Faith: Evangelical Discourse and the Discipline of Composition Studies." *College Composition and Communication* 52, no. 3 (2001): 349–67.

Reeves-Ellington, Barbara. *Domestic Frontiers: Gender, Reform, and American Interventions in the Ottoman Balkans and the Near East*. Amherst: University of Massachusetts Press, 2013.

Reeves-Ellington, Barbara, Kathryn Kish Sklar, and Connie Anne Shemo, eds. *Competing Kingdoms: Women, Mission, Nation, and the American Protestant Empire, 1812–1960*. Durham, NC: Duke University Press, 2010.

Reitano, Joanne. "Working Girls Unite." *American Quarterly* 36 (1984): 112–34.

Religious Leaders for Sensible Priorities. "President Bush, Jesus Changed Your

Heart. Now Let Him Change Your Mind." Advertisement. *New York Times,* December 4, 2002.

Richter, David, ed. *The Critical Tradition: Classic Texts and Contemporary Trends,* 2nd ed. Boston: Bedford, 1998.

Ringer, Jeffrey M. "The Consequences of Integrating Faith into Academic Writing: Casuistic Stretching and Biblical Citation." *College English* 75, no. 3 (January 2013): 270–97.

Robert, Dana L. *American Women in Mission: A Social History of Their Thought and Practice.* Macon, GA: Mercer University Press, 1996.

———. "The Influence of American Missionary Women on the World Back Home." *Religion and American Culture: A Journal of Interpretation* 12, no. 1 (2002): 59–89.

Rogow, Faith. *Gone to Another Meeting: The National Council of Jewish Women.* Tuscaloosa: University of Alabama Press, 1993.

Rohan, Liz. "A Woman's Guide to Wholeness: The Diaries of Janette Miller, 1879–1969." *WILLA (Women in Literature and Life Assembly)* 8 (Fall 1999): 21–36.

Roosevelt University. *English Composition Program: Philosophy and Goals.* February 24, 2013. Available online at http://www.roosevelt.edu/CAS/Programs/LIT/Composition/Philosophy.aspx.

Rosaldo, Renato. "Grief and a Headhunter's Rage." In *Literacies: Reading, Writing, Interpretation,* 2nd ed., edited by Terence Brunk, Suzanne Diamond, Priscilla Perkins, and Ken Smith, 469–87. New York: Norton, 2000.

Royster, Jacqueline Jones. "When the First Voice You Hear Is Not Your Own." *College English* 47, no. 1 (1996): 29–40.

Salliant, John. "Antiguan Methodism and Antislavery Activity: Anne and Elizabeth Hart in the Eighteenth-Century Black Atlantic." *Church History* 69, no. 1 (2000): 86–115.

Sanders, E. P. *Jesus and Judaism.* Philadelphia: Fortress, 1985.

———. *Paul and Palestinian Judaism: A Comparison of Patterns of Religion.* Philadelphia: Fortress Press, 1977.

Schilb, John. *Rhetorical Refusals.* Carbondale: Southern Illinois University Press, 2007.

Schnabel, Landon. "Former Head of National Council of Churches Speaks at Andrews Seminary Symposium—Part II." *Spectrum,* February 2, 2012. Available online at http://spectrummagazine.org/blog/2012/02/02/former-head-national -council-churches-speaks-andrews-seminary-symposium.

Scott, Anne Firor. *Natural Allies: Women's Associations in American History.* Urbana: University of Illinois Press, 1991.

Seat, Karen K. *"Providence Has Freed Our Hands": Women's Missions and the American Encounter with Japan.* Syracuse, NY: Syracuse University Press, 2008.

Segal, Phillip. *The Halakhah of Jesus of Nazareth According to the Gospel of Matthew.* Atlanta, GA: Society of Biblical Literature, 2007.

Seidler, Victor. "Language and Masculinity." In *Literacies: Reading, Writing, Interpretation,* 2nd ed., edited by Terence Brunk, Suzanne Diamond, Priscilla Perkins, and Ken Smith, 627–43. New York: Norton, 2000.

Semmel, Bernard. *The Methodist Revolution.* New York: Basic Books, 1973.

Shaver, Lisa J. *Beyond the Pulpit: Women's Rhetorical Roles in the Antebellum Religious Press.* Pittsburgh: University of Pittsburgh Press, 2012.

Shipps, Jan. *Marketing Mormonism: The LDS Church's Use of Public Relations and Advertising Techniques to Represent Themselves and Sell Their Message to the World.* Atlanta, GA: American Society of Church History, January 1996.

———. *Mormonism: The Story of a New Religious Tradition.* Chicago: University of Illinois Press, 1987.

Shuger, Debora K. *Sacred Rhetoric: The Christian Grand Style in the English Renaissance.* Princeton, NJ: Princeton University Press, 1988.

Smith, Christian. *Souls in Transition: The Religious and Spiritual Lives of Emerging Adults.* New York: Oxford, 2009.

Snow, Eliza R. "An Address." *Woman's Exponent,* September 15, 1873, 62–63.

———. "Position and Duties." *Woman's Exponent,* July 15, 1874, 28.

———. "To Every Branch of the Relief Society in Zion." *Woman's Exponent,* April 1, 1875, 164–65.

Spencer, Benjamin. *The Quest for Nationality: An American Literary Campaign.* Syracuse, NY: Syracuse University Press, 1975.

Stanley, Christopher. "Paul's 'Use' of Scripture: Why the Audience Matters." In *As It Is Written: Studying Paul's Use of Scripture,* edited by Stanley E. Porter and Christopher D. Stanley, 125–55. Atlanta, GA: Society of Biblical Literature, 2008.

Stegner, William Richard. "Romans 9.6–29: A Midrash." *Journal for the Study of the New Testament* 22 (1984): 37–52.

Stenberg, Shari. "Liberation Theology and Liberatory Pedagogies: Renewing the Dialogue." *College English* 68, no. 3 (2006): 271–90.

Stowers, Stanley K. *The Diatribe and Paul's Letter to the Romans.* Chico, CA: Scholar's Press, 1981.

———. *A Rereading of Romans: Justice, Jews, and Gentiles.* New Haven, CT: Yale University Press, 1994.

Strand, Kenneth A. "The Sabbath and Sunday from the Second through Fifth Centuries." In *The Sabbath in Scripture and History,* edited by Kenneth A. Strand, 323–32. Washington, D.C.: Review and Herald, 1982.

Strong, Tom. 2003. "Getting Curious about Meaning-Making in Counselling." *British Journal of Guidance and Counselling* 31, no. 3 (2003): 259–73.

Sullivan, Regina D. *Lottie Moon: A Southern Baptist Missionary to China in History and Legend.* Baton Rouge: Louisiana State University Press, 2011.

Syme, Eric. *A History of SDA Church-State Relations in the United States.* Mountain View, CA: Pacific Press, 1973.

Taft, Zachariah. *Biographical Sketches of the Lives and Public Ministries of Various Holy Women.* 2 vols. Vol. 1, London: Kershaw, 1825; vol. 2, Leeds: Cullingworth, 1828.

———. *The Scripture Doctrine of Women's Preaching.* High-Ousegate, UK: N.p., 1820.

Tennyson, Alfred. *In Memoriam, A.H.H.* In *The Norton Anthology of English Literature,* vol. 2, edited by M. H. Abrams et al., 750–69. New York: W. W. Norton, 1962.

Terrell, Mary Church. "1904 Presidential Address to National Association of Colored Women." In *Righteous Discontent: The Women's Movement in the Black Baptist Church, 1880–1920,* edited by Evelyn Brooks Higginbotham, 206–7. Cambridge, MA: Harvard University Press, 1993.

Tobin SJ, Thomas H. *Paul's Rhetoric in Its Contexts: The Argument of Romans.* Peabody, MA: Hendrickson, 2004.

Tolar Burton, Vicki. *Spiritual Literacy in John Wesley's Methodism: Reading, Writing, and Speaking to Believe.* Waco, TX: Baylor University Press, 2008.

Tompkins, Jane. *Sensational Designs: The Cultural Work of American Fiction, 1790–1860.* New York: Oxford University Press, 1985.

Toulmin, Stephen. From *The Uses of Argument.* In *The Rhetorical Tradition: Readings from Classical Times to the Present,* 2nd ed., edited by Patricia Bizzell and Bruce Herzberg, 1410–28. Boston: Bedford/St. Martins, 2001.

Towner, W. S. "Hermeneutical Systems of Hillel and the Tannaim: A Fresh Look." *Hebrew Union College Annual* 53 (1982): 101–35.

Turner, James. "Secularization and Sacralization: Speculations on Some Religious Origins of the Secular Humanities Curriculum, 1850–1900." In *The Secularization of the Academy,* edited by George M. Marsden and Bradley J. Longfield, 74–106. New York: Oxford University Press, 1992.

Underwood, Grant. "Mormonism as a Historical Concept." Quoted in Carol Cornwall Madsen, "Schism in the Sisterhood: Mormon Women and Partisan Politics, 1890–1900." In *New Views of Mormon History: A Collection of Essays in Honor of Leonard J. Arrington,* edited by Davis Bitton and Maureen Ursenbach Beecher. Salt Lake City: University of Utah Press, 1987.

Valenze, Deborah M. *Prophetic Sons and Daughters: Female Preaching and Popular Religion in Industrial England.* Princeton, NJ: Princeton University Press, 1985.

Vander Lei, Elizabeth, and Lauren Fitzgerald. "What in God's Name? Administering the Conflicts of Religious Belief in Writing Programs." *WPA: Writing Program Administration* 31, nos. 1–2 (2007): 185–95.

Van Wagenen, Lola. "In Their Own Behalf: The Politicization of Mormon Women and the 1870 Franchise." In *Battle for the Ballot: Essays on Woman Suffrage in*

Utah, 1870–1896, edited by Carol Cornwell Madsen, 60–75. Logan: Utah State University Press, 1997.

Vermes, Geza. *Jesus the Jew.* Minneapolis, MN: Fortress Press, 1981.

Volf, Miraslov. "Forgiveness, Reconciliation, and Justice: A Christian Contribution to a More Peaceful Social Environment." In *Forgiveness and Reconciliation: Religion, Public Policy, and Conflict Transformation,* edited by Raymond G. Helmick SJ and Rodney L. Peterson, 27–49. Philadelphia: Templeton Foundation Press, 2001.

————. "Indefensible War." *Christian Century,* September 25, 2002, 35.

Wald, Priscilla. *Constituting Americans: Cultural Anxiety and Narrative Form.* Durham, NC: Duke University Press, 1995.

Walsh, Brian J. "Worldviews, Modernity, and the Task of Christian College Education." *Faculty Dialogue* 18 (Fall 1992): 13–35.

Walsh, Brian J., and J. Richard Middleton. *The Transforming Vision: Shaping a Christian World View.* Downers Grove, IL: InterVarsity Press, 1984.

Weeks, Jeffrey. "Values in an Age of Uncertainty." In *Literacies: Reading, Writing, Interpretation,* 2nd ed., edited by Terence Brunk, Suzanne Diamond, Priscilla Perkins, and Ken Smith, 709–24. New York: Norton, 2000.

Weisenfeld, Judith. "Introduction: We Have Been Believers: Patterns of African-American Women's Religiosity." In *This Far By Faith: Readings in African-American Religious Biography,* edited by Judith Weisenfeld and Richard Newman, 1–18. New York: Routledge, 1996.

Welter, Barbara. "The Cult of True Womanhood, 1820–1860." *American Quarterly* 18, no. 2, part 1 (Summer 1966): 151–74.

White, Ellen. *The Great Controversy.* Nampa, ID: Pacific Press, 1950.

White, Jean Bickmore. "Woman's Place Is in the Constitution: The Struggle for Equal Rights in Utah in 1895." *Utah Historical Quarterly* 42 (1974): 344–69.

Wigger, John H. *Taking Heaven by Storm: Methodism and the Rise of Popular Christianity in America.* New York: Oxford University Press, 1998.

Wilson, D. R. "'Thou Shal[t] Walk with Me in White': Afterlife and Vocation in the Ministry of Mary Bosanquet Fletcher." *Wesley and Methodist Studies* 1 (2009): 71–85.

Woman's Missionary Friend. Boston: Woman's Foreign Missionary Society of the Methodist Episcopal Church, 1896–1924. Accessed through the United Methodist Archives, Drew University, Madison, NJ.

Woman's Work for Woman and Our Mission Field. Philadelphia: Woman's Foreign Missionary Society of the Presbyterian Church, 1886. Accessed through the Library of Congress, Washington, D.C.

Worsham, Lynn. "Going Postal: Pedagogic Violence and the Schooling of Emotion." *Journal of Advanced Composition* 18, no. 2 (1998): 213–45.

CONTRIBUTORS

—

AESHA ADAMS-ROBERTS received her PhD from Pennsylvania State University. Her dissertation, "As the Spirit Gives Utterance: The Language and Literacy Practices of Black Women Preachers," includes Aesha's own experiences as an ordained minister. She is currently a blogger and raising her two children, Amani and Roy, at home.

THOMAS AMOROSE is a professor of English at Seattle Pacific University. He has published in the areas of rhetoric and the liberal arts and what he calls "the rhetoric of ultimate things." The latter has taken him into the rhetoric of religion, material rhetoric, and literary nonfiction.

BETH DANIELL is a professor of English at Kennesaw State University in the North Atlanta suburbs, where she teaches rhetorical theory to undergraduates and research methods to graduate students. She serves as director of the general education program in the English department and as director of the writing-across-the-curriculum program in the College of Humanities and Social Sciences. She is the author of *A Communion of Friendship: Literacy, Spiritual Practice, and Women in Recovery* and editor, with Peter Mortensen, of *Women and Literacy: Local and Global Inquiries for a New Century*.

ROSALYN COLLINGS EVES teaches at Southern Utah University, where she coordinates the writing fellows program. Her research interests include nineteenth-century women's rhetorics and rhetorics of space. She was the recipient of the Rhetoric Society of America dissertation award, and her work has appeared in *Rhetoric Review* as well as in a handful of edited collections. New work is forthcoming in *Legacy*.

ANNE RUGGLES GERE is Arthur F. Thurnau Professor and Gertrude Buck Collegiate Professor at the University of Michigan, where she serves as director of the Sweetland Center for Writing and as co-chair of the Joint PhD in English and Education. Author of a dozen books and more than seventy-five articles, she is a past chair of CCC.

BRUCE HERZBERG is a professor of English and media studies and director of the Writing and Communication Program at Bentley University, where he teaches courses in the Bible, composition, and public speaking. His publications include *The Rhetorical Tradition* as well as articles on composition teaching, service learning, and rhetoric. In biblical studies he recently published "Isaac's Blindness" in *Narrative*, "Deborah and Moses" in the *Journal for the Study of the Old Testament,* and "Samson's Moment of Truth" in *Biblical Interpretation.* He is at work on a study of the function of miracles in legal discourse in the New Testament and rabbinic literature.

PRISCILLA PERKINS teaches composition and American literature at Roosevelt University. She is co-author of *Literacies: Reading, Writing, Interpretation* and has published on hermeneutic approaches to teaching evangelical college students, general education reform, and eugenics in the writings of Gertrude Stein and Theodore Dreiser. She is currently studying how Bernard Lonergan's philosophy can be used to encourage more holistic undergraduate learning in the humanities.

LIZABETH A. RAND is an associate professor of rhetoric at Hampden-Sydney College, a liberal arts college in Virginia for men, where she also serves as the director of the Rhetoric Program and the associate director of the Writing Center. She teaches basic writing, research writing, creative nonfiction, and rhetorical theory. Her primary research interest is the study of illness, identity, and argument, but she is also interested in rhetorics of religiosity, especially within the Seventh-day Adventist church.

LIZ ROHAN is an associate professor of composition and rhetoric at the University of Michigan–Dearborn. Her articles have appeared in such journals as *Rhetoric Review, Composition Studies,* and *Reflections.* With Gesa Kirsch she edited *Beyond the Archives: Research as a Lived Process.*

KAREN K. SEAT is associate professor of religious studies and director of the Religious Studies Program at the University of Arizona. Her book, *"Providence Has Freed Our Hands": Women's Missions and the American Encounter with Japan,* examines nineteenth-century Protestant women's mission movements and their impact on American ideologies regarding gender, race, Christianity, and civilization.

Vicki Tolar Burton is a professor of English at Oregon State University, where she teaches courses in rhetoric, writing, and pedagogy and directs the Writing Intensive Curriculum Program. She is the author of *Spiritual Literacy in John Wesley's Methodism: Reading, Writing, and Speaking to Believe*. She has published articles in *College English, College Composition and Communication,* and *Rhetoric Review* and has written chapters for a number of anthologies.

Elizabeth Vander Lei is a professor of English at Calvin College, where she co-chairs the English department and directs the written rhetoric program. With bonnie kyburz she co-edited *Negotiating Religious Faith in the Composition Classroom,* and with Dean Ward she co-authored *Real Texts: Reading and Writing across the Disciplines.* She has published articles in *College Composition and Communication, College English, WPA,* and elsewhere.

INDEX

—

abolitionism, 49, 66, 162n25

academia, 58, 80; avoiding religion, 98; responses to Christian fundamentalism in, 92–94; univocalism in, 98

African Americans, women's clubs of, 8–9

agency, of rhetors, 138, 140–43

Allen, Danielle, 101

American dream, 20

Anderson, Chris, 152n20

Andrews University, ecumenism speech at, 26–27

Angola, Miller's mission work in, 54–57

Anthony, Susan B., 12

antifoundationalism, 148

Antigua, 49, 161n18; Hart sisters working in, 45–46; histories of Methodism in, 45, 47; missionaries in, 47–48

Anti-Polygamy Society, 7

apologias: forensic, 37; Mary Bosanquet using rhetoric of, 36–37; "Tina's," 80

apostles, as role models for community, 51

apostolic rhetoric, 45–46, 147; of Anne Hart, 47–48; authority through, 48–49, 51; of Eliza Snow, 52–54; of Janette Miller, 54–57; relation to community, 52, 54, 57–58; translation as, 54–57

Aquinas, Thomas, 111

Areopagitica (Milton), 112

argument: Jewish forms of, 120–31; treated as warfare, 91–92

Arrington, Leonard, 153n7

Ashworth, Peter, 81, 88

Athanasius, Bishop of Alexandria, 111

Augustine of Hippo, 111, 140–42

authority: gaining rhetorical, 45; for interpretation of sacred texts, 143–44; rhetoric in claiming, 47; sources of, 79; to speak, 138; through apostolic rhetoric, 46, 48–49, 51–52, 54

Bacchiocchi, Samuele, 19

Baker, Frances J., 59, 63, 68

Barnes, Elizabeth, 153n2

Bauthumley, Jacob, 113

Baxter, John, 47, 51, 162n25

"belief-as-narrative," 78, 81

Benson, Joseph, 51

Berry, Wendell, 97–98

the Bible, 37; dramatistic narratives in, 109; in history of Christianity, 110–13; interpretations of, 110, 115–16, 175n12; Jewish interpretation of, 119–20; literal interpretations of, 84–86, 94, 114, 173n40; Methodist speech genres and, 33–34; Old Testament rhetoric in, 140; as sacred text, 108; truth of, 106

Bizzell, Patricia, x, 115

blue laws, as state-legislated Sabbath observance, 20–25
Bok, Edward, 155n23
Borg, Marcus, 107, 113–15, 173n40
Brown, Earl Kent, 33–34
Brown, Isabel Cameron, 12
Buckley, James Monroe, 61–62
Bull, Malcolm, 20–21
Burke, Kenneth, 53, 139; on God as the Word, 136–37; on scientistic *vs.* dramatistic language, 109
Bush, George W., 99–100
Butler, William, 65–66

Calvin, John, 112
Cameron, Averil, 139
Campbell, Karlyn Kohrs, 32
Carter, Shannon, 101
Carter, Stephen L., 25, 98
Ceppi, Elisabeth, 56
Chappell, Virginia, 103
Chicago Exposition (1893), Mormons at, 12–13, 156n29
Chilton, Bruce, 133
Christianity: attitudes toward worldviews in, 138–39, 146–49; in churchstate separation, 18; disrupted by Reformation, 143–44; gender equality as ideal of, 69; history of, 110–13, 136; interpretation of sacred texts in, 143; Jews and, 126–30, 175n14; relation to rhetoric, 137, 143–145; responses to fundamentalism in, 92, 152n20; rhetoric of, 136, 139; stagnation *vs.* change in, 145–46; Sunday Sabbath in, 19–20
Church of England, Methodism and, 32, 38–39
Church of the Latter Day Saints. *See* Mormons
church-state separation, 18–19, 23

civic discourse, incivility in, 91–92
class, social, 48
classical rhetoric, 81
Coke, Thomas, 47–48
common sense, Lonergan's sense of, 80–81, 167n19
communities, 45, 121; apostles as role models for, 51; avoiding conflict, 98–99; boundaries of, 93; common good of, 80–83, 100; Mary Bosanquet's, 34–35; Miller serving American and African, 55–57; narratives of, 50, 96; relation of apostolic rhetoric to, 46, 57–58; sacred texts in context of, 108; women strengthening through apostolic rhetoric, 46–47, 52, 54
Congregationalism, Miller's mission work for, 54–56
consent, as issue in polygamy and slavery, 5
conversion narratives, 47, 49–50
Coppe, Abiezer, 113
Cottrell, Raymond F., 17
critical thinking, students moving toward, 105, 107
Croly, Jennie June, 10–12
Crosby, Sarah, 34
Crowley, Sharon, xi, 91, 93–94, 108
"Cult of True Womanhood," 61, 69
culture: education as agent of hegemony in, 115; worldview underlying, 146–47
"culture wars," 91–92

Dante, 111–12
Daube, David, 174n5
Davies, W. D., 175n11
deliberative argument, 38
democracy, deliberative *vs.* participative, 102–3
DePalma, Michael-John, 76

Derr, Jill Mulvey, 14, 52–53
DiMattei, Steven, 134
diversity, welcoming, 99–101
doctors, Mormon women as, 7–8
Donawerth, Jane, 34
Downs, Doug, 92–93
Durbin, John Price, 63

Ebenezer Orphanage, 56
ecumenism, SDA and, 26–27
Edmunds-Tucker law, 7
education: as agent of cultural hegemony,
   115; effects of evangelism on students',
   87–88; emotions in, 91, 96–97; by Hart
   sisters, 46; by Janette Miller, 56–57; for
   male itinerant preachers, 39; by Mary
   Bosanquet, 34–35; Mormon women's
   activism on, 7; need for respect in,
   105–6; pedagogical violence in, 96–97;
   responses to students' fundamentalism in, 92–94, 152n20; secularization
   and, 15; by women's clubs, 9
Ehrman, Bart D., 107
Ellis, E. Earle, 132–33
Emerson, Ralph Waldo, 16
emotions: in education, 91, 96–97; as rhetorical tools, 141–42; in truth, 139–41
Enlightenment, effects of, 114, 144
equality: gender, 69; racial, 47, 50
ethos, in rhetorical pedagogy, 75–76, 84
ethos orientation, 84–86
evangelism, 55, 62; ethos orientation in,
   84–85; by Mormon women, 13–14;
   by students, 76, 79–80; women's
   effectiveness in, 47, 51
Everything's an Argument (Lunsford and
   Ruszkiewicz), 75
exhortation, 33, 159n8
expounding, as opportunity for women's
   public speech, 33–34

family, 35; ideology of, 4, 60, 153n2; missionaries trying to spread Christian,
   60, 62, 65–66; slavery's effects on, 51,
   162n25; threats to Christian conception of, 61–62
Feldman, Stephen M., 18–19, 24
Female Refuge Society, 50–51
Female Relief Society, 13, 45–46
Fish, Stanley, 112–13, 148
Fishbane, Michael, 121
Fletcher, John, 42–43
Fletcher, Mary Bosanquet, 31; angst over
   call to preach, 41–42; background of,
   34–36; defense of women's preaching
   by, 36–38, 160n18; marriage of, 42–43;
   objections to preaching by, 36–37;
   rhetorical genres of, 32, 35–36; Wesley
   and, 31, 35
Flowers, Montaville, 64
force and criteria, 109–10
forensic apologia, 37
Foucault, Michel, 116
Frudd, David, 43

Gadamer, Hans-Georg, 81
Gager, John, 133–34
Gates, Susa, 4
Geiger, T. J., II, 96
gender: concerns about slavery and, 5;
   in "Cult of True Womanhood," 61;
   doubts about women's abilities, 60;
   equal moral standards for, 14; genres
   and, 49; in Mormon society, 52–53;
   preaching and, 31–32, 36–37, 42; in
   visions of family, 4
gender ideology: missionaries appropriating and undermining, 60–61;
   separate spheres in, 61–63, 69
gender roles: delineation of, 4; missionaries appropriating and undermining,
   61, 65–68; Mormon, 163n42, 163n45;

gender roles (*cont.*): Mormon women resisting and accepting, 4, 14–15; women as moral anchors, 62; women's missionary societies outside, 60

genres, rhetorical: blending of, 32, 36–38, 43–44; gender and, 31–32, 49; in Hart sisters' histories of Methodism, 47; opportunities for women's public speech in, 33–34

Gere, Anne Ruggles, 52

Gilbert, Anne Hart, 46, 51; apostolic rhetoric of, 47–48, 58; concern about slavery's effects on morality, 50–51; history of Methodism by, 45–47, 51

God: associated with the Word, 136–37, 139; rhetors as mediators with, 142

Gordon, Sarah Barringer, 5

government: "blue laws" of, 20–25; church-state separation and, 18–19, 23; SDA conflict with, 21–23

Grand, Sarah, 14

Greco-Roman rhetoric, 122; influence on Paul, 119–20, 131–32

Gregory, Pope, 20

Gunning, Sandra, 153n8

Hansen, Kristine, 98

Harline, Craig, 20, 23–24

Harpham, Geoffrey Galt, 139

Hart, Anne. *See* Gilbert, Anne Hart

Hart, Elizabeth. *See* Thwaites, Elizabeth Hart

Hauerwas, Stanley, 95–98

Haughey, John C., 75

Haupt, John, 153n7

Hays, Richard B., 132–33, 177n28

The Heathen Woman's Friend, 60, 62, 66–67

Hillel, Rabbi, 174n5; exegetical principles by, 122, 125, 132

Himes, Michael J., 84–85

hospitality, in welcoming diversity, 99–103

immigrants, 4–5, 9

Iraq War, theologians' efforts to prevent, 99–100

Irenaeus, Bishop of Lyons, 111

Jamieson, Kathleen Hall, 32

Jeffrey, Julie Roy, 52

Jesus, and Pharisees, 174n9

Jews: gentiles and, 126–30, 175n14; as Other in development of Christianity, 18–19; Sunday Sabbath as Christian split from, 19–20; women's clubs of, 8–9

Josephus, 121

Judaism: influence on Paul's rhetoric, 119, 126–32, 133–34; Paul's relation to, 132–33, 177nn31–32; rhetorical practices in, 120–31

Kennedy, George A., 140

Kim, Johann, 133

Kinneavy, James, 139

Kugel, James, 174n4, 175n12

language, 139; in Christian tradition, 136–37; relation to faith, 145; scientistic *vs.* dramatistic, 109; truth and, 105, 110

Lawler, Peter, 87

Lawrence-Hammer, Lesley, 20

Lears, T. J. Jackson, 15

Liberty (SDA publication), 22–23

literature: anti-Mormon, 5–6, 153n7; missionary, 59–60, 66–67; Mormon clubwomen studying, 11, 13; SDA publishing and printing of, 22–23

Lockhart, Keith, 20–21

logos, 84–85

Lonergan, Bernard, 74–75, 79; on affective conversion, 83–84; on common sense, 80–81, 167n19; on self-appropriation, 84–88

Lundin, Roger, 144

Lunsford, Andrea, 75

Luther, Martin, 112

Maccoby, Hyam, 174n9

marriage, 4, 6. *See also* polygamy

Marsden, George, 15

"Marty," 94, 98, 103; alternatives for conversation with, 101–2; experience of writing assignments, 89–90

maternal ethos, women's use of, 53, 58

meaning: faith and, 137–38; reader making from text, 112–13; worldview and, 146

Melchin, Kenneth, 80–81

Methodism, 48–49; formal ban on women preaching in, 40–41, 43; Hart sisters' histories of, 45–47, 51; lay preachers in, 38–39; Mary Bosanquet and, 34, 36–38; opportunities for women's public speech in, 32–34; women preachers of, 31, 34, 36–38, 40–41; Women's Foreign Mission Society of, 59–60

Middleton, J. Richard, 146–49

Miller, Janette, 46, 54–58

Miller, William, 18

Milton, 112–13

missionaries: in Antigua, 47–48; challenging preconceptions about race, 63–65; corruption of, 45, 48–49; expanding career options for women, 65–68; expanding home communities' worldviews, 61, 70; Janette Miller as, 46, 54–57; promoting women's rights, 66–70; trying to spread Christian

family, 62, 65–66; women as, 60–63, 68–69

mission societies, women's, 59, 62–63, 164n1

modernism, worldview of, 146

Montgomery, Helen Barrett, 68–70

Moody, Jocelyn, 58

morality: blacks' criticized, 51, 162n25; Christian families providing, 65–66; defense of black women's, 48–49; effects of slavery on, 50–51; Mormon women on, 11, 14; required of missionaries, 48–49; women's role as anchors of, 62

Morissy, Lee, 112–13

Mormons: antipolygamy novels and, 6, 153n7; discrimination against, 10, 16; Eliza Snow's leadership in, 52–54; gender roles of, 4, 163n42, 163n45; patriarchal principles of, 6; polygamy and, 4–5, 8, 154n17; public relations efforts by, 156n29; support for woman suffrage, 12; in Utah, 3, 5; in Utah's struggle for statehood, 6–7; women of, 4, 15; women's clubs of, 8–14

motherhood, metaphors of, 41–42, 44

Mutz, Diane, 100–103

naming, as hortatory device, 53

narratives: Bible, 109, 114; metaphorical, 115; nesting of, 96–98; religious traditions and, 95–96; in sacred texts, 107–8; students reexamining, 105–6; univocal, 98

National Council of Women, 12

National Reform Association (SDA), 23

Neusner, Jacob, 133

newspapers, Mormon women's, 7

Noahide laws, 130

Nott, Josiah C., 64
Nowacek, Rebecca, xiii–xv

Olson, Gary A., 148
Oral Law, Jewish, 120–22, 127
O'Reilley, Mary Rose, 90, 95, 96–97

paganism, in Sunday Sabbath, 19
Pagels, Elaine, 111
patriarchy, women challenging, 58
Pattison, Richard, 46, 48
Paul: influences on rhetoric of, 119–20,
    122, 131–32; Jewish rhetoric of, 126–31,
    133–34, 175n11; as a Pharisee, 119–21,
    133; relation to Judaism, 132–33, 177n31,
    177n32; rhetoric of, 176n17, 176n27;
    scriptural interpretation by, 123–25;
    on status of Gentiles, 126–30
Perelman, Chaim, 110
personhood, in apprehension of truth,
    140–42
persuasion, rhetoric as, 81, 83
Pharisees: Jesus and, 174n9; rhetorical
    practices of, 119–22, 129–31, 133
Polaski, Sandra Hack, 47–48, 51
politics, in deliberative vs. participative
    democracy, 101–3
polygamy, among Mormons, 154n17;
    antipolygamy novels and, 5–6; effects
    of, 8, 16; non-Mormon opposition
    to, 4–7; slavery concerns blended
    with, 5–6; woman suffrage in Utah's
    relation to, 6–7
postcritical naiveté, 115
postmodernity, 114–15, 143–44
Pratt, Mary Louise, 9
Pratt, Romania, 7
prayer, Mary Bosanquet's method of, 35
preaching: associated rhetorical genres
    and, 33–34; Augustine on, 111; as male
    genre, 31–32; by male laymen, 32, 39;

Mary Bosanquet's, 35–37, 41–42; Mary
    Bosanquet's defense of women's,
    36–38; objections to women's, 36–37,
    41; Snow's, 53; Wesley on, 37, 39–40,
    44; women's, 31, 34, 36–41, 43–44, 53
precritical naiveté, 107, 114, 173n40
"problem of meaning," 82, 86
prophetic voice, vs. apostolic rhetoric, 46
Protestants: ideology of social order of,
    60–61; modernists vs. fundamental-
    ists in, 55; women's mission societies,
    164n1
public life, religion in, 15–16
pulpit, preaching in alternatives to, 43

race, 47, 101, 161n18; Hart arguing for
    equality of, 47, 50; missionaries
    challenging preconceptions about, 60,
    63–65; morality and, 48–49
race suicide, fear of, 4–5
reading: in history of Christianity, 110–13;
    levels of, 111–12; multiple methods of,
    106–7, 113–15; regulation of, 113; sacred
    texts' history of, 110–13
reason, and emotion, 139–41
Reformation, 138, 143–44
religion, 54, 69, 139; academia avoiding,
    58, 80, 98; alternatives for conversa-
    tion with students on, 101–2; blue laws
    ruled secular vs., 24–25; in "culture
    wars," 91–92; freedom of, 22–23, 144;
    history of Christianity, 110–13, 136;
    history of multiple interpretations of
    texts in, 115–16; in Mormon women's
    clubs, 13; narratives in, 95–96, 106; as
    private vs. public, 15–16, 98–99; re-
    sponses to Christian fundamentalism,
    92, 152n20; role in society, 25, 99–100;
    role in women's involvement in public
    life, 15–16; sacred texts in, 107–8, 113,
    136; secularization of society and,

15; of students, 87–88; in students' identity, 85, 88, 108; students' relation to, 96, 106; in students' writing, 78–79, 81–86, 90, 102, 152n20; tendency to homogenize, 93–94, 151n8; traditions of, 95–96; women's writing on, 58. *See also specific religions*

repentance, Snow calling for, 53–54

rhetorical genre theory, 32

rhetorical refusal, 27

rhetoric pedagogy, 75–76, 110; argument as warfare in, 91–92; truth in, 105

rhetors: agency of, 138, 140–43; effectiveness of, 142–43, 148; role of, 137–38, 143

Richter, David, 111

Ringer, Jeffery, 102

Ringer, Jeffrey, 76

Rome, in development of church-state separation, 18–19

Royster, Jacqueline Jones, 94

Ruszkiewicz, John, 75

Ryan, Sarah, 34

Sabbath: as defining issue, 21, 25–26; in development of Christianity, 19–20; for non-Seventh-day Adventists, 18; for Seventh-day Adventists, 17–18, 25, 27; state-legislated observance of, 21–25

sacred texts, 139; in Abrahamic religions, 107–108, 136; expectation of interpretation of, 120–21; history of reading, 110–13; interpretation of, 143–44, 174n4, 175n12; Jewish, 119–22, 134; multiple interpretations of, 115–16, 134

Sanders, E. P., 132–133

Satan, SDA perception of, 22

Schnabel, Landon, 26

scholastic diatribe, 131–32

self-appropriation, 74, 76, 81, 84–88

Seventh-day Adventists (SDA), 147;

development of, 17–18; discrimination against, 213–24; ecumenism and, 26–27; oppositional stance of, 22–23, 27; publishing and printing by, 22–23; Sabbath as defining issue for, 21, 25–26; Sabbath beliefs of, 17, 25, 27

Sewall, May Wright, 12–13

sexuality, concern about black women's, 50–51

Shaver, Lisa J., xii, 33

Shipp, Ellis, 12

Shipps, Jan, 156n29

Shuger, Debora K., 141

slavery, 49; effects of, 50–51, 162n25; Elizabeth Hart's critique of, 49, 162n25; polygamy concerns blended with, 5–6

slaves, 46; Mormon women compared to, 4–5, 163n42; non-Christian women equated to, 66

Smith, Christian, 96

Smith, Joseph, 163n41

Snow, Eliza R., 6–7, 45–46; apostolic rhetoric of, 52–54, 58; rhetoric of, 53, 163n45

social reform/service: by Mary Bosanquet, 34–36; by Mormon clubwomen, 10–11; by Seventh-day Adventists, 18; through mass conversions, 55

spiritual letter, rhetoric of, 36

spiritual mothers, Hart sisters as, 51

Stanley, Christopher, 176n17

Stenberg, Shari, 94

Stone, Lucy, 7

Strand, Kenneth, 19–20

suffrage. *See* woman suffrage

Taft, Mary Barritt, 40–41

Taft, Zechariah, 40

Talmud: on argumentative procedures, 122; interpretations of, 110, 122–25, 132; as written form of memorized Oral Law, 129 testimony, 33, 159n8

Thiselton, Anthony C., 144

Thwaites, Charles, 162n25

Thwaites, Elizabeth Hart, 49–50, 162n25

"Tina," 76; relations with classmates, 77, 79–80, 82–83, 86–87; two personas of, 79–80, 85, 87

Tobin, Thomas, 133, 177n31

Tompkins, Jane, 5–6

Torah, 130, 174n9; expectation of interpretation of, 120–21; oral and written, 120–22; on status of Gentiles, 126–30

Toulmin, Stephen, 109–10

Toward Civil Discourse (Crowley), 91, 93–94

Towner, W. S., 132

translation, in Miller's mission work, 54–57

trivialization, rhetorical power of, 93, 95

truth: Bible's, 111, 114–15; effort required in discerning, 112–13; emotion and reason in, 139–41; force and criteria of, 109–10; interpretation to discover, 143; language and, 105, 110; metaphor *vs.*, 115; multiple, 115–16; of sacred texts, 113; will to, 116

Twaites, Elizabeth Hart, 45; apostolic rhetoric of, 58; conversion narrative of, 47; history of Methodism by, 46–47, 51; on slavery's effects on morality, 50–51

Underwood, Grant, 154n17

Utah: anti-Mormonsim in, 10; Mormons settling in, 3, 163n41; struggle for statehood, 4–8, 14, 154n17; woman suffrage in, 6–7, 12; women's clubs in, 8–11

Utah Women's Press Club (UWPC), 9

violence: causes of, 90–91, 95; intellectual, 90–91, 93; religion linked to, 99; self-control to avoid, 96–98; in students' lives, 90

Volf, Miroslav, 99–102

Wald, Priscilla, 4

Walhout, Clarence, 144

Walsh, Brian J., 146–49

Warren, Earl, 24

Washington, George, 20

Weisenfeld, Judith, 49

Wells, Emmeline, 9, 11–13

Welter, Barbara, 61

Wesley, John: forensic apologia by, 37–38; Mary Bosanquet and, 31, 35; Mary Bosanquet's defense of women's preaching to, 36–38, 160n18; on preachers, 32, 37, 39; response to Mary Bosanquet's defense of women's preaching, 38–40; on women preaching, 39–40, 44

White, Ellen, 18, 21–22, 26

White, James, 18

Wigger, John H., 33

Wilson, D. R., 34

The Woman's Exponent, 7, 10–13, 52

woman suffrage: Mormon support for, 6, 12; in Utah, 6–7, 12; women missionaries promoting, 70

women: black, 48–51; consent of, 5; criticized for challenging gender roles, 61–62; discrimination against, 39, 63; involvement in public life, 15–16; as missionaries, 47, 54–57, 62–63; missionaries expanding career options for, 65–66; missionary societies of, 59, 62–63, 164n1; omitted from Methodist histories, 45, 51; opportunities for public speech by Methodist, 32–34;

opposition to polygamy, 4, 7, 153n7;
preaching by, 31, 34, 36–41, 43–44,
53; religious writing of, 58; rhetorical
genres and, 31–34, 49, 68–69; status
of, 6, 66; strengthening communities
through apostolic rhetoric, 46–47,
52, 54, 57–58; in Utah's struggle for
statehood, 6–7; as victims, 66–67,
69–70; women missionaries focusing
on, 63, 65–66

women, Mormon, 153n8; activism of,
7, 14–15; Eliza Snow's leadership of,
52–54, 163n45; loyalty to religion,
6, 13–14, 163n42; role of, 3–4, 14–15,
52–53; stigmatization of, 4, 14, 52; in
women's clubs, 8–14

women's clubs, 155n23; African American, 8–9; Jewish, 8–9; Mormons in,
8–14

Women's Foreign Mission Society
(WFMS), 59–60, 63

women's rights, 4, 7, 67–70

Woodruff, Wilford, 8

worldviews: Christian attitudes toward,
138–39, 146–49; missionaries expanding home communities', 61, 70;
post-Enlightenment rationality, 114;
students' vs. schools', 115

Worsham, Lynn, 90–91

writing pedagogy, 74–75; in deliberative
vs. participative classrooms, 103;
essay assignments in, 77–79; hermeneutic understanding through, 81;
renovation of, 94–96; rooting in the
personal, 95; students' experience
of, 89–90, 102; students' religion in,
81–86, 102

Yochanan, Rabbi, 125, 130

Young, Brigham, 3, 52–54